EDUCATION, INCOME, AND HUMAN CAPITAL

NATIONAL BUREAU OF ECONOMIC RESEARCH
CONFERENCE ON RESEARCH IN INCOME AND WEALTH

EDUCATION, INCOME, AND HUMAN CAPITAL · EDITED BY

W. LEE HANSEN · UNIVERSITY OF WISCONSIN

Studies in Income and Wealth · VOLUME THIRTY-FIVE
by the Conference on Research in Income and Wealth

NATIONAL BUREAU OF ECONOMIC RESEARCH

NEW YORK · DISTRIBUTED BY COLUMBIA UNIVERSITY PRESS

NEW YORK AND LONDON 1970

Printed in the United States of America

RELATION OF THE NATIONAL BUREAU DIRECTORS TO
PUBLICATIONS REPORTING CONFERENCE PROCEEDINGS

Since the present volume is a record of conference proceedings, it
has been exempted from the rules governing submission of manu-
scripts to, and critical review by, the Board of Directors of the
National Bureau.

PREFATORY NOTE

THIS volume of *Studies in Income and Wealth* contains most of the papers presented at the Conference on Education and Income held at the University of Wisconsin on November 15-16, 1968 and jointly sponsored by the University's Department of Economics and the Conference on Research in Income and Wealth. We are indebted to the University for making its facilities available to us for these sessions; to the National Science Foundation for its support; to the Program Committee consisting of W. Lee Hansen (chairman), Gary S. Becker, Sam Bowles, Albert Fishlow, Alice Rivlin, and Theodore W. Schultz; to the Editorial Committee composed of Messrs. Bowles, Hansen (conference editor), and Schultz; to Roger Kopstein who prepared the manuscript for publication; and to H. Irving Forman, for charting.

CONTENTS

EDUCATION AND HUMAN CAPITAL IN INTERNATIONAL ECONOMICS

CONFERENCE OVERVIEW

EDUCATION, INCOME, AND HUMAN CAPITAL

INTRODUCTION • W. LEE HANSEN •
UNIVERSITY OF WISCONSIN

THE objective of these conference papers is to take stock of our knowledge on a subject of rapidly growing interest—the relationships between education and income and the role of the human-capital approach in illuminating these relationships. This stock-taking follows more closely than usual on the heels of a prior conference, the Universities-National Bureau Exploratory Conference on Capital Investment in Human Beings held in late 1961.[1] The expanding volume and diversity of work, stimulated in large part by that previous conference, argued for an early attempt to pull together what had been learned and to plot some of the directions that future research on this subject should take.

The rapid growth of research in this general area is remarkable, as can be determined from Blaug's bibliography.[2] Of the approximately 800 items listed, only 45 appeared prior to 1961, and another 53 appeared from 1951 to 1955. But in the next five-year period, 1956-60, almost 200 items appeared. And for the period 1961-65, almost 500 items are listed. Three mimeographed supplements listed another 300 items for 1966-67. This pattern of extremely rapid growth clearly parallels that in many of the more publicized and rapidly expanding scientific fields where discussions of the knowledge explosion are rampant. This work on education, income, and human capital spills over into a wide range of fields, among them economic theory, production economics,

[1] *Investment in Human Beings,* NBER Special Conference 15, Supplement to *Journal of Political Economy,* October 1962.
[2] Mark Blaug, *Economics of Education: A Selected Annotated Bibliography,* 1966 (also mimeographed supplements, 1966, 1967, and 1968).

1

public finance, labor economics, and development. Running through much of this work are two underlying themes: (1) there are important links between education and productivity—and therefore income, and (2) the role of education can be explored fruitfully when viewed as an income-generating form of human capital.

The conference at which these papers were presented was held at the University of Wisconsin in November 1968. The conference brought together a substantial number of the small but expanding group of scholars undertaking research in this area. The papers and some of the more pertinent discussion are summarized in the section below.

The opening paper by Bowles is an effort to go behind the education-income relationship so as to explore what is known about how education is produced. Bowles reasons that if education has the productivity- and income-enhancing effects that have been so widely noted, we should be able to learn through an analysis of the production function for education just what factors do contribute to increased learning in the schools. Given the absence of a theory of learning, not to mention the lack of requisite data, Bowles concentrates on examining the conceptual and econometric problems involved in estimating educational production functions. In addition to a discussion of the choice of the appropriate form of the production function, he gives extensive consideration to the measurement of output, the value-added problem, and the input structure of the schools and their associated environmental characteristics. The final pages of his paper are devoted to some applications of his ideas and draw upon data from the Equal Educational Opportunity Survey. The empirical results, for black twelfth-grade students and for Northern and Southern twelfth-grade students, are interesting in that they reveal the complexity involved in identifying the factors which explain achievement levels.

One important point raised by both discussants—Brandl and Hause —is that because school administrators may be maximizing something quite different from any of the conventional school output measures (such as achievement scores), it is going to be difficult to learn what kinds of production techniques are most effective. Indeed, Brandl goes so far as to argue that only through carefully controlled individual demonstration projects are we likely to build up the type of information needed before we can prescribe for the schools; the conventionally used survey data will at best describe what is currently going on without telling much about possible alternatives. Hause also raises a question as to the most appropriate way to take account of the effect of previous educational experience on the kinds of inputs needed for the next stage of the educational process.

Zvi Griliches's paper has a somewhat broader orientation than Bowles's in that it explores the role of education variables in aggregate production functions. Opening with a section on growth accounting, he moves on to consider alternative definitions of the education variable and alternative production functions. This leads him to consider the appropriate level of aggregation in view of the many labor quality dimensions. The remainder of the paper explores the education-ability-income relationship in an effort to throw light on a variety of issues, among them the apparent constancy of education-income differentials, increases in the demand for educated labor, and possible complementarities between human and physical capital. Griliches offers a number of useful leads and suggestions on these various issues. He concludes that although more work must be done before we can understand the processes of production of human capital and the determinants of rates of return, we are in reasonably good shape in measuring the contribution of education.

In his comment Conlisk develops the implications of two alternative methods of including the education or human-capital variable—that is, as a separate factor versus as a labor-augmenting factor. He concludes that the latter treatment can be more easily reconciled with the literature on growth models, thereby opening up a link between growth theory and work on the economics of education and human-capital theory. Conlisk provides some additional suggestions regarding the handling of the ability factor. Nelson argues for a quite different approach to the role of education in production functions; he sees education as being important because it acts to enhance the quality of decision making rather than to increase the quantity of learning as such.

The thrust of Ben-Porath's paper differs greatly from that of the first two papers. In expanding on some of his earlier work, he examines the path of the production of human capital over the life cycle. The particular problem he focuses upon is the extent to which the accumulation of human capital affects the accumulation of human capital in the future, given the fact that past human-capital accumulation increases the opportunity cost of acquiring additional human capital. Using the model developed, he tests it with data from an earlier study by Mincer; somewhat mixed results are obtained.

Mincer offers a number of perceptive comments on Ben-Porath's model and on the empirical test of it. In particular, he discusses some of the implications of the "neutrality hypothesis" which is embodied in the model. In addition, he speculates on the role of variable depreciation and also notes that additional human investment can extend both the age of retirement and the length of life. Thurow, on the other hand, believes that the model provides too simple an explanation of lifetime human investment patterns. He spells out what he terms the "peculiarities" of human capital and tries to show how they affect the pattern of investment. In particular, he stresses the importance of the time constraint in making the human-capital market inherently imperfect. It seems quite clear that though some progress has been made in understanding the impact of obsolescence, other lines of attack are also needed.

In addition to having an impact on growth and earnings, education also affects the distribution of income. Chiswick's paper addresses an aspect of this broad topic as he seeks to explain the skewness of the income distribution, a relatively neglected topic. He sets forth a model which shows that the distribution of schooling itself would cause positive skewness in the distribution of income. But this skewness is further accentuated by the pattern of rates of return to schooling and by a variety of other schooling parameters. He finds empirical support for his model in an analysis of data for the United States and Canada.

The discussants take issue with Chiswick on several points. Mary Jean Bowman argues that skewness is the result of a number of factors which affect the shape of the entire distribution, that some of Chiswick's empirical results are not fully consistent, and that his measure of the rate of return is not equivalent to the internal rate of return as customarily defined. Foley questions Chiswick's failure to test alternative functional forms (other than the log-linear form) and the interpretation of the residual in his regression. Finally, and most important, he sees the need for a much more detailed and well-articulated model to fully explore the role of education in affecting the distribution.

The final two papers represent a shift of orientation to the role of education and human capital in the explanation of international trade and mobility patterns. The education-income relationship, while less direct in these two papers, is nonetheless important in affecting gains from trade and the profitability of moving from one country to another.

Kenen sets himself the task of dealing with two questions: What do we know about the role of skills, human capital, or knowledge in determining comparative advantage and thereby the structure of external trade? And what are the implications of what we know and what else do we need to know? The accumulating evidence seems to indicate that skill differences and research-development variables are both useful in explaining comparative advantage. Given that the skills hypothesis appears to have a slight edge, Kenen goes on to develop some of the major questions which this raises. What determines the disparities in the amounts of skill and of physical capital possessed by different countries? Why do some countries seem to have an advantage in the acquisition of human capital? How does human capital enter the production function? The final section of the paper discusses some of the normative questions that are raised through this approach. Two appendixes expand upon the empirical and theoretical issues which are touched upon in the body of the paper.

The comments of the discussants make clear that a great many issues must be cleared away in bringing the role of human capital to bear upon explanations of comparative advantage. Both Krueger and Baldwin are concerned about the human-capital measures used. Krueger believes that the R & D variables reflect flows rather than stocks of knowledge and that the skill indexes typically used make implicit and limiting assumptions about skill-substitution possibilities. Krueger goes on to point out several critical theoretical and empirical problems likely to be encountered in pursuing some of Kenen's proposed lines of inquiry, while Baldwin presents a brief summary of some of his own research on this same topic.

The migration of human capital and its impact is the subject of Scott's paper. Actually, he focuses on the "brain drain" phenomenon— the movement of one of the most valued types of human capital, highly-educated and trained personnel—which has been a subject of increased concern in recent years. The bulk of his attention is given to exploring the major strands of this research: the decision to migrate, the valuation of human capital embodied in migrants, and the policy questions posed by this type of migration.

Holtmann in his comments tries to throw added light on the possible importance of the "dead-weight loss" relative to the income distribution effect, to consider another aspect of the externalities problem, and to suggest some directions for future work. Sjaastad elaborates on the nature of the transfers produced through migration and on the nature of the externalities. Although like Scott in believing that little of significance has been turned up by the brain drain research, Sjaastad suggests that the change in factor proportions resulting from intentional migration and its consequent effects does merit further study.

The final paper in the volume is by T. W. Schultz whose writings and direct encouragement played such an important role in stimulating research in human capital, and more specifically, in education as a form of human capital. He discusses the problems of definition and aggregation in grappling with issues in the human capital area and touches upon some of the important omissions in the work on education as a form of human capital.

Of the topics covered by the conference, the most clear-cut progress appears in those that endeavor to incorporate education into production functions and to explain international trade patterns using the human-capital approach. This progress is no doubt attributable to a general resurgence of interest in production-function analysis in recent years and to the vigorous efforts of international economists to seek explanations for Leontief's paradox. The least understood and most difficult subject to handle analytically seems to be human-capital obsolescence and its counterpart, the process of human-capital accumulation. Much the same kind of appraisal applies to education's effect upon income distribution, although the growing and ever-richer body of survey data may make this subject more amenable to future empirical investigation. Finally, and surprisingly, the topic of international migration evoked the least interest from both a theoretical and empirical standpoint. It may be that migration *within* countries rather than *among* countries provides a more attractive entree to the subject, because it is tidier, both analytically and empirically, and because it avoids some of the political issues that so often becloud "brain drain" discussions.

The general conclusion that seemed to emerge from this conference is that though the human-capital concept provides a highly useful analytical framework for attempting to understand the relationship between education and income, our understanding of these relationships is still very sketchy both at the conceptual and the empirical levels. In part, this arises from the fact that this is still a relatively new area of inquiry, and so a great deal of work remains to be done; in part, from the fact that the data we have to work with are still quite limited in both quantity and quality. But most important of all is the fact that the underlying theory with which we work—both in economics and in related fields—is not yet rich enough and our knowledge of the underlying processes is not yet adequate to overcome some of the major stumbling blocks.

In the light of this state of affairs, the virtue of the papers and comments in this volume is that they make explicit efforts to identify the questions and issues that require analysis and, where possible, they attempt to give a notion of research priorities. There is no necessity to repeat or even try to summarize these questions here—they are best expressed in the context of each contributor's own remarks.

Any conference must necessarily limit its scope, with the result that a number of topics received little or no attention. A few of the more important research questions that need to be tackled are set out below.

1. What are the determinants of the demand for schooling? We know that for individuals there are both investment and consumption components of their demand for schooling. While considerable progress has been made in exploring the investment returns, much less is known about the more elusive consumption returns. What is the nature of these returns, how can they best be approached analytically, and, finally, how can they be measured? We seem to be equally ignorant in our understanding of the determinants of the derived demand for labor with different amounts of schooling. It is clear that, in general, employers offer higher pay to more highly educated workers, but our knowledge of what elements or ingredients of schooling make people more productive is scanty. Is it what they have learned in school, as measured by test scores? Or is schooling valuable for the patterns and modes of thought and behavior it develops in people? Or does schooling merely serve as a screening device that identifies the more able, highly motivated young people in our society?

2. What forces explain the persistence of differences in earnings and rates of return by level of schooling despite marked increases in the average level of, and some rather dramatic shifts in the distribution of, educational attainment? Many writers have commented on this point, among them Griliches in his paper. Have relative shifts in the supply of, and demand for, educated manpower been such as to neutralize each other over most of the past several decades? Or have there been offsetting shifts in age-education-earnings patterns and in the relative distribution of people in the various age-education groups? Or is it possible that we have the illusion of relative stability in the return to schooling because our data are not particularly good? As yet we know little about how the labor market for educated people works, i.e., about the interrelationships between price and quantity of labor and the nature of adjustments to market shifts.

3. Although there is much to be learned about the role of education in explaining human investment decisions and associated labor-market and income-distribution phenomena, it is equally important to inquire about the impact of education on people's decisions regarding the disposition of their incomes. To the extent that education provides people with vastly more information, their attitudes toward risk and uncertainty may be affected in perceptible ways. These changes may in turn influence patterns of consumption and savings. To what extent do savings patterns differ by level of educational attainment? How is the distribution among various forms of savings affected? What are the implications for family savings of the distribution of income over the life cycle for people of different educational attainment? In what ways are their consumption patterns affected both at a point in time and over time?

4. Closely related to the above questions is the role of education in affecting intergenerational patterns of human-capital accumulation, wealth holdings, and income distribution. Through the decision of parents to transfer wealth to the next generation via the purchase of more education, rather than via cash gifts or bequests, there may have been a speeding up of intergenerational transfers. If so, this has no doubt affected the distribution of income and wealth among generations as well as the relative shares of wages and nonwages. With the growing availability of income and wealth data, it should soon be possible to begin probing these relationships.

EDUCATION AND
PRODUCTION FUNCTIONS

TOWARDS AN EDUCATIONAL PRODUCTION FUNCTION •

SAMUEL BOWLES • HARVARD UNIVERSITY

1 INTRODUCTION

EDUCATION occupies an important position in every major economy of the world. In the United States over 6 per cent of gross national product is annually spent on formal schooling alone, and the amount is increasing at a rate more than twice that of the economy as a whole.[1] According to Machlup's estimates for the year 1958, the resource costs of education and training, broadly defined, amounted to over 12 per cent of the value of GNP.[2] Education is called upon to accelerate the rate of growth and to equalize the distribution of income. In the poor countries schools are regarded as a central element in the economic infrastructure. In the United States, schooling and training programs receive the lion's share of the funds of the war on poverty. Everyone seems to have accepted James Mill's dictum that "if education cannot do everything, there is hardly anything it cannot do." The growing popular interest in education has been paralleled by the development of an immense literature on the role of human capital in economic growth and the distribution of income. And yet nobody really knows how education is produced.

NOTE: I should like to acknowledge the competent research assistance of Matthew Lambrinides, and the helpful comments of Susan Contratto, Herbert Gintis, Christopher Jencks, Henry Levin, Arthur MacEwan, Stephan Michaelson, Christopher Sims, Lester Thurow, and Thomas Weiskopff. In preparing this paper, I received financial support from the U. S. Office of Education and the National Science Foundation.

[1] Council of Economic Advisers [15], p. 143. The figures do not include foregone earnings; they refer to the year 1966 and the previous decade.

[2] Fritz Machlup [49], pp. 354 and 362. The resource costs of education and training include foregone earnings, and expenditures on training on the job, as well as in the army and other institutions. The gross national product figure is adjusted to include items counted as educational costs, but not normally included in the national income accounts.

11

This paper is a discussion of the educational production process. An educational production function is the relationship between school and student inputs and a measure of school output. This method of representing the educational production process is likely to be of particular value both in descriptive studies of human capital formation and in normative investigations to determine optimal educational resource allocation.

If schooling does have a unique effect on labor productivity or earnings, we should be able to trace this effect to the development of cognitive skills and attitudes in school. We may also be able to relate the development of productive skills and attitudes to school policies concerning the allocation of scarce resources. A production function relating school inputs to the development of productive capacity should give us a better indication of why the more educated are better qualified for productive roles. Moreover, differences in production functions for different racial and social class groups, as well as differences in educational inputs for these groups, may help explain an important aspect of the determination of the distribution of personal earnings.

In setting school policy and in long-range educational planning, knowledge of the educational production function is essential to efficient resource allocation. This is true whether the decision unit is pursuing the objective of growth or of equality, or a combination of these and other (perhaps noneconomic) goals. Without an estimate of the technology of education (the production function) the relationship between the opportunity cost and expected benefits of particular policies must be little more than guesswork.

In this paper, I will concentrate on the relationship between school inputs and conventional measures of school outputs, such as achievement scores. An explanation of the relationships between scholastic inputs and achievement, on the one hand and economic performance on the other, would have been more germane to the theme of this conference—education and income. In fact, much, though not all, of the economic relevance of what follows depends on there being some systematic relationship between scholastic achievement and economic performance. For the present, however, I can only present results based on the educational evaluation of the schools' outputs.

An educational production function is defined as follows:

$$A = f(X_1, \ldots, X_m, X_n, \ldots, X_v, X_w, \ldots, X_z) \tag{1}$$

where

A = some measure of school output—for example, a score on a scholastic achievement battery;

$X_1, \ldots, X_m$ = variables measuring the school environment. The variables here would typically include the amount and quality of teaching services, the physical facilities of the school, and the length of time that the student is exposed to these inputs;

$X_n, \ldots, X_v$ = variables representing environmental influences on learning outside the school—e.g., the parents' educational attainment; and

$X_w, \ldots, X_z$ = variables representing the student's ability and the initial level of learning attained by the student prior to entry into the type of schooling in question.

We are interested in estimating the structural parameters of the function f. It will be seen later that, although we cannot estimate the equation in the form presented, some progress can be made with a slightly modified version.

The data at our disposal are ordinarily based on a cross-section of students. Although I dwell at length on the deficiencies of our particular data, the information generally available for the purposes of estimating educational production functions is, in some respects, superior to that available for estimating economic production functions: we have data at the "firm" level and therefore avoid the problem of making "technological" inferences based on industrial, state, or national averages; most of our input data are measured directly, rather than in monetary aggregates; and we have ample data on the quality of the factors of production— e.g., teachers, principals, and other school personnel.

The crucial deficiency is not in the lack of data but the absence of a theory of learning to guide us in establishing a model for our estimation. The engineer can tell us exactly what technical processes are necessary for the production of particular physical commodities; these processes, in turn, suggest appropriate specifications of the production function, as well as some a priori limits on plausible estimates. In education, the psychologist replaces the engineer or agronomist as the source of technical information on the production process, and, despite fruitful developments in learning theory, we still know very little about the underlying technology. Nonetheless, a reasonable a priori model of the production of scholastic achievement *can* be specified on the basis of existing theory, and preliminary estimates based on this model are encouraging.

Although attempts to measure the relationship between school inputs and outputs have occupied the attention of a number of educational researchers over the last half-century, the estimation of the structural parameters of a production function similar to (1) is a relatively new approach.[3] The results of these studies are difficult to summarize, in part because of the variety of measurements used, and because of the diversity of findings. In any case, the purpose of this paper is not primarily to present empirical estimates of production functions but rather to explore some of the conceptual and econometric problems involved in this type of estimation. The results of some of these studies, as well as my own results, are included as examples.

Section 2 includes a discussion of the behavioral assumptions underlying the usual production function estimates and the particular difficul-

---

[3] Herbert Kiesling [45, 46] used data generated by the Quality Measurement Project of New York State to estimate school production functions for various communities in New York. Martin Katzman [43] estimated production functions for a variety of school outputs of elementary schools in Boston. As a part of the study which gave rise to the report of the Central Advisory Council for Education (the Plowden Report) in England, G. F. Peaker estimated a series of production functions for British elementary education. Thomas Fox, John Holland, and Jesse Burkhead have estimated production functions for a wide range of school outputs for Atlanta and Chicago, as reported in Burkhead [9]. I have not included in this list the study of Finis Welch [66], as he relies on highly aggregated inputs and his estimates can only be identified as educational production functions by some stretch of the imagination. Eric Hanushek [30] and David Armor [2] have used U.S. data on the sixth grade to estimate production functions for elementary education. The International Project for the Evaluation of Educational Achievement, under the direction of Torsten Husén, has estimated similar functions for the determination of mathematics achievement in a sample of twelve countries [36]. A considerable amount of additional work is now in progress. Larry Posner (at Harvard) is currently estimating production functions for on-the-job training.

ties encountered when such concepts are applied to schools. Sections 3 and 4 are devoted to the measurement of school outputs and student inputs. The measurement and interpretation of school inputs are discussed in Section 5, and some preliminary illustrative results are presented in Section 6.

2   ESTIMATING A PRODUCTION MODEL FOR SCHOOLS

IN A statistical investigation using nonexperimental data, the most we can expect is to discover some relationship among measurable dimensions of the process, based on the particular configuration of the data in our sample. In this we are limited both by the preconceptions of the researchers who selected the sample and obtained the data and by the patterns of variation which school decision-making processes have brought about in the sample of schools chosen. To use the apt analogy of Marshak and Andrews [50], we are in the position of neither the agronomist nor the meteorologist. The agronomist seeks to understand production relations in agriculture with a mind to increasing productivity; he can experiment, varying his inputs systematically and in any desired combination and thus, under ideal conditions, predict the effect on productivity of specific changes in inputs. The meteorologist relies on nonexperimental data, but seeks only to predict normal behavior—not to affect events. We have the worst of these worlds. We seek to affect educational output by altering school inputs, and our data are generated by decision-making units and student responses entirely beyond our control. Thus our ability to calculate the consequences of changes in existing educational processes is very limited indeed.[4] But the limited ability to vary and control school inputs which occur in our data is just one of many difficulties.

---

[4] A considerable amount of educational research has used experimental techniques. See, for example, Gray and Klaus [25] and Kirk [47]. These methods hold some promise for empirical determination of the educational production function, particularly when we seek to estimate the consequences of major departures from existing technologies.

Assume for the moment that we seek to estimate the production function (1) in the form:

$$A_i = f_0 + f_1 X_{1i} + f_2 X_{2i} + \ldots + f_z X_{zi} + u_i \qquad (2)$$

where

A_i = the achievement score (or other output measure) for the ith student;

$f_0, \ldots, f_z$ = the parameters of the production function to be estimated;

X_{ji} = the amount of input j devoted to observation i's education, $j = 1 \ldots z$; and

u_i = the disturbance term.

The least squares technique yields unbiased estimates of the regression coefficients only if the independent variables, X_{ji}, are exogenous—i.e., only if they are uncorrelated with the disturbance term, u_i. We may, however, expect the school inputs to be endogenous to some system— for example, a system of equations based on the school administrators' preference function, the educational production function(s) and an educational budget constraint. In this case, we are faced with the problem of simultaneous equation bias which plagues the estimation of production functions at the firm level;[5] a single equation approach to the estimation of (2) will yield inconsistent estimates of the structural parameters f_j.

The basic implausibility of the above behavioral model provides one way out of this difficulty. Given that school administrators know very little about the underlying production processes and are subject to a wide variety of political and legal constraints, we can assume that they do not select or alter school inputs with a mind to optimizing any well-defined function of school outputs. Therefore, we can assume for purposes of estimation that the X_j's are exogenous.

Rejection of an optimizing decision model for school administrators alleviates at least one simultaneity problem (there will be others), but it deprives us of the usual interpretation of the estimated parameters of (2) as a production function—a relationship which in conventional usage indicates the *maximum* output consistent with a given set of inputs.

[5] See Marshak and Andrews [50] and Nerlove [54] for a discussion.

If school administrators follow no systematic optimizing behavior, then the observations on which our estimates are based are not generally technically efficient. (It may be possible to produce the same output with less than the observed level of all inputs.) Thus we arrive at some sort of *average* production function. Only if the absolute degree of technical inefficiency is uncorrelated with the level of factor inputs (which seems unlikely) will the estimates of f_j from (2) represent unbiased estimates of the true production relationship.[6]

Moreover, the school output is multidimensional, and the relative valuation of different outputs—say, mathematical competence as opposed to citizenship—differs among school districts. For this reason, technical inefficiency may result neither from inadvertence nor from the absence of optimizing behavior but rather from the conscious pursuit of objectives not adequately measured in any single index of school output. The appearance of technical inefficiency in this context can occur whenever school administrators are able to vary the composition of the school output by exercising choice about the allocation of *a given set* of resources within the school. As long as the levels of factor inputs measured in our production function do not completely determine the composition of school output, the failure to produce the maximum possible level of one dimension of output with a given set of inputs may reflect a relatively low valuation of that output by the school personnel.

A perfectly analogous problem arises because students differ in the aspects of the school output which they most successfully acquire. Not all students seek to maximize their scholastic achievement. For this reason, we may observe low achieving schools whose technical inefficiency results from the fact that the students have chosen to emphasize the noncognitive aspects of personal development. Given the possibility of making this kind of tradeoff, it is not surprising that McDill, Meyers, and Rigsby [52] found that a measure of the degree of intellectualism and achievement orientation in the predominant value systems of schools is a good predictor of scholastic achievement.[7]

---

[6] Of course, the constant term will be biased downward. If we had a number of different observations on inputs for the same school, perhaps from different grades, or years, or tracks, we might be able to use school dummy variables to eliminate this "management bias." See Massell [51] and Hoch [32].

[7] Of course, it is virtually impossible to establish the causal relationship between intellectual values and scholastic success.

Differences in student valuation of scholastic success and other dimensions of output present serious difficulties in the measurement of output as well as the interpretation of the estimated production function. We use the score on any achievement test as an output index to measure some underlying competence purportedly learned in school. However, in order for the test to be an adequate measure of the level of competence, it must be the case that children try equally hard to do well on the test, or more simply that they tell all that they know. Yet to some children the reward of doing well on the test is by itself sufficient to call forth the maximum effort, while for others the testing situation does not elicit full concentration. Zigler and DeLabry [72], for example, found that, although there were significant differences in middle-class and lower-class students on a set of tests given in normal conditions, when each group was tested under the reward conditions which had been found to be optimal for that group, there were no group differences in performance. Likewise, Terrell, Durkin and Wiesley [61] found that material-reward conditions produced better performance in lower-class children, and nonmaterial reward proved more effective with middle-class children. Thus the importance of the social class of the student's family in our production functions is probably not a pure measure of a direct influence on learning, but represents a proxy for motivation in test-taking as well. If this is the case, the structural parameters of (1) relating to the student's social background will be upward-biased estimates of the effect of social class on school learning.

While some school inputs can perhaps be regarded as exogenous to our system, one set of inputs—student attitudes—must be endogenous. Student attitudes toward self and toward learning are a consequence of past and present achievement (as well as other influences) and are important determinants of achievement. Thus we have to rewrite equation 2 as

$$A = f(X_1, \ldots, X_z, \text{attitudes}) \qquad (3)$$

and,

$$\text{Attitudes} = g(X_1, \ldots, X_z \text{ achievement—past and present}) \qquad (4)$$

In this case simultaneity seems unavoidable. Estimates based on (3) will certainly be biased, since attitudes will in general be correlated with the disturbance term. The solution is to return to (2). Although this equation does not directly incorporate attitudes (the explanatory variables being those which are exogenous), it incorporates the effects of attitudes indirectly, as they are related to the set of exogenous variables. Unless we are specifically interested in increasing scholastic achievement by changing student attitudes directly, we lose little if we exclude attitude variables from the equation.[8]

The dearth of knowledge concerning the learning process makes any a priori specification of form for the estimation of educational production relationships particularly difficult. The notion of diminishing marginal product is appealing, although not well established in the field of education. A function linear in the logarithms of the variables would seem somewhat superior, particularly in view of the possibility of positive interactions between inputs. Nevertheless, the restrictions of the Cobb-Douglas function are severe.[9] An analysis of variance designed to identify the nature of the interaction between inputs would seem a prerequisite for the adequate specification of the form of the educational production function. In the work below, I will use the simple linear additive form presented in (2) above.[10] I have not been able to compare my results with those generated with alternative forms of (2).

Children do not learn in the same way, nor do they learn the same things. Lesser and Stodolsky, for example, found dramatic differences in the patterns of scholastic proficiency on four different dimensions of learning among Chinese, Jews, Negroes, and Puerto Ricans.[11] When we find consistent differences in patterns of response to school inputs, we have good grounds for grouping students according to these patterns and

---

[8] Nonetheless, in my results I present both the reduced form and the (biased) estimates of the structural equation including attitudes.

[9] Particularly important, to my mind, is the fact that the cross derivatives among any pair of inputs, each of which is positively related to output, must also be positive. This would require, for example, that an increase in the quality of teachers be more effective on children of well educated parents than on the children of illiterate parents.

[10] The choice is dictated largely by data considerations. My regressions are estimated from correlation tables, not from the raw data. Thus I was unable to make the necessary logarithmic transformations. Hanushek [30] found that the logarithmic form gave slightly better significance for the estimates of the parameters of his production functions.

[11] Stodolsky and Lesser [60].

estimating a number of different technologies. Casual inspection of the results of Hanushek's, Kiesling's and my own work suggests that it is useful to think of distinct educational production technologies—at least for the four-way classification of students—black/white and rich/poor.[12] The need to stratify the population by race and class reflects the primitive level of our inquiry. In a completely specified model the differences in the behavior among these subpopulations ought to be attributable to characteristics of these groups which are relevant from the standpoint of learning theory.

Based on recent findings in the study of economic growth, we may anticipate that the major changes in productivity of schools will be effected not by a more rational input structure within the existing technology, but by changes in production functions themselves—including changes in the relationship between home background and achievement, as well as the more conventional input-output relationships. If our goal is to effect such changes, we should identify "best practice" schools and attempt a quantitative explanation of their superiority.

3 THE MEASUREMENT OF OUTPUT

WHAT DO schools produce? They perform two primary economic functions: selection and socialization. The socialization process may be broadly construed as the preparation of youths to fill adult roles. This involves the transmission of skills and perhaps even more important, the indoctrination of values and commitments appropriate to successful adult participation in life. Many dimensions of school output are directly relevant to economic performance, others are valued for different reasons. Both are economically important.

We would like to measure school output by post-school economic or social performance or by indexes of valued characteristics thought to be acquired in school. Unfortunately, our indexes of school output are based largely on tests administered in school and designed to measure

---

[12] However, I have seen no statistical test of the hypothesis that the underlying subpopulations differ significantly. I have estimated functions for black twelfth-grade students separately, as well as black twelfth-grade students stratified by region.

scholastic achievement. These achievement scores must, then, be considered proxies for, or, perhaps, influences on, later economic behavior. Scholastic achievement is, presumably, not valued per se, but only as input to subsequent measures of performance. Therefore, although we use achievement, A, as the measurement of output, our rationale for this is that many socially or individually valued characteristics are themselves functions of scholastic achievement. As an illustration, we may consider the capacity to earn income, E, as such a valued attribute and investigate the function:

$$E = E(A). \tag{5}$$

There are indications (at least for some groups) of a significant relationship between scholastic achievement and earnings. Wolfle [71], for example, found that among persons with the same number of years of schooling, percentile class rank in high school, and other measures highly correlated with school learning (IQ scores) showed positive relationships to annual earnings. Weisbrod and Karpoff [67] found a strong relationship among college grades and earnings in a large sample of employees of a nationwide firm. When Weiss [68] measured years of schooling in achievement units rather than calendar years, the significance of his estimates of the relationship between earnings and schooling improved.[13] Hansen, Weisbrod, and Scanlon [29] also found a highly significant relationship between earnings and scores on the Armed Forces Qualification Test—a measure highly correlated with school learning; and Duncan [19] reports similar findings for a somewhat more representative sample.[14] The apparent unimportance of scholastic achievement in the

[13] His study refers to white male workers in the North Central region of the United States, and is based on the 1/1000 sample of the 1960 Census. Years of schooling for each subcategory of workers were translated into achievement years based on evidence in Coleman [13], on mean "years" of achievement for groups of individuals classified by place of schooling (urban, rural, north, south, etc.). An "achievement year" is a norm based on the average achievement scores attained in each year of school by white students in the urban northeastern United States.

[14] Some additional evidence is surveyed in Griliches [26]. It should be pointed out that in the Hansen-Weisbrod-Scanlon [29] sample of draft *rejects,* the relationship was remarkably small; and in Weiss' study of black workers, only *one* age group exhibited a significant relationship between years of schooling (measured in achievement units) and earnings. Weiss reported similar results using a direct measure of years of schooling completed.

determination of earnings of some categories of workers (black, for example) may indicate that our present schools are economically ineffective for these groups. However, it is also possible that other dimensions of school outputs such as aspects of personality development not reflected in achievement scores have a more direct bearing on economic performance. In this case we have selected the wrong dependent variable in our investigation.

Most educational processes may be thought of as producing intermediate goods for use in other educational or training activities. Virtually all workers receive some on-the-job training, above and beyond the general education received in school. And most forms of schooling are a direct input into yet higher levels of education. In the empirical work presented below, we are particularly interested in education at the twelfth grade. At the present time in the United States, about half of the high school graduates move on to further education. Thus the evaluation of the school output must not be confined to the direct effects of schooling on the productivity of the worker—the effects on the efficacy of vocational training and further schooling must also be considered. Here we have strong evidence that success in vocational training as well as in higher education is significantly related to the initial level of scholastic achievement.[15] It may be that the main economic importance of scholastic achievement in secondary school is not its direct contribution to production, but rather its effect in increasing the "trainability" of workers and consequently in reducing the costs of further human capital accumulation at the post-secondary school level.[16]

Scholastic achievement, of course, is not the only dimension of school output. Literally hundreds of tests have been devised to measure "achievement" alone, and this is only one aspect of the effect of schooling on cognitive skills and personality. In addition to economic performance in the post-school years, schooling may affect an individual's self-concept and his sense of control over his environment. These and other aspects of personality development may be valued per se, and additionally may be important determinants of post-school economic performance.

---

[15] Jensen [39], Ghiselli [24] and Astin [3].

[16] In the above discussion of these issues, I have drawn heavily on the unpublished work of Herbert Gintis.

TABLE 1

Zero-Order Correlations Among Measures of School Outputs,
Twelfth-Grade Boys, United States

	2	3	4	5	6
1. Information total	.23	.65	.76	.54	.19
2. Self-confidence		.17	.19	.09	.11
3. English total			.67	.46	.26
4. Mathematics total				.57	.20
5. Abstract reasoning					.19
6. Clerical checking					

NOTE: Based on a sample of 3,027.
SOURCE: J. C. Flanagan, *et al., Project Talent,* Pittsburgh (1962), Table 2–7j. (Description of test scores accompanies table.)

It is safe to say that there are fewer independent dimensions of school output than there are test instruments to measure them. But if we rely on the (unsatisfactory) evidence of zero-order correlations among individual test scores (see Table 1), we find that the relationship between some of these measures is rather weak.

Thus the output of schools is multidimensional with a vengeance, and to complicate matters, there are no convenient sets of "prices" with which to aggregate the output. Moreover, the technologies for the production of each dimension of the output are blatantly dissimilar. For example, my estimates of the reduced-form equation (2) in which the dependent variable is scholastic achievement, differ considerably from estimates in which the dependent variable is an index of the student's sense of control over his environment.[17] My preliminary results indicate that for twelfth-grade black students in the United States the verbal ability of teachers is the most important explanatory variable in the former equation, while the racial composition of the school and the experience of the teaching staff is more important in the latter.[18]

[17] The measurement of this variable is described in the appendix to this paper.
[18] In the latter equation teacher experience and the proportion of school enrollment which is black are positively related to a crude measure of the student's sense of control over his environment.

Apparently, then, schools are multiproduct firms; and the composition of output is highly sensitive to the particular combination of inputs used. The school production function must be represented by a number of equations, each relating the school inputs to a different dimension of output. The choice of an optimal input structure thus depends on the relative valuation of the different school outputs and on the rates of transformation among these outputs implicit in this system of production equations.

For the purposes of educational policy making, we are particularly interested in the structural parameters of production function (2), for under ideal conditions they may be interpreted as the marginal products of the inputs in question—that is, $MP_j = \partial A / \partial X_j = f_j$. If we know the social opportunity costs of inputs, p_j, we may use this information to move in the direction of optimal input proportions as defined by the conditions[19]

$$\frac{\partial A / \partial X_j}{\partial A / \partial X_k} = \frac{\hat{f}_j}{\hat{f}_k} = \frac{p_j}{p_k} \qquad \text{(for all pairs, } j, k\text{)} \tag{6}$$

However, difficulties arise when we seek to compare the marginal products of the same input for two different groups of students. We find, for example, that the estimate of the structural parameter relating to the verbal ability of teachers as an input into an achievement production function is considerably greater for black twelfth graders in the United States than for whites. Can we infer from this that verbally adroit teachers ought to be shifted from white to black districts? The answer is no.

The output measure is ordinal; there is no zero point and no well-defined unit of measurement for achievement.[20] Thus, while the marginal rate of substitution in production—represented in the additive linear form by the ratio of regression coefficients of any two input factors—is still a valid analytical concept, the absolute magnitude of the marginal product is not. Among students scoring at very different parts of the

---

[19] Of course, we are here accounting for only one output.

[20] At least one writer has constructed a cardinal index of achievement based on the size of vocabulary Bloom [5], pp. 103–04. Whether words known is linearly related to anything important is not known.

scale of measurement, equal units of increase in scores are not comparable; for example, it may be "easier" to make gains at the lower end of the scale than at the upper end due to a so-called "ceiling effect."[21] We really need to know the relationship between our output measure A and measurements of directly desired performance, such as earnings. The studies by Weiss, and Hansen, Scanlon and Weisbrod, mentioned earlier, suggest a linear relationship between their measurements of achievement (in one case achievement years, in the other the AFQT score).[22] Although this evidence is encouraging, it is certainly not sufficient to justify much confidence in a cardinal interpretation of academic measurement of school learning.

A further problem remains. Our output indexes are subject to some error—that is, test score = "true measure" + error, and, consequently, var(test score) = var(true measure) + var(error). We have no idea of the validity of the test—that is, its correlation with a hypothetical true measure. But some idea of the magnitude of the error may be gained from estimates of the reliability of the tests.[23] The reliability of our tests is in the neighborhood of .9. Taking this as an upper estimate of the validity, at least 19 per cent of the variance of the test scores is due to test errors. Assuming that the errors in test measurement are uncorrelated with our explanatory variables, even if our explanatory variables predict the true measure with perfect accuracy, a validity of .9 imposes an absolute maximum proportion of variance explained by our equations of .81. It will be seen below that the actual R^2's are considerably lower.

---

[21] "Most frequently, aptitude and achievement tests are constructed in such a way that it is harder to secure significant changes on one part of the scale than on another. This unevenness stems from the combined effect of a ceiling on the tests as well as the greater difficulty of the test items which can make the difference at the high end of the scale." *Ibid*.

Also, Chausow [11] indicates that among a relatively homogenous group of individuals, students who are initially high on a test characteristically make smaller gains than students who are initially low.

[22] For white males Weiss found that the linear relationship was superior to a logarithmic or polynomial one.

[23] Although there are various ways of measuring test reliability, we may convey the essential meaning as the zero order correlation between scores on the odd and even number questions of the same test or the zero order correlation between two versions of the test given to the same individual at roughly the same time.

4 THE VALUE-ADDED PROBLEM

AN ACHIEVEMENT SCORE must be considered a measure of *gross* output. Our goal is to estimate the relationship between school inputs and *net* output, or value added. For this we need a measure of the raw material inputs, i.e., student ability, or, alternatively, the level of learning upon entry to the school in question. (Without such a measure our efforts are like attempting to measure the effectiveness of a beauty parlor without knowing what the clientele looked like to begin with.)

The problem is that all measures of relevant student "ability" are hardly distinguishable from measures designed explicitly to test scholastic achievement.[24] According to a survey of the evidence by Bloom, simple correlation coefficients between intelligence and achievement scores (when both tests are administered at the same age) are ordinarily in the neighborhood of .85.[25]

There are a number of possible interpretations of this close association between measured achievement and intelligence. First, it may be that the tests simply measure the same thing. There is strong evidence that intelligence as measured by the usual instruments is a developmental concept, measuring general learning.[26] Moreover, most IQ tests depend heavily on verbal facility, which is probably a good reflection of general school learning.[27] A second explanation is that the tests measure different dimensions of competence, but that they both are sensitive to variations in the school environment. Evidence that abilities as measured by IQ tests are significantly influenced by the educational environment is available in the data from a study of identical twins separated prior to the age of three and reared apart (see Table 2). Results not reported there showed that over 60 per cent of the variance in the IQ differences between paired identical twins can be explained by differences in the educational environment; alone, the differences in the physical and social environments

---

[24] Duncanson [20] and Cohen [12].

[25] Kelley [44], pp. 193–213; Bloom [5], pp. 102–03; Coleman and Cureton [14]; Duncanson [20], and Cohen [12]. All of these studies use correlations corrected for test reliability. Jensen [39] reports lower correlations, although no references are given.

[26] See Hunt [35].

[27] Bloom [5], pp. 71 and 104.

TABLE 2

The Effect of Environmental Differences on IQ
Differences Among Paired Identical Twins Reared Apart

Environmental Difference	Effect[a]	*t* Statistic
Educational	.66	4.2
Social	.25	1.6
Physical	.19	1.3
R^2:	.70	
$\|X'X\|$:	18	
Number of observations:	18	

[a]Normalized regression coefficient of the environmental difference in an equation predicting I Q differences.

SOURCE: Data from F. N. Freeman; H. H. Newman; and K. J. Holzinger; *Twins: A Study of Heredity and Environment,* Chicago, 1937.

explain less than a third of the variance.[28] A third interpretation holds that there is little casual relationship between intelligence and achievement, but that for some reason the bright children go to good schools, receive especially sympathetic attention of school personnel within their schools, and consequently achieve well. Although evidence on this interpretation is fragmentary, data from the U.S. Office of Education's Equality of Educational Opportunity Survey suggests that skepticism is in order. The relationship at grade one between a measure of verbal ability and the two school inputs found to be most important in the determination of scholastic achievement is very weak. The zero order correlations between verbal ability and a measure of the teacher's verbal ability are .05 and .02 for blacks and whites, respectively; the correlation between student verbal ability and a proxy for the adequacy of the school's physi-

---

[28] The evaluation of the social, physical, and educational environments was a subjective assessment by a panel of judges who were not cognizant of each others' evaluations or of the twins' test scores. Although the judges were in close agreement, we have little knowledge of what they took into account in their evaluation. See Freeman, *et al.* [23].

cal plant was −.07 and −.02. Moreover, in an equation including measures of the parents' level of schooling and other social class dimensions no school input measures were significantly related to grade-one verbal ability among black students.[29] Finally, it is possible that achievement and intelligence tests measure distinct abilities but that intelligence is the primary influence on the acquisition of scholastic knowledge.

Of course, elements of each interpretation are consistent with parts of the others. What is important here is that, to the extent that either of the first two explanations is correct, it is illegitimate to include a measure of IQ in the production function as an independent variable, as the importance of the school input variables will thus be underestimated. Note, however, that if *both* the third and fourth interpretations are correct, the exclusion of the intelligence measure from our equations will bias upwards the estimated effect of school resources.

On balance, the evidence seems strong enough to reject the use of a contemporaneous IQ score as the measure of the student "raw material" input into the production process. What are the alternatives? As we are interested in measuring school learning, it would seem reasonable to use tests of learning administered at grade one as a measure of raw input. Because these first grade tests clearly measure the combined effects of genetic ability and environmental influences prior to age six, they are exactly what we need. Thus, our basic equation (1) becomes

$$A_{12} = f(X_1, \ldots, X_v, A_1) \tag{7}$$

where subscripts on the achievement variable refer to the grade at which the test is taken. In order to estimate a function of this type, we need individual test scores for students at two different levels of schooling. While some data of this type are currently available, and more is on the way, we are generally forced to rely on cross-sections.

If (7) is the correctly specified relation, and we are forced to work with data which do not include the first grade scores (A_1), we may be able to estimate the unbiased regression coefficients of (7) if we have independent evidence on $b_{1,12}$, the regression coefficient of A_1 in equation 7, as well as the estimated equations:

[29] The data are from volume II of Coleman [13].

$$A_{12} = f^{12}(X_1, \ldots, X_v) \tag{8}$$
$$A_1 = f^1(X_1, \ldots, X_v) \tag{9}$$

The unbiased estimates of the regression coefficients of (7).
are then

$$b^*{}_j = \hat{b}_j{}^{12} - b_{1,\,12}\hat{b}_i{}^1 \tag{10}$$

where $\hat{b}_j{}^{12}$, $\hat{b}_j{}^1$ are the estimated regression coefficients of X_j in equations
(8) and (9), respectively. This approach is equivalent to Theil's method
of estimating the bias due to specification error.[30]

I have assumed that the relationship between first grade and twelfth
grade scores is such that a student scoring one standard deviation above
the mean at grade one will, *ceteris paribus*, score .5 standard deviations
above the mean at grade twelve. Thus,

$$b_{1,\,12} = .5 \left(\frac{\sigma_{12}}{\sigma_1}\right) \tag{11}$$

where σ_1 and σ_{12} are the standard deviation of achievement scores at
grades one and twelve, respectively. This figure is somewhat arbitrary.
It is based on two sets of data. First, longitudinal studies of scholastic
achievement scores suggest a simple correlation between early and late
test scores in the neighborhood of .6 to .9. Most of the studies cover substantially less than twelve years, so we may suspect that the simple correlation of scores at grades one and twelve would be somewhat lower.[31]
Moreover, the simple correlation is not the appropriate evidence, as we
seek an estimate of the partial effects of differences in A_1 on A_{12}. To the
extent that students who initially score high on tests are exposed to a
better learning environment in either home or school, the size of the

---

[30] Theil [62]. Our method is based on the assumption that the function f accurately
represents the relationship between each X_j and first grade scores which prevailed at
the time of entry into school, and that the vector $V_1, \ldots, X_r$ is the same for a given
student at grades one and twelve.

[31] Based on forty-one longitudinal achievement score correlations reported in
Bloom [5], pp. 106–09. The correlations for more widely separated years occupy the
lower end of this range.

above-reported correlations exaggerates the normalized partial relationship between initial endowments and later scholastic achievement.[32]

A study by John Conlisk, using longitudinal data on students' intelligence scores, provides additional evidence.[33] Using a sample of seventy individuals in Berkeley, California, Conlisk estimated the following regression equations:

$$IQ_{18} = 4.77 + .490 \ IQ_{1-5} + 1.514 \ YrsSch \qquad R^2 = .45$$
$$\quad \quad (6.44) \ (.099) \qquad (.358)$$

$$IQ_{18} = 8.11 + .527 \ IQ_{6-8} + 1.051 \ YrsSch \qquad R^2 = .49$$
$$\quad \quad (5.74) \ (.093) \qquad (.367)$$

where IQ_{t-u} = score on IQ test administered between ages of t and u, and YrsSch = number of years of school attended.

The IQ measures are standardized indexes with identical means and standard deviations; the standard errors of the estimated regression coefficients are in parentheses. Although the correct equation for our purpose would predict scholastic achievement and would include measures of school inputs, the biases are likely to be small unless there is a strong association between the early IQ measure and the quantity of school resources.

We assume that the function f^1 (equation 9) will consist entirely of arguments relating to the social class and home background of the student, since school inputs could hardly affect scores on tests taken at the beginning of grade one.[34] For this reason, correction of this specification bias will involve reductions in the estimates of the coefficients of variables which measure the student's social class and home environment. Some difficulties in implementing this correction for specification bias will be discussed in the concluding section.

---

[32] All of the achievement measures are subject to error. At grade 1 the reliability of the achievement score used (verbal ability) is .78. If the validity of this score is only slightly below its reliability, the portion of variance in A_1 due to random error is .5. Thus our method is equivalent to assuming that the normalized partial relationship between the *true* measure of initial endowments and A_{12} is 1.

[33] Conlisk kindly allowed me to use his unpublished results.

[34] There is ample evidence that grade one achievement scores are associated with measures of student social class. See Bereiter [4] and Gray and Klaus [25].

5 THE INPUT STRUCTURE OF THE SCHOOL AND OTHER LEARNING ENVIRONMENTS

WE WANT to estimate the effect of school inputs on the value added of schools. In order to isolate this effect, however, we must specify, as fully as possible, all the environmental influences on learning—home, community, peer groups, and school. A complete specification of the model is particularly important in view of the specification bias likely to arise because of the close statistical association usually found between school and home environments that are highly conducive to learning.

We may derive some suggestion of the relative effects of various dimensions of environment on learning from another study of identical twins reared apart. In this case the differences in paired identical twins' scores on Stanford Achievement Tests are the measure of differential learning; the relationship between environment and learning based on this study of twins is illustrated in Table 3. Comparing the contents of Table 3 with Table 2, we see that the educational environment is of

TABLE 3

The Effect of Environmental Differences on Scholastic Achievement Differences Among Paired Identical Twins Reared Apart

Environmental Difference	Effect[a]	*t* Statistic
Educational	.899	7.69
Social	.024	0.21
Physical	.001	0.01
R^2:	.82	
$\lvert X' X \rvert$:	.86	
Number of observations:	19	

[a]Normalized regression coefficient of the environmental difference measure in an equation predicting achievement differences among paired identical twins.

SOURCE: Based on data of Freeman, Newman, and Holzinger (see Table 2).

considerably greater importance in the explanation of achievement differences than of IQ differences. Educational environment alone explains more than 80 per cent of the difference in scholastic achievement between paired identical twins. While this is hardly surprising, the insignificance of the social and physical environment among genetically equivalent individuals is striking.[35] Of course, this may well be due to the imperfect measures of the environments in question, but it alerts us again to the dangers of specification bias in equations which do not include some measurement of initial endowment and suggests that much of the importance of social class to school learning apparent from cross-section studies may reflect genetic differences associated with the educational and social characteristics of the student's family.

Let us begin by asking which aspects of the student's environment could have some effect on learning. A brief survey of the literature on learning suggests that the major environmental influences on school achievement (in addition to general intelligence) include:

    a. The quantity of verbal interaction with adults[36]

    b. The quality of verbal interaction with adults[37]

    c. The motivation for achievement and understanding in the environment[38]

    d. The richness of the physical environment.[39]

The available measures of these dimensions of the environment are far from adequate. However, data exist which allow us to attempt an empirical implementation based on the above a priori specifications. Moreover, a number of relations in sociological and psychological research will assist us in implementing the model.[40]

---

[35] Alone they explain only .13 of the variance of achievement differences.

[36] Anastasi [1].

[37] For example, see Olim, Hess, and Shipman [55], and Jackson, Hess, and Shipman [37].

[38] See Dave [16].

[39] Particularly for very poor children, the level of family income may have a strong causal relation to the development of intelligence and scholastic achievement. See, for example, Harrell, *et al.* [31].

[40] There are some grounds for believing that the student's peers exercise an effect on learning. I have not included this discussion of the learning environment as I have been unable to find adequate measures of the peer group environment in the data which I am currently using.

Let us begin with the nonschool environment. We may use a measure of parental education to represent the quality of the verbal interaction between child and adult;[41] and family size (as well as the number of adults living at home) provides a rough measure of the quantity of interaction and communication.[42] If we restrict ourselves to variables which can be regarded as largely exogenous, the motivation for achievement may be measured in terms of parental attitudes toward schooling[43] as well as in terms of the potential objective importance of education to the student. Race, for example, may constitute a logical measure of expected returns: we have compelling evidence that the economic returns to schooling, at the elementary and secondary levels, are significantly less for black than for white children.[44] The physical environment of the home may be measured by the quantity of reading material in the home, the parents' occupation or income, or proxies for these variables, such as quantity of consumer durables, etc. Evidence of a relationship between malnutrition (primarily protein deficiency) and learning difficulties suggests that some measurement of the physical environment may substitute for a measure of the physical development of the child as related to learning, particularly for very poor children.

A number of authors have attempted to account for the familial and social environment by stratifying their analyses according to social class.[45] Available evidence suggests that while this technique is certainly useful in reducing the multicollinearity among the explanatory variables, it is a thoroughly inadequate representation of nonschool effects on learning. Peterson and DeBord [57], for example, found that *within* two refined

[41] On the importance of language models, see Olim, Hess, and Shipman [37], and Jackson, Hess, and Shipman [55].

[42] Anastasi [1].

[43] Although we are not able to include this variable in our analysis below, as we have no adequate measures in our sample, at least one study which sampled the parents as well as the children, has confirmed the importance of parental attitudes. See Peaker [56]. Of course, parental attitudes toward schooling must depend in some degree on the particular school in which the child is enrolled. Thus parental attitudes are not unambiguously exogenous.

[44] See Michaelson [53], Weiss [68], Hanoch [28]; some of the data are summarized in Bowles [6]. Differences in family interest in schooling and its associated impact on children's motivation is, in part, a cultural phenomenon, likely to vary among ethnic groups. For convincing evidence in one case, see Gross [27].

[45] For example, Kiesling [46] and the U.S. Commission on Civil Rights [63], in their study of the effect of racial integration on scholastic achievement.

TABLE 4

*A Model for the Estimation of the Environmental
Influences on Learning*

Underlying Influence on Learning	Empirical Representation in the Model	
	Home	School
1. Quality of verbal interaction with adults	a. education of parents	a. educational level of teachers b. other measures of teacher "quality", such as verbal-ability c. school policies d. teacher attitudes
2. Quantity of verbal interaction with adults	a. family size b. one or both parents absent	a. class size
3. Motivation for achievement in school	a. parental attitudes toward education b. race, ethnic group c. objective returns to schooling	a. community support of education
4. Richness of the physical environment	a. family income or occupation, consumer durables in the home b. reading material in the home	a. school facilities, labs, libraries, texts, etc.

substrata (white and black lower-class urban children in the South), variables measuring home environment and parent-child interaction explained .56 (white) and .66 (black) per cent of the variance in achievement scores.[46] The predictive power of dimensions of home environment *within* narrowly defined social strata suggests that an analysis using no other control for social environment will be subject to serious specification bias.[47]

We may proceed in roughly the same manner (although with less confidence) with the empirical measurement of the school environment. The quality of interaction between child and adult may be represented by a measure of the educational level or verbal proficiency of the teachers. The quality of the interaction may depend somewhat on school policy, which may be represented by a host of imperfect measures of such aspects of school environment as breadth of curriculum, amount of extracurricular activities, etc. (Although there is some evidence—e.g., Chausow [11]—that methods of teaching make a difference, the available data do not allow even a rough measure of this variable.[48]) The physical environment of the school may be represented by measures of special facilities—labs and libraries—as well as overcrowding, makeshift classrooms, and so on.

Table 4 summarizes our model of the environmental influences on learning.

Notice that even this partial specification of the learning environment includes fourteen measures, many of which are highly correlated. Thus serious multicollinearity problems arise. In the estimation of a full model of the type specified for twelfth-grade black students in the United States, the determinant of the $X'X$ matrix, which is probably the best

---

[46] Of course, the Peterson and DeBord findings could result from collinearity between the home environment and school inputs to which the children were exposed. This probably will not explain the entire result, however. Within a group of black sixth-grade students in the third socio-economic quartile, Levin found that in addition to various school input measures a number of home measures were significantly related to scholastic achievement.

[47] The strength of the measured relationship between school inputs and achievement observed by Kiesling may be due in part to this bias.

[48] For an exception, see Peaker [56], who found in many cases that an assessment of the teacher's proficiency by an inspector was significantly related to scholastic achievement.

single measure of the presence of multicollinearity, fell to .0005.[49] Similar problems arise for whites and for other grades. In order to estimate the above model, we need to reduce the number of variables so as to simplify the presentation and bring the multicollinearity problem within tolerable limits. That is, we would like to replace the equation

$$A = f(X_1, \ldots, X_v) \tag{12}$$

with

$$A = F[g_1(X_1, \ldots, X_v), g_2(X_1, \ldots, X_v), \ldots, g_h(X_1, \ldots, X_v)] \tag{13}$$

where $h < v$.

Thus we may wish to define a new variable, e.g., "teacher quality," as an aggregate of individual variables measuring verbal ability, years of schooling, experience, certification, and so on. If a significant degree of multicollinearity arises from intercorrelations *within* each set of variables forming an aggregate variable, the problem will be reduced; the new aggregate variables, represented by $g_1, \ldots, g_h$, may be sufficiently orthogonal to allow successful estimation of the relationship. The choice of a precise grouping of factors is determined by more than the desire to reduce multicollinearity; however, the usual aggregation rules do not seem particularly helpful here, as we have no knowledge of the matrix of second derivatives and cross-derivatives which would allow us to make use of them.

We have no previous results or compelling theory to use as a guide as to how to aggregate. In situations where all inputs are priced in the market, and where the assumption of maximizing behavior is somewhat more plausible, we ordinarily use factor or commodity prices as the basis of aggregation, as in the measurement of "capital" or intermediate inputs. Failure to appreciate the importance of these assumptions in the validity of any monetary aggregate in production theory has led to the frequent use of what might be called spurious factors of production, such as expenditure per pupil and teachers' salaries. In my own empirical work

---

[49] See Farrar and Glauber [21]. X is the matrix of normalized observations. The determinant of the $X'X$ matrix varies between 1, indicating complete orthogonality of the variables, and 0, indicating linear dependence of at least two vectors of observations. See also Bowles and Levin [7].

(for black twelfth graders), whereas teachers' salaries explain only .0085 of the variance in achievement, the two variables most closely related to variations in teachers' salaries—teachers' verbal ability and years of schooling—explain over four times as much.[50]

Similarly, Kiesling [46] found a "disappointingly weak" relationship between expenditure per pupil and achievement; in a later paper [45] he found that variables which together explain most of the variance in expenditure per pupil are very strongly related to achievement. All of this simply suggests that school administrators are not using their resources efficiently as far as the production of scholastic achievement is concerned. The relative market prices used to aggregate inputs in the expenditure measure are apparently significantly different from the marginal products of the inputs.[51] Thus the use of monetary aggregates is unfounded in theory.

In our situation the best method seems to be to attempt to identify the underlying dimensions of the input structure by both a priori and empirical methods. This done, we would select a variable, or an index based on a number of variables, to represent each dimension. Our a priori specification of the school environment suggests that we have four important dimensions of the school environment: teacher quality, teacher quantity, school policy, and physical facilities. One procedure would be to assume that these represent the dimensions of the input structure and to select from each set a variable to represent the underlying input. Thus we could represent teacher quality by the teacher's score on a verbal ability test (at least when we are predicting verbal achievement), and so on.

Alternatively, we may combine our preconceptions based on previ-

[50] In each case I am referring to the increase in the coefficient of determination in an equation already including measures of social background and nonteacher school inputs, as in equation 8. See Levin [48] for an analysis of the relation between teacher quality and teacher salary. These two teacher attributes (verbal ability and years of schooling) explain 60 per cent of the variance in teachers' salaries in the sample reported in the next section.

[51] This inference is supported by a comparison of the estimated marginal products f_j and the supply prices for various teacher attributes. (See Levin [48].) Calculations of the cost of unit increase in achievement through increases in each factor based on these estimates show that for the sample under consideration increases in teacher's verbal ability are more efficient than any other dimension of teacher quality, by a wide margin.

ous research and learning theory with an empirical analysis of the structure of our data, using principal components analysis.[52]

Leaving the problem of aggregation in this unsatisfactory state, let me ask how well we have measured the environmental influences on learning, particularly as they relate to the school. The answer "not very well" stems primarily from three problems: (a) the home and school variables fail to capture the complexity and richness of the interaction processes relevant to learning; (b) we have ignored significant qualitative differences in education available *within* a school; and (c) we have measured inputs at only one point in time, while the learning process must certainly be cumulative and therefore dependent on past inputs.

Turning to the first problem, our measures of social class, family size, class size, teacher quality, and school facilities do not measure the quantity and quality of interaction as relevant to learning. Our input measures are merely circumstantial evidence of a few of the opportunities for such interaction. Two recent studies suggest that these crude measures are a poor substitute for measures of actual patterns of interaction. On the basis of detailed interviews with sixty parents, Dave [16] and Wolf [70] found that their measurement of home environment explained .57 and .64 of the variance in intelligence and achievement, respectively.[53] The crude home environment measures used in our study explain only 10 per cent of the variance in individual achievement scores. Presumably, analogous detailed studies of actual classroom interaction would reveal that our school measures are an equally poor representation of our basic learning model.

The second problem arises particularly where tracking is widespread and the differences in the educational opportunities within a single institution are so great that we really have two or three schools in one.[54] Also, differences in teacher and administrator attitudes and expectations may differ considerably within a school and even within a classroom.[55]

---

[52] This is the method used by Kiesling.

[53] Recall, also, the Peterson and DeBord (1963) study, *op. cit.*

[54] Differences in the quality and quantity of school inputs received within the same school are documented in Hollingshead [34].

[55] See Davis and Dollard [17], pp. 284–85, and Warner, Havinghurst and Loeb [65], as well as more recent studies by Deutsch [18] and Wilson [69].

One recent study (Rosenthal and Jacobson [58]) suggests that teacher expectations have a significant effect on learning, at least in the early years of school. Failure to measure these in-school and in-class differences in inputs results in a specification error which is particularly serious because of the correlation of these differences with other of our explanatory variables. Because low social class and minority racial or ethnic status are closely associated with intraschool deprivation of school inputs,[56] the estimates of the parameters reflecting the impact of social class and race are biased upward. Further, because of the serious errors introduced by the school-wide aggregation of the variables measuring school inputs, the estimated effect of the school environment is biased downward.[57]

Our third objection, against the sole use of contemporary input measures, would not be serious if children did not move from school to school and inputs were roughly uniform throughout all of the grades up to the one for which the production function is being estimated. Of course, the world is simply not like that, and I think we sometimes underestimate the seriousness of this problem. In a sample of black sixth-grade students in a Northeastern metropolis, 57 per cent had attended more than one school since grade one, and 29 per cent had attended more than two.[58] Evidence from a number of studies of the phasing of learning development over the school years suggests that this problem is particularly serious, as patterns of achievement are apparently established with a high degree of stability in the early grades. Scannell [59], for example, found that scores on fourth-grade tests (Iowa Tests of Basic Skills) explained half the variance in test scores (Iowa Tests of Educational Development) in the twelfth grade.[59] Cardinal measures of scholastic achievement based on vocabulary tests suggest that about two-thirds

---

[56] See the evidence in Hollingshead [34] and the more recent studies cited in Rosenthal and Jacobson [58].

[57] In a study in which within-school variations were measured, Peaker [56] found that school inputs were considerably more important in the determination of school achievement (relative to other influences such as home background) when within-school variations in these inputs were taken into account.

[58] Work in progress by Henry Levin and Stephen Michelson.

[59] Scannell [59]; Bloom [5] summarizes the evidence on the stability of achievement.

of what is known in grade twelve was already known in grade six. On the presumption (which seems to have currency among educational psychologists) that the effects of environment on learning are potentially greater during periods in which the most learning takes place, it would seem that measurement of the inputs in the early grades would be essential to the prediction of achievement at the higher levels.[60]

The importance of the early years in the learning process suggests one last question: how much impact can we expect schools to have on learning?

The mental ability commonly called intelligence is probably the single most important determinant of scholastic achievement. Studies of the degree of hereditability of the characteristics measured by scholastic achievement tests are, to some extent, contradictory—the very wide range of estimates does not allow any simple summary of the results.[61] Nonetheless, it is safe to conclude that a sizable portion of the variance in scholastic achievement is associated with genetic differences. Thus, even in an otherwise perfectly specified and perfectly measured model, unless we are able to take account of genetic differences, we are likely to be unable to account for all of the variance of scholastic achievement. Of course, if the genetic component in intelligence is related to social class (through inheritance), our social background measures in the learning model will take account of some of the genetic differences in mental abilities among our students. Thus, the residuals in the estimation of the education production function cannot be unambiguously identified as the influence of student ability differences.[62]

Given the importance of genetic influences on scholastic achievement the possible impact of schools on achievement is severely limited. But

---

[60] In the absence of a time series of school inputs, it might be advisable to concentrate on the estimation of production relations in the early grades.

[61] See Jensen [39], Burt [10], Vandenberg [64], and Jensen [38].

[62] There is evidence of a significant genetic component in the observed social class differences in measured intelligence. For example, the IQ's of children adopted in early infancy show a much lower correlation with the social class status of their adopting parents than do the IQ's of children reared by their own parents; the IQ's of children reared in an orphanage from infancy and who have not known their parents show only slightly lower correlations with their true father's occupational status than that found for children reared by their own parents. See Jensen [40], pp. 1–2 and references.

this reasoning still overstates the importance of schooling, as the classroom is only a small part of the learning environment of the child. During the elementary and high-school years, children ordinarily spend considerably less than one-fourth of their waking hours in school. In addition, Bloom [5] suggests, about one-third of adult learning is achieved before age six.

Jensen [39] suggests that the impact of well-designed and well-executed "enrichment" and "cognitive stimulation" programs is ordinarily between 0.5 and 2.0 standard deviations on specific achievement tests. These rough estimates place broad limits on the expected maximum effect of either a very good or a very bad school as opposed to an average one. Of course, our estimations are based on a cross-section of representative schools, not well-endowed experimental programs designed to raise scholastic achievement. This fact plus the severe deficiencies in the measurement of the learning environment suggest that the impact of extreme school environments estimated from our production functions are likely to fall short of Jensen's estimates.

6 AN EDUCATIONAL PRODUCTION FUNCTION

THE FOLLOWING results are presented here to illustrate the discussion in the previous section of educational production functions. Their empirical substance must be treated with extreme caution.

The estimates are for black students enrolled in the twelfth grade in the fall of 1965. The data were collected by the U. S. Office of Education as part of the Equal Educational Opportunity Survey. Some of the results of this survey have been reported in *Equality of Educational Opportunity,* known popularly as the Coleman Report, after its principal author.[63] The sample and a number of serious shortcomings of the data are described in detail elsewhere.[64] Any reader adventuresome

---

[63] Coleman, *et al.* [13]. Our estimations are based on the correlation tables and mean and standard deviation of each variable, as reported in Vol. II of *Equality of Educational Opportunity*.

[64] In addition to the report itself, see also Bowles and Levin [7], Hanushek [30], and Hanushek and Kain [42].

enough to take seriously my preliminary results is urged to consult these sources.

The variables used in the empirical implementation of the model, along with their means and standard deviations, and a table of zero order correlations appear in the appendix. A listing of all other variables which were used in the experimental stage also appears there. A total of thirty-six variables were tested for significance in the educational production function. The equations presented below include all of the variables which

TABLE 5

An Educational Production Function (Reduced Form),
Black Twelfth-Grade Students

Independent Variable[a]	Regression Coefficient (*t* in parentheses)	Beta
1. Reading material in the home	1.9284 (2.5847)	0.0822
2. Number of siblings (positive = few)	1.8512 (4.3411)	0.1316
3. Parents' educational level	2.4653 (4.4660)	0.1431
4. Family stability	0.8264 (1.6938)	0.0494
5. Teacher's verbal-ability score	1.2547 (7.1970)	0.2222
6. Science lab facilities	0.0505 (2.5821)	0.0784

Constant:	19.4576 (5.1887)
R^2 :	0.1708
$|X' X|$:	0.6628
Number of observations:	1,000

[a]Dependent variable is verbal achievement.

made sense on the basis of the learning model, and which proved to be significantly related to achievement.

The estimate of our basic equation of the educational production function (8) appears in Table 5. Note that the estimated parameters are consistent with our suggested model of learning. With one exception, all of the estimates, including those for the school environment, are significantly different from zero at the 99 per cent level.[65] The quality and quantity of interaction with adults, as well as motivation for schooling and the richness of the home environment, are all represented (at least symbolically) in the four nonschool environment variables.

Note also that the estimated parameters of the school inputs are consistent with the suggested model of learning. The very significant estimate of the influence of teacher quality (represented by the teacher's verbal ability score) is not surprising, since the teacher is the single most important school input.[66] The importance of teacher quality, which our estimate demonstrates, has also been confirmed by other work on educational production functions.[67] The failure of the class-size variable to appear in the equation may reflect severe errors in the measurement of this variable.[68] Although a number of studies have suggested that class size is not a significant influence on achievement (e.g., Hanushek [30] and Levin [work in progress]), Kiesling did find a highly significant rela-

[65] The family-stability variable is significant only at the 90 per cent level. The regression coefficients of the reduced-form equation, excluding attitudes, is virtually unaffected by the removal of the absent father variable.

I have fewer schools than individuals, and because of the strong possibility of there being unmeasured school effects, the variance-covariance matrix of the error term is not diagonal: the off-diagonal elements reflect the covariance of the residuals among students in the same school. As a result I have probably underestimated the standard errors of the estimates of the regression coefficients. Without school identifications for each observation, I am unable to estimate the extent of this bias.

[66] The teacher's verbal ability test consists of only 30 questions and is self-administered. If, as seems likely, the variance of the error component in this measure is larger than the variance of the error component in the dependent variable, the estimate of the associated regression coefficient may be biased seriously downward. The same reasoning, of course, applies to the other inputs.

[67] See Kiesling [45]; Hanushek [30]. In addition to these results, Levin found that two measures of teacher quality (verbal score and type of college attended) were highly significant in explaining verbal achievement among sixth-grade black students of the third socio-economic quartile in a large Northeastern metropolitan area.

[68] See Bowles and Levin [7].

TABLE 6

Educational Production Function (Reduced Form), with School Policy and Community Support Proxies, Black Male Twelfth-Grade Students

Independent Variable[a]	Regression Coefficient (t in parentheses)	Beta
1. Reading material in the home	1.6579 (2.2193)	0.0707
2. Number of siblings (positive = few)	1.7583 (4.1322)	0.1250
3. Parents' educational level	2.4519 (4.4575)	0.1423
4. Family stability	0.8339 (1.7174)	0.0499
5. Teacher's verbal-ability score	1.0419 (5.5605)	0.1845
6. Science lab facilities	0.0373 (1.8824)	0.0580
7. Average time spent in guidance	1.4803 (2.3652)	0.0804
8. Days in session	0.2032 (1.9213)	0.0582

Constant: −14.2214 (−0.7529)

R^2 :   0.1804

$|X'X|$:   0.4477

Number of observations: 1,000

[a]Dependent variable is verbal achievement.

tionship between students-per-teacher and achievement.[69] It is somewhat more surprising that the very crude representation of the physical facilities of the school—science laboratories—appears to be significantly related to achievement.

Note that the explained variance is very small. This is to be expected, given the crudeness of our measures, and it points to our failure to specify adequately a model of school achievement. In addition to the poor measurement of our variables we have certainly omitted altogether some important influences on learning.

The absence of a measure of school policy, which would help to indicate the quality of student-teacher interaction, is explained by the profusion of imperfect measurements of this input dimension. When we entered eleven school policy and environment variables (see Table A.1) into the above equation, we could not accept the hypothesis that the entire set of regression coefficients for these variables were zero.[70] In order to represent the influence of school policy variables, we have introduced a proxy variable, representing the extent of guidance counseling in the school. We have further added a days-in-session variable to represent the general level of community interest in and support of education. The resulting equation appears in Table 6.

Both of these proxy variables are highly correlated with measures indicating over-all support for education—e.g., teachers' salaries and system-wide expenditure per pupil. In addition, both are positively asso-

[69] My preliminary results with a different sample of black twelfth-grade students in the Northeast and Central United States reveal a significant negative relationship between class size and achievement. The positive relationship between class size and a measure of school output found by Welch [66] is almost certainly a reflection of the smaller classes in rural schools and the failure to take account of the negative influences on learning associated with a rural home and community environment. The negative association between student-teacher ratio and tenth-grade verbal scores in twenty-two Atlanta public schools estimated by J. W. Holland and J. Burkhead [9] is difficult to interpret, as the equation in which this finding is reported includes a measure of per pupil expenditure (plus a number of insignificant variables). This seems to suggest that even with a given level of expenditure, reduction in class size produces sufficiently strong effects on achievement to more than offset the associated opportunity costs.

[70] The F value leading to the rejection of the hypothesis was 2.39 with 11 and 984 degrees of freedom. Thus the hypothesis was rejected at the 99 per cent level of significance.

ciated with such school policy variables as extracurricular activities and foreign language courses (though days in session is less closely associated than is guidance counseling.)[71]

Regressions similar to that reported in Table 6 were estimated separately for different samples of 1,000 students each in the North and in the South. The estimated equations (which are presented in an appendix) are remarkably similar to those estimated for the national sample.[72]

Thus far we have been working with a model which takes no explicit account of students' endowments at the beginning of school. The resulting biases in our estimates are suggested by the following exercise, based on equations (9), (10), and (11). We have attempted to explain a similar achievement score in grade one using our set of explanatory variables. The resulting equation and the calculation of the specification bias appear in Table 7. At the first-grade level, coefficients of the school input variables were never significantly different from zero (at conventional levels).

Given the crudeness of both the measurements and the technique, the particular numerical estimates are subject to considerable error. The effect of correcting for this specification bias is to reduce the apparent influence of social class on school learning. Of course, as long as we use an additive linear model with no interaction effects and plausibly find no relationship between school inputs and initial scores, there can be no estimated bias of the school inputs.

It is likely that some of the remaining influence of social class and home background is a reflection of genetic differences. This is certainly a plausible interpretation of the results, given the apparent unimportance

---

[71] Of course, the days-in-session measure may simply reflect urban-rural differences, as there is evidence that rural schools are open for fewer days per year. (See Coleman [13].) As a test of this hypothesis, we added a variable measuring the size of the senior class to the equation. This new variable was insignificant, and, although its introduction lowered the estimated regression coefficient for days in session by about 10 per cent, the latter variable was still significantly different from zero at the 95 per cent significance level. The remainder of the equation was altered only slightly. The importance of guidance counseling is equally difficult to interpret, as an abundance of counselors may be associated with a large fraction of college-bound students in the school, or severe discipline problems, or both.

[72] In both North and South, only one school policy-community support variable is significant: days in session in the North and average time spent in guidance in the South. The very large difference in the constant term in the two equations is due to the absence of the days-in-session variable in the southern equation.

of class and home environment on scholastic achievement among pairs of genetically equivalent identical twins. (See Table 3.)

Although in Table 7 the corrected regression coefficients of all background variables are positive, in general the predicted effect of social class and family environment on the difference in scores at grade one and grade twelve is ambiguous. This is because the grade-one scores in

TABLE 7

Correction For Specification Bias Due to Omitted Initial Endowments in the Educational Production Function, Black Twelfth-Grade Students

Independent Variable (dependent variable is verbal achievement)	Regression Coefficients		Corrected Regression Coefficients[c] (3)
	At Grade Twelve[a] (1)	At Grade One[b] (2)	
Reading material in the home	1.657	.348 (1.97)	1.029
Number of siblings (positive = few)	1.758	—	1.758
Parents' educational level	2.451	.884 (5.85)	.856
Family stability	.833	—	.833
Teacher's verbal ability score	1.041	—	1.041
Science lab facilities	.037	—	.037
Average time spent in guidance	1.480	—	1.480
Days in session	.203	—	.203

[a]From Table 6.

[b]t ratios are in parentheses; the coefficient of determination for the equation was .05.

[c]Column 3 = Column 1 – Column 2 × $b_{1,12}$, where $b_{1,12}$, the regression coefficient of A_1 in equation 7, is assumed to be

$$.5\left(\frac{\sigma_{12}}{\sigma_1}\right), \text{ or } 1.806.$$

equation (7) measure the initial level of learning and not the student's capacity to learn. There is evidence that among below-average achieving children with similar IQ scores in the elementary school grades, learning capacity on some tasks varies widely, and *inversely* with social class. That is, lower-class students with an IQ of 90 learn faster than upper-class students with equivalent IQ scores on tasks which do not depend on previous learning.[73] Thus it would not be anomalous to find a negative relationship in equation (7) between twelfth-grade scores and social background, at least for some background variables.

The main difficulty with the above method arises because of the social selectivity of the dropout phenomenon. The students tested in the fall of the twelfth grade are not the full complement of those who began in grade one. The fact that low achieving, low-social-class children are much more likely to drop out than other children, clearly biases downward the estimated coefficients of the social class variables in equation (8).[74]

Turning now to a second problem of specification bias, recall that equation (2) represented our reduced form. Yet a complete specification of the learning environment must include student attitudes. As mentioned earlier, these attitudes are represented in two ways: student self-concept and student sense of control over environment.[75] Measurements of these are added to the equation and the resulting estimates are presented in Table 8.

In the new equation, the structural parameters of school inputs change very little, which suggests that in this case the simultaneous-equation bias is relatively small. The attitude variables are powerfully related to achievement—the proportion of variance explained is almost doubled by their inclusion.

---

[73] Jensen [41]. Of course, much of school learning does depend on prior learning, but a major portion of it probably is not strictly cumulative once the rudimentary communications skills have been learned.

[74] The seriousness of this bias is difficult to determine, although experiments using a similar equation for grade-nine students (who have not had the opportunity to drop out) may suggest the order of magnitude of the bias. Of the four regression coefficients for the relevant social-background variables in an equation predicting ninth-grade achievement (rescaled to take account of the different units of measurement of the achievement variable), two are similar to those in the twelfth-grade equation and two are about 50 per cent larger than the downward biased estimates at grade twelve.

[75] The measurement of these variables is described in the appendix.

7   CONCLUSION: THE EFFECTS OF SCHOOLING

IMPERFECT measurement, limited exposure to the educational environment, and our fundamental ignorance of how children learn establish the presumption that estimated effects of different schools upon scholastic

TABLE 8

*Educational Production Function with Student Attitudes Measured,
Black Male Twelfth-Grade Students*

Independent Variable (dependent variable is verbal achievement)	Regression Coefficient (t in parentheses)	Beta
1. Reading material in the home	0.4982 (0.7169)	0.0212
2. Number of siblings (positive = few)	1.5287 (3.8885)	0.1087
3. Parents' educational level	1.8746 (3.6768)	0.1088
4. Family stability	0.3818 (0.8489)	0.0228
5. Science lab facilities	0.0355 (1.9383)	0.0552
6. Days in session	0.1814 (1.8571)	0.0519
7. Teacher's verbal-ability score	1.1100 (6.4133)	0.1966
8. Average time spent in guidance	1.7747 (3.0644)	0.0964
9. Student's control of environment	4.4059 (8.2159)	0.2334
10. Student's self-concept	4.2721 (7.4439)	0.2108

Constant:	−12.1269 (−0.6949)	
R^2 :	0.3036	
$|X'X|$:	0.3764	
Number of observations:	1,000	

TABLE A.1

Full List of Variables Used

Dependent variable:
    Verbal score

Nonschool environment:
    Consumer durables in the home
    Family stability
    Foreign language at home
    Number of siblings
    Parents' educational level
    Preschool attendance
    Reading material in the home
    Student urbanism of background

General school environment:
    Accelerated curriculum
    Amount of homework
    Average time spent in guidance
    Comprensiveness of curriculum
    Days in session
    Extracurricular activities
    Freedom of movement between tracks
    Length of academic day
    Number of foreign language courses
    Number of mathematics courses
    Number of twelfth-grade students in school
    Promotion of slow learners
    Proportion of students transferring in and out
    Teacher turnover
    Tracking

Teacher quality:
    Degree received (teacher)
    Experience (teacher)
    Localism (teacher)
    Number of absences (teacher)
    Quality of college attended by teacher
    Salary (teacher)
    Teacher's socio-economic status
    Teacher's verbal-ability score

Teacher quantity:
    Total pupils in school / total teachers in school

(continued)

Table A.1 (concluded)

School facilities:
  Science laboratory facilities
  Volumes per student in the school library
Student attitudes:
  Student self-concept
  Student sense of control of environment

achievement will be quite limited. Our equation (Table 6) suggests that, for the individuals represented by our sample, a uniform improvement of 10 per cent in *all* school inputs (in the neighborhood of the mean) would raise achievement by 5.7 per cent. (This cannot be construed as the effect of a uniform improvement in the school environment, as we have not measured some of the important school inputs.) Put somewhat differently, the difference in achievement between students in schools with inputs one standard deviation below the mean for our sample, compared with students in schools one standard deviation above the mean, is slightly over two-thirds of a standard deviation on our achievement scale.[76]

Given the limited nature of the sample and the inadequate opportunity to explore the available data, I will refrain from generalizing from these initial encouraging results. We are still a long way from estimating a satisfactory educational production function. However, we have successfully identified a number of school inputs which do seem to affect learning. Further studies of the educational production function may contribute to making schools more nearly equal for those now deprived of a constructive learning environment, and more effective for all children.

[76] This is roughly equivalent to two years of scholastic progress, using the performance of white urban Northeastern children as the norm. For the purposes of these calculations, the variable "length of school year" is considered a community variable, not a school input.

TABLE A.2
Means, Standard Deviations and Zero-Order Correlations Among Variables Used in Estimates

Variable[a]	Mean	Standard Deviation
Dependent variable		
Verbal achievement scale score[b]	49.2202	14.4512
Home environment [c]		
Reading material in the home	-0.1091	0.6159
Number of siblings (positive = few)	-0.3334	1.0275
Family stability	-0.1691	0.8645
Parents' educational level	-0.1672	0.8389
School environment		
Teacher's verbal-ability score	21.2211	2.5593
Science lab facilities (index)[d]	89.4083	22.4557
Average time spent in guidance	1.8528	0.7847
Number of days in session	179.8984	4.1359
Size of the senior class	264.3718	212.7663
Student attitudes		
Sense of control of environment[e]	-0.1265	0.7654
Self concept[f]	0.0460	0.7132

[a]Further definition of these variables, as well as the survey instruments on which they were based, is available in J. S. Coleman *et al., Equality of Educational Opportunity* [13], Vol. II.

[b]The verbal-ability score is based on the School and College Ability test scores of the Educational Testing Service.

[c]The home environment and student attitude variables have been normalized to mean = 0 and standard deviation = 1 for the national sample taken as a whole.

[d]Range = 0-99. A score of 33, 66, or 99 indicates that the school has one, two, or all of the following types of laboratories: biology, chemistry, and physics.

[e]The sense of control variable is based on the student agreement or disagreement with three statements: "Good luck is more important than hard work for success; Every time I try to get ahead, something or somebody stops me;" and "People like me don't have much of a chance to be successful in life."

[f]The self-concept variable is based on the student's responses to the following items: (1)"How bright do you think you are in comparison with the other students in your grade?" (2)"Sometimes I feel that I just can't learn" (agree – disagree); (3) "I would do better in school work if teachers didn't go so fast" (agree – disagree).

TABLE A.3

Zero Order Correlations Among Variables

Variables	1	2	3	4	5	6	7	8	9	10	11	12
1. Verbal achievement scale score	1.000	.220	.225	.044	.261	.308	.188	.254	.153	.262	.350	.282
2. Reading material in the home		1.000	.178	.107	.363	.204	.152	.218	.106	.216	.161	.117
3. Number of siblings			1.000	-.049	.263	.152	.122	.134	.108	.173	.089	.042
4. Family stability				1.000	-.020	-.019	.001	-.010	.009	-.018	.094	.044
5. Parents' educational level					1.000	.198	.136	.174	.050	.205	.112	.115
6. Teacher's verbal-ability score						1.000	.280	.453	.179	.506	.054	-.053
7. Science lab facilities							1.000	.295	.170	.263	.078	-.039
8. Average time spent in guidance								1.000	.287	.522	.063	-.071
9. Number of days in session									1.000	.304	.058	-.026
10. Size of the senior class										1.000	.070	-.065
11. Sense of control of environment											1.000	-.309
12. Self-concept												1.000

APPENDIX

The final specifications of the educational production functions were based on analysis of data on a much larger number of variables. These are listed in Table A.1. The means and standard deviations of the variables appearing in the final specifications appear in Table A.2., and the zero order correlations among these variables appear in Table A.3. All

TABLE A.4

Estimated Production Function for Samples of Northern U.S. Twelfth-Grade Students

Independent Variable[a]	Regression Coefficient (*t* in parentheses)	Beta
1. Reading material in the home	1.279 (1.601)	.052
2. Number of siblings (positive = few)	1.660 (3.700)	.116
3. Parents' educational level	2.655 (4.626)	.151
4. Family stability	.899 (1.675)	.051
5. Teacher's verbal-ability score	.721 (3.193)	.097
6. Science lab facilities	.059 (2.137)	.067
7. Days in session	.189 (1.971)	.062

Constant:	−2.585 (−0.1462)
R^2 :	.090
$\lvert X' X \rvert$:	.730
Number of observations:	1,000

[a]Dependent variable is verbal achievement.

of the basic data in these appendix tables is based on the Equality of Education Survey of the U. S. Office of Education. The correlation coefficients, means and standard deviations are from J. S. Coleman [13]. The form and specification of the educational production function which is developed in the text and estimated for a national sample of 1,000 students was tested on different samples of 1,000 students each in the North and the South. The results of this estimation appear in Tables A.4, and A.5.

TABLE A.5

Estimated Production Function for Samples of Northern U.S. Twelfth-Grade Students

Independent Variable[a]	Regression Coefficient (*t* in parentheses)	Beta
1. Reading material in the home	1.841 (2.629)	.083
2. Number of siblings (positive = few)	1.794 (4.438)	.135
3. Parents' educational level	2.185 (4.181)	.132
4. Family stability	.823 (1.858)	.053
5. Teacher's verbal-ability score	1.097 (6.593)	.210
6. Science lab facilities	.027 (1.724)	.052
7. Average time spent in guidance	2.017 (3.266)	.102

Constant:	20.373 (6.247)
R^2:	.1961
$|X'X|$:	.519
Number of observations:	1,000

[a]Dependent variable is verbal achievement.

REFERENCES

1. Anastasi, Anne, "Intelligence and Family Size," *Psychological Bulletin,* vol. 53, no. 3 (August, 1956), 187–209.
2. Armor, David J., "School Effects on Negro and White Achievement: A Re-Examination of the USOE Data," 1968 (mimeo.).
3. Astin, A. W., "Undergraduate Achievement and Institutional Excellence," *Science,* vol. 161, August 16, 1968, 661–68.
4. Bereiter, C., *et al.,* "An Academically-Oriented Pre-School for Culturally Deprived Children," Paper presented at AERA meeting, Chicago, February 1965.
5. Bloom, Benjamin S., *Stability and Change in Human Characteristics,* New York, 1964.
√ 6. Bowles, Samuel S., "Towards Equality of Educational Opportunity?" *Harvard Educational Review,* vol. 38, no. 1, (1968), 89–99.
7. Bowles, Samuel S., and Henry M. Levin, "More on Multicollinearity and the Effectiveness of Schools," *The Journal of Human Resources,* vol. III, no. 3, (Summer) 1968, 393–400.
8. ————, The Determinants of Scholastic Achievement—An Appraisal of Some Recent Evidence," *The Journal of Human Resources,* vol. III, no. 1, (Winter) 1968.
9. Burkhead, Jesse, Thomas G. Fox, and John W. Holland, *Input and Output in Large-City High Schools,* Education in Large Cities Series. Syracuse, New York, 1967.
10. Burt, C., "The Evidence for the Concept of Intelligence," *British Journal of Education,* vol. 25, (1945), 158–77.
11. Chausow, H. M., "The Organization of Learning Experience to Achieve More Effectively the Objective of Critical Thinking in the General Social Sciences Courses at the Junior College Level," unpublished Ph.D. dissertation, University of Chicago, 1955.
12. Cohen, J., "The Factorial Structure of the WISC at Ages 7–6, 10–6, and 13–6," *Journal of Consultative Psychology,* vol. 23, (1959), 285–99.
√ 13. Coleman, James S., *et al., Equality of Educational Opportunity,* 2 vols. Washington, D. C., 1966.

14. Coleman, W., and E. E. Cureton, "Intelligence and Achievement," *Educational and Psychological Measurement,* vol. 14, (1954), 347–51.

15. Council of Economic Advisers, (*Annual Report*), Washington, D. C., 1967.

√ 16. Dave, R. H., "The Identification and Measurement of Environmental Process Variables That Are Related to Educational Achievement," unpublished Ph.D. dissertation, University of Chicago, 1963.

17. Davis, A., and J. Dollard, *Children of Bondage,* American Council on education, Washington, D.C., 1940.

√ 18. Deutsch, M., "The Disadvantaged Child and the Learning Process," in A. H. Passow (ed.), *Education in Depressed Areas,* New York, 1963.

19. Duncan, O. D., "Achievement and Ability," *The Eugenics Quarterly,* 1968.

20. Duncanson, J. P., "Learning and Measured Abilities," *Journal of Educational Psychology,* vol. 57, (1966), 220–29.

21. Farrar, Donald E., and Robert R. Glauber, "Multicollinearity in Regression Analysis: The Problem Revisited," *Review of Economics and Statistics,* (February 1967), 98–99.

22. Flanagan, John C., *et al., Project Talent,* Pittsburgh, vol. 1, 1962; vol. 2, 1964.

23. Freeman, F. N., H. H. Newman, and K. J. Holzinger, *Twins: A Study of Heredity and Environment,* Chicago, 1937.

24. Ghiselli, E. E., "The Measurement of Occupational Aptitude," *University of California Publications in Psychology,* vol. 8, no. 2, (1955).

25. Gray, Susan W., and R. A. Klaus, "An Experimental Preschool Program for Culturally Deprived Children," *Child Development,* vol. 36, (1965), 887–98.

26. Griliches, Zvi, "Notes on the Role of Education in Production Functions and Growth Accounting," this volume.

27. Gross, Morris, *Learning Readiness in Two Jewish Groups,* New York: Center for Urban Education, 1967.

√ 28. Hanoch, G., "Personal Earnings and Investment in Schooling." unpublished Ph..D. dissertation, University of Chicago, 1965 (mimeo.).

29. Hansen, W. Lee, Burton A. Weisbrod, and William J. Scanlon, "Schooling and Earnings of Low Achievers," *American Economic Review,* vol. 60, no. 3, (June 1970).

30. Hanushek, Eric A., "The Education of Negroes and Whites," unpublished Ph.D. dissertation, Massachusetts Institute of Technology, 1968.

31. Harrell, Ruth F., Ella Woodyard, and A. I. Gates, *The Effect of Mothers' Diets on the Intelligence of the Offspring,* New York, 1955.

32. Hoch, Irving, "Estimation of Production Function Parameters Combining Time-Series and Cross-Section-Data," *Econometrica,* vol. 30, no. 1, (January 1962), 34–53.

33. ————, "Simultaneous Equation Bias in the Context of the Cobb-Douglas Production Function," *Econometrica,* vol. 26, no. 4, (October 1958), 566–78.

34. Hollingshead, A. B., *Elmtown's Youth,* New York, 1949.

35. Hunt, J. McV., *Intelligence and Experience,* New York, 1961.

36. Husén, Torsten (ed.), *International Study of Achievement in Mathematics,* vol. I, New York, 1967.

37. Jackson, J. D., R. D. Hess, and Virginia Shipman, "Communication Styles in Teachers: An Experiment," Paper presented at AERA meeting, Chicago, (February 1965).

38. Jensen, Arthur R., "Estimation of the Limits of Hereditability of Traits by Comparison of Monozygotic and Dizygotic Twins," *Proceedings of the National Academy of Sciences,* vol. 58, (1967), 149–57.

39. ————, "How Much Can We Boost IQ and Scholastic Achievement?" *Harvard Educational Review,* vol. 39, no. 1, (1969).

40. ————, "Patterns of Mental Ability and Socioeconomic Status," *Proceedings of the National Academy of Sciences,* (August 1968).

41. ————, "Social Class, Race, and Genetics: Implications for Education," *American Educational Research Journal,* vol. 5, no. 1, (January 1968).

42. Kain, John F., and Eric A. Hanushek, *On the Value of Equality of Educational Opportunity as a Guide to Public Policy,* Program on Regional and Urban Economics. Discussion Paper no. 36, Harvard University, May 1968.

43. Katzman, Martin T., *Distribution and Production in a Big City*

Elementary School System, Ph.D. dissertation, Yale University, 1967.

44. Kelley, T. L., *Interpretation of Educational Measurement,* Yonkers, New York, 1927.

45. Kiesling, Herbert J., "Educational Production Functions in New York State," 1968 (mimeo.).

46. ————, "Measuring a Local Government Service: A Study of School Districts in New York State," *The Review of Economics and Statistics,* vol. XLIX, no. 3, (August 1967), 356–67.

47. Kirk, S. A., *Early Education of the Mentally Retarded,* Urbana, Illinois, 1958.

48. Levin, Henry M., *Recruiting Teachers for Large City Schools,* Studies in Social Economics, Washington, D. C., June 1968.

√ 49. Machlup, Fritz, *The Production and Distribution of Knowledge in the United States,* Princeton, New Jersey, 1962.

50. Marschak, Jacob, and William H. Andrews, Jr., "Random Simultaneous Equations and the Theory of Production," *Econometrica,* vol. 12, nos. 3–4, (July-October 1944), 143–205.

51. Massell, Benton F., "Elimination of Management Bias From Production Functions Fitted to Cross-Section Data: A Model and An Application to African Agriculture," *Econometrica,* vol. 35, nos. 3–4, (July-October 1967), 495–508.

52. McDill, Edward L., Edmund D. Meyers, Jr., and Leo C. Rigsby, "Institutional Effects on the Academic Behavior of High School Students," *Sociology of Education,* vol. 40, no. 3, (1967), 181-99.

√ 53. Michelson, Stephan, *Incomes of Racial Minorities,* Studies in Social Economics, Washington, D. C., September 1968.

54. Nerlove, Marc, *The Estimation and Identification of Cobb-Douglas Production Functions,* 1967.

55. Olim, E. G., R. D. Hess, and Virginia Shipman, "Relationship Between Mothers' Abstract Language Style and Abstraction Styles of Urban Pre-School Children," Paper presented at the Midwest Psychological Association meeting, Chicago, April 1965.

56. Peaker, G. F., *et al., Children in Their Primary Schools,* Report of the Central Advisory Council for Education (England), vol. II, London, 1967.

57. Peterson, R. A., and L. DeBord, "Educational Supportiveness of the Home and Academic Performance of Disadvantaged Boys,"

IMRID Behavioral Science Monograph, no. 3, Nashville, Tenn., 1966.

58. Rosenthal, Robert, and Lenore Jacobson, *Pygmalion in the Classroom,* New York, 1968.

59. Scannell, D. P., "Differential Prediction of Academic Success, from Achievement Test Scores," unpublished Ph.D. dissertation, State University of Iowa, 1958.

60. Stodolsky, Susan S., and Gerald Lesser, "Learning Patterns in the Disadvantaged," *Harvard Educational Review,* vol. 37, no. 4, (1967), 546–93.

61. Terrell, G., Kathryn Durkin, and M. Wiesley, "Social Class and the Nature of Incentive in Discrimination Learning," *Journal of Abnormal Social Psychology,* vol. 59, (1959), 270–72.

62. Theil, H., "Specification Errors and the Estimation of Economic Relationships," *Revue Institute Internationale de Statistique,* vol. 25, (January 3, 1957), 41–51.

63. U. S. Commission on Civil Rights, *Racial Isolation in the Public Schools,* Washington, D. C., 1967.

64. Vandenberg, S. G., "Hereditary Factors in Psychological Variables in Man, with a Special Emphasis on Cognition," in J. S. Spuhler (ed.), *Genetic Diversity and Human Behavior,* Chicago, 1967.

65. Warner, W. L., R. J. Havighurst, and M. B. Loeb, *Who Shall Be Educated?* New York, 1944.

66. Welch, Finis, "Measurement of the Quality of Schooling, The Economics of Education," *American Economic Review,* vol. LVI, no. 2, (May 1966), 379–92.

67. Weisbrod, Burton A., and Peter Karpoff, "Monetary Returns to College Education, Student Ability, and College Ability," *Review of Economics and Statistics,* vol. 50, no. 4, (November 1968), pp. 491–497.

68. Weiss, Randall Dunn, "The Effect of Education Upon the Earnings of Whites and Blacks: Experiments with Single Equation and Recursive Models," *Review of Economics and Statistics,* May, 1970.

69. Wilson, A. B., "Social Stratification and Academic Achievement," in A. H. Passow (ed.), *Education in Depressed Areas,* New York, 1963.

70. Wolf, R. M., "The Identification and Measurement of Environmental Process Variables Related to Intelligence," unpublished Ph.D.

dissertation, University of Chicago, 1963.

71. Wolfle, Dael, and Joseph Smith, "The Occupation Value of Education for Superior High School Graduates," *Journal of Higher Education,* (April 1956), 201–13.
72. Zigler, E., and J. DeLabry, "Concept Switching in Middle-Class, Lower-Class and Retarded Children," *Journal of Abnormal Social Psychology,* vol. 65, (1962), 267–73.

COMMENTS

JOHN E. BRANDL

OFFICE OF THE SECRETARY, DEPARTMENT OF HEALTH,
EDUCATION, AND WELFARE

Sam Bowles has written a discerning, discouraging paper. He has explicitly shown the gap between what estimators of education production functions have been doing (mostly least-squares regressions of achievement or even income on a host of explanatory variables), and what they could be doing with the econometric tools now available. The paper hints at the desirability of a system of simultaneous relations over a uniequational model, cleverly manipulates and combines variables to lessen the difficulties associated with collinearity, mentions that production functions should recognize that "schools are multiproduct firms," makes a start at giving some theoretical content to education production functions, produces some impressive estimates, and, in general, shows the way toward more respectable econometric analysis in this field that has been characterized by shabby statistics.

The paper is discouraging to me, however, for it leaves little room for hope that estimations of education production functions from survey data can be very useful for policy purposes in the foreseeable future. The remainder of this comment consists of two parts: the first outlines my reasons for taking this pessimistic position, and the second offers some observations on policy making given such a state of affairs. As the lone bureaucrat participating in this conference I am looking for answers to the question, "How can education expenditures be allocated more efficiently now?"

NOTE: Dr. Brandl is now Director, School of Public Affairs, University of Minnesota.

WHY PROSPECTS ARE BLEAK

Consider Bowles' regression equation (p. 13)

$$\hat{A} = \hat{f}_0 + \hat{f}_1 x_1 + \hat{f}_2 x_2 + \ldots + \hat{f}_n x_n$$

where $\hat{A}$ is a measure of "output," such as an achievement test score, the x_i are "input" measures, and the $\hat{f}$'s are constants. This is the typical specification of education "production functions," and it is used by Bowles despite his own cogent and compelling reservations. The implications of such a relationship for a policy-maker are disconcerting. As Bowles notes, optimum conditions for resource allocation are

$$\frac{\partial A}{\partial X_j} \bigg/ \frac{\partial A}{\partial X_k} = \frac{\hat{f}_i}{\hat{f}_k} = \frac{p_i}{p_k}$$

(where p_i is the price of x_i) or, alternatively, $\dfrac{\hat{f}_i}{p_i} = \dfrac{\hat{f}_k}{p_k}$, or achievement gain per marginal dollar expended should be identical for all factors.

The $\hat{f}$'s are constant by definition, and for any single decision-making body in this country (probably including the federal government since its contribution to education is relatively small) the p's probably are, too. Policy-makers are being told, then, that their job is to determine the highest ratio of $\hat{f}$ to p for any variable over which they have control and to expend all available funds in that direction. That conclusion is enough to disenchant any educator or bureaucrat—many of whom are already wary of economists that they think intend to show them up.

The following are some reasons why I believe such incredulity to be justified.

1. Surely the "production function" is misspecified. The argument against linear production functions already mentioned is at least as strong on a priori grounds as that suggested by Bowles against the Cobb-Douglas.[1]

---

[1] The Cobb-Douglas function would require, as Bowles mentions, "that an increase in the quality of teachers be more effective on children of well-educated parents than on the children of illiterate parents," i.e., that $\dfrac{\delta^2 A}{\delta x_j \delta x_k} > 0$. See Bowles (p. 19, note 9).

2. A variation on this specification theme is that we know and desire that our schools produce more than ability to achieve high scores on standardized achievement tests. Failure to include others of the joint outputs gives no indication of the effect of an input change on those other outputs. More importantly, it means that the regression coefficients do not even necessarily indicate the most efficient way to produce an impact on the single measure chosen, since the relative weightings of the several outputs in the preference functions of administrators are not known.

This leads to a third objection which I consider to be a critical blow to the usefulness of production functions of this sort. But to make myself clear, let me assume away the econometric problems alluded to—specification, simultaneous equations, multicollinearity (and others such as the absence of good time series data).

3. Even if we could overcome these statistical problems, the meaning of our estimates would be in doubt. Local, state, and federal school administrators and decision makers are maximizing neither "achievement" nor any other known combination of outputs, or rather, it is likely that different decision makers weigh the several outputs in different ways. Survey or longitudinal data which aggregate information resulting from the maximization of dozens, hundreds, or thousands of different objective functions will not yield an answer to the question posed in the beginning of this comment: "How can education expenditures be allocated more efficiently?"

WHERE DO WE GO FROM HERE?

If we had a well-defined theory giving us grounds for choosing particular variables as the inputs and outputs to be included,[2] and which provided guidance in the choice of functional form, then perhaps at least negative results of estimated production functions could be used to prod an embarrassed education community into doing better. That is, indications that marginal products of some inputs approach zero might be a goal to improve. As it is, tentative results showing little improvement

---

[2] Presumably the outputs could be chosen on either consumption or investment grounds. At present we are not able to relate our test measures either to the fun of being in school or to the financial gains of having been educated.

on achievement tests after injection of Head Start or Title I (of the Elementary and Secondary Education Act) funds[3] are often shrugged off by educators on the grounds that that's not what they are trying to do.

We are, then, in a pre-Newtonian (or perhaps even pre-Ptolemaic!) state where we not only lack theory, but have at least some grounds for believing that the best technology is not widely used.[4]

My personal reaction to this state of affairs can be summarized as follows:

a. Estimation of efficient technological relationships might be more readily accomplished through examination of exemplary and demonstration programs than through scrutiny of data from large national surveys—this not only because the objectives of such programs are more easily determined than are the objectives of a conglomeration of systems, but also because the statistical problems of managing data are not as great when one can influence selection of control and experimental groups, variables on which data will be collected, types of tests administered, and so on.

b. We economists tend to find more maximizing than exists. Just as the problem of X-efficiency[5] in firms has been neglected until very recently (with economists assuming that firms operate on their efficiency frontiers) our usual approach for estimating education production functions ignores not only the existence of joint products, but the possibility that our schools may not be efficient users of resources. Thus, survey data (such as that collected by the Coleman Commission, or the reams of material obtained each year through the survey of school districts receiving Title I ESEA funds) can be of more value for *describing* the present state of education, than for *prescribing* what might be done.

c. Attempts should be made to determine what it is that school

---

[3] See *Evaluation of Title I,* Office of Program Planning and Evaluation, Office of Education, Department of Health, Education, and Welfare, Washington, D. C., 1968.

[4] *Ibid.,* for unimpressive results of the present school system. Scattered examples of impressive results indicate the possibility that superior technology may exist but, for whatever reason, not be widely disseminated. See *A Study of Selected Exemplary Programs for the Education of Disadvantaged Children,* American Institute for Research in the Behavioral Sciences, Palo Alto, California, September 1968.

[5] See H. Leibenstein, "X-Efficiency vs. Allocative Efficiency," *American Economic Review,* June 1966.

authorities are trying to accomplish, first, in order to find out whether they are attaining their objectives, and second, so that the questions of whether to change those objectives and provide incentives to do so can be considered.

d. In addition to fostering research to find out what works and how to get people to use it, we should recognize that our current ignorance has implications for how we allocate money to existing programs. For example, in the field of higher education, there is a growing consensus (both inside the government and out) that federal assistance to students is preferable to the government's buying *inputs* (such as buildings, teaching paraphernalia, or teachers). That is, for the time being we cannot relate pompons per cheerleader to lifetime income or graduate record exam score, so perhaps assisting students directly—and letting them choose where (and to some extent, how) to spend the money— has some advantages.

Sam Bowles, cosmetologist,[6] has beautified considerably what was a most unattractive client. Unfortunately, she is still not very helpful around the house.

JOHN C. HAUSE
UNIVERSITY OF MINNESOTA

In the following comment Bowles' interesting, exploratory paper will be discussed under three headings: first, some important aspects of his general analytic framework; second, several specific problems arising in the execution of the study; and finally, a few of the main issues the study raises for future research.

I. GENERAL FRAMEWORK OF THE STUDY

Bowles sets for himself the task of devising a systematic and sensible framework for studying the relationship between inputs and outputs of schools. In addition, he presents some initial attempts to estimate

[6] See Bowles (p. 26).

crude structural parameters of relationships implied by this framework. The motivation of the study appears to be essentially normative—presumably to aid in improving allocation in the educational sector. It is not concerned with how or why school administrators currently allocate educational resources as they do.[1] Indeed, Bowles explicitly assumes that "they do not select or alter school inputs with a mind to optimizing any well-defined function of school outputs." As the author recognizes, this implies that the estimated dependence of educational outputs on inputs may significantly understate what could be achieved if the inputs were allocated in an efficient way.[2] One might perhaps examine in greater detail schools with large positive residuals from regressions in hopes of determining additional factors that "explained" why these schools were especially productive. But cross-sectional studies of the average observed relationships between inputs and outputs do not appear to be very promising as a way of getting at optimal techniques in the current regime. However, Bowles considers that the most serious difficulty is the lack of a theory of learning that would aid in specifying the production function. I shall discuss the implications of this problem.

One important omission in Bowles' general analysis is a careful discussion of the appropriate level of aggregation for carrying out the study of the production of education, especially if the results are intended to held guide the decisions of school administrators. As the author recognizes, the lengthy process of educating a child is very complex, and the measurable inputs applied by school administrators vary greatly in magnitude and importance during this process. He stresses the important role of value added analysis for appropriately imputing the returns from education, but does not adequately emphasize the main methodological issues that depend on the use of a value added framework. Consider a

---

[1] One might argue that positive economic analysis of resource allocation in the public sector is at least as deficient as relevant normative analysis. Modification of existing incentives and constraints in this sector may at times be as important as presenting confused administrators with better normative theories to aid them in their decisions.

[2] Bowles provides some indirect evidence which suggests current inefficiencies. For the educational outputs he is concerned with, instructional costs per pupil are less strongly related to output than specific characteristics of the inputs, which in turn can also "explain" much of the variance of expenditures per pupil.

child who has been "in process" in the educational system for a number of years. Is it possible to measure his current status by means of achievement, aptitude, and interest tests and thereby determine the additional inputs that will efficiently help him achieve additional, well-defined educational objectives? Or is the educational process so interdependent that the full, detailed history of the child's previous educational experience critically affects the appropriate inputs for the next stage of development? The task of improving the technology of education is greatly simplified if extensive decomposition of the education production function is possible for a least two reasons. First, it permits a degree of decentralization and the assignment of limited, but well-defined responsibilities to teachers and administrators who are directly concerned with only a small part of the whole educational process. Second, if such decomposition of the educational process is feasible, it may help to identify certain kinds of achievement and attitudes which are exceptionally important for subsequent educational development. It seems possible that a significant increase in educational expenditures on such key elements would yield high returns if they could be identified.

The extent to which such temporal disaggregation of the educational production function is useful is essentially the same question as the extent to which detailed value added analysis is feasible. This is currently an open question. Bowles cites an article by Jensen that indicates possible pitfalls in trying to specify the current status of a child that would be appropriate for a value added analysis. Jensen mentions some evidence that students from lower social-economic backgrounds with a given IQ learn faster than students from higher backgrounds with the same IQ when confronted with tasks that are not dependent on former learning. Thus IQ information alone might lead to inappropriate groupings of young pupils for some purposes.

Even if it is impossible to disaggregate the detailed education production function very far, it is not clear how much normative guidance can be obtained from a highly aggregated model. The statistical experiments an economist can carry out depend, of course, on the data available to him. Still, an explicit discussion of the appropriate level of aggregation might be useful to other people studying these problems.

II. SEVERAL TECHNICAL PROBLEMS.

Although Bowles considers the empirical calculations reported in the study to be preliminary, several issues deserve comment. A key difficulty stems from the lack of explicit variables for controlling initial ability (or achievement). The author acknowledges that such a variable would be desirable, but it is not available in his cross-section data. As a partial adjustment, he adjusts home environment regression coefficients for twelfth graders by the corresponding coefficients for first graders. The motivation for this procedure is not very clear, and the modification in any case seems to be of dubious value. This adjustment would seem to be relevant for discussing the following question. Given the influence that home environment has already exerted on a child by the time he has entered the first grade, how much additional influence does it have on his achievement test score by the time he is in the twelfth grade? It is not obvious what issue is clarified by such an imputation even if it were legitimate. The procedure does not seem appropriate because the home environment variables are surely correlated with omitted variables (including genetic factors) that are determinants of first grade "ability" or achievement. Strong (and implausible) assumptions are required to justify interpreting the adjusted coefficient as a measure of the net *additional* influence of home environment after the child has entered the first grade.

The limited predictive power of Bowles' initial regressions is of course due primarily to the unavailability of control for initial ability. Nevertheless, the relationships of central importance for this study are those between school environment and education output variables. It is not clear how much the coefficients of these variables will be biased by inability to control for initial ability and this issue is more important than the values of the coefficients of determination obtained in the reported regressions. It seems quite possible that inefficiencies in the current allocation of educational resources may be empirically the more important cause of understating the size these coefficients would have if the resources were appropriately organized.

The general variables that seem appropriate determinants of the educational production function are not directly observable. This raises the problem of the appropriate way of aggregating less satisfactory proxy variables into indexes representing the general factors. The difficulty with including all the specific factors is that multicollinearity makes the estimates of the individual coefficients unstable and difficult to interpret. Bowles does not attempt to resolve this issue. He mentions two alternatives—selecting a single proxy variable to represent each general variable or adopting some formal statistical procedure such as principal components analysis—and opts for the former in this study. The following very simple procedure might be more appropriate than either of these suggestions. Associate the specific variables that seem to be reasonable proxies for a general factor with that factor, run an ordinary multiple regression including all these specific variables, and test only groups of coefficients, where each group includes the specific variables associated with a particular general factor. The test corresponding to the usual t-test for a coefficient being significantly different from zero is to test the vector of specific variable coefficients corresponding to a general factor to see whether it differs significantly from a zero vector. Multicollinearity will often lead to imprecise estimates of the coefficients of some specific variables, but it is presumably the influence of the general factor that is of interest. This procedure amounts to accepting the linear function determined by the coefficients of each group of specific variables as an appropriate index serving as a proxy for the general factor.

III. SOME IMPLICATIONS AND PROBLEMS FOR FUTURE RESEARCH.

Bowles recognizes that such educational "outputs" as achievement scores in tests do not represent the ultimate outputs that one hopes the educational system will generate. Specific levels of proficiency may indeed provide minimal standards of achievement which are useful tools for school administrators. Bowles discusses briefly the importance of trying to relate the educational process to such outputs as earnings capacity. The implicit conclusion appears to be that it is necessary to analyze how the more specific, readily measured educational outputs are related to these more important outputs. This raises the question whether the analysis of the relationship between the "ultimate" outputs and inputs allocated by school administrators should attempt to establish a direct relationship or whether these variables should be related only by intermediate output variables such as test scores. At this stage of research into the economics of education, this is an unresolved issue. Certain inputs may generate so many joint products of intermediate educational output that the appropriate imputation of ultimate returns to school-administered inputs will be an unmanageable task if the analysis must proceed through the mechanism of the intermediate level outputs of education. At least this possibility should be considered before any major attempt is made to analyze the ultimate outputs in an educational production function framework.

A second important issue for future research was raised in the discussion in the first part of this comment: the levels of aggregation that will be most fruitful for improving the technology of education. The magnitude of sub-optimal decisions currently made by administrators may seriously limit the relevance of statistical analyses based on typical, current practices for improving current technology.

NOTES ON THE ROLE OF EDUCATION IN PRODUCTION FUNCTIONS AND GROWTH ACCOUNTING • ZVI GRILICHES •

HARVARD UNIVERSITY

I INTRODUCTION

THIS paper started out as a survey of the uses of "education" variables in aggregate production functions and of the problems associated with the measurement of such variables and with the specification and estimation of models that use them. It soon became clear that some of the issues to be investigated (e.g., the relative contributions of ability and schooling to a labor quality index) were very complex and possessed a literature of such magnitude that any "quick" survey of it would be both superficial and inadvisable. This paper, therefore, is in the form of a progress report on this survey, containing also a list of questions which this literature and future work may help eventually to elucidate. Not all of the interesting questions will be asked, however, nor all of the possible problems raised. I have limited myself to those areas which seem to require the most immediate attention as we proceed beyond the work already accomplished.

As it currently stands, this paper first recapitulates and brings up to date the construction of a "quality of labor" index based on the changing distribution of the U. S. labor force by years of school completed. It then

NOTE: The work on this paper has been supported by National Science Foundation Grants Nos. GS 712 and GS 2026X. I am indebted to C. A. Anderson, Mary Jean Bowman, E. F. Denison, R. J. Gordon, and T. W. Schultz for comments and suggestions.

surveys several attempts to "validate" such an index through the estimation of aggregate production functions and reviews some alternative approaches suggested in the literature. Next, the question of how many "dimensions" of labor it is useful to distinguish is raised and explored briefly. The puzzle of the apparent constancy of rates of return to education and of skilled-unskilled wage differentials in the last two decades provides a unifying thread through the latter parts of this paper as the discussion turns to the implications of the ability-education-income interrelationships for the assessment of the contribution of education to growth, the possible sources of the differential growth in the demand for educated versus uneducated labor, and the possible complementarities between the accumulation of physical and human capital. While many questions are raised, only a few are answered.

II THE QUALITY OF LABOR AND GROWTH ACCOUNTING

ONE of the earliest responses to the appearance of a large "residual" in the works of Schmookler [50], Kendrick [39], Solow [56] and others was to point to the improving quality of the labor force as one of its major sources. More or less independently, calculations of the possible magnitude of this source of economic growth were made by Schultz [53, 54] based on the human capital approach and by Griliches [22] and Denison [16] based on a standardization of the labor force for "mix-changes." Both approaches used the changing distribution of school years completed in the labor force as the major quality dimension, weighting it either by human capital based on "production costs" times an estimated rate of return, or by weights derived from income-by-education data.[1]

At the simplest level, the issue of the quality of labor is the issue of the measurement of labor input in constant prices and a question of correct aggregation. It is standard national-income accounting practice

---

[1] Kendrick [39] had a similar "mix" adjustment based on the distribution of the labor force by industries. Bowman [10] provides a very good review and comparison of the Denison and Schultz approaches.

to distinguish classes of items, even within the same commodity class, if they differ in value per unit. Thus, it is agreed (rightly or wrongly) that an increase of 100 units in the production of bulldozers will increase "real income" (GNP in "constant" prices) by more than a similar numeric increase in the production of garden tractors. Similarly, as long as plumbers are paid more than clergymen, an increase in the number of plumbers results in a larger increase in total "real" labor input than a similar increase in the number of clergymen. We can illustrate the construction of such indexes by the following highly simplified example:

| | Number | | Base Period |
Labor Category	Period 1	Period 2	Wage
Unskilled	10	10	1
Skilled	10	20	2
Total	20	30	

The index of the unweighted number of workers in period 2 is just $N_2 = 30/20 = 1.5$. The "correct" (weighted) index of labor input is $L_2 = \dfrac{10 + 2 \times 20}{10 + 2 \times 10} = \dfrac{50}{30} = 1.67$. The index of the average quality of labor per worker can be defined either as the ratio of the second to the first measure or equivalently as the "predicted" index of the average wage rate, based on the second period's labor mix and base period wages:

$$\bar{w}_1 = 1.5, \ \overset{*}{w_2} = \frac{10 + 2 \times 20}{30} = 1.67, \ E_2 = \frac{1.67}{1.5} = L_2/N_2 = 1.113.$$

Note that we have said nothing about what happened to actual relative wages in the second period. If they changed, then we could have also constructed indexes of the Paasche type which would have told a similar but not numerically equivalent story. It is then more convenient, however, and more appropriate to use a (chain-linked) Divisia total-labor-input index based on a weighted average of the rates of growth of different categories of labor, using the relative shares in total labor compensation as weights.[2] To represent such an index of total labor input,

---

[2] See Jorgenson and Griliches [37], from which the following paragraph is taken almost verbatim, for more detail on the construction of such indexes, and Richter [48] for a list of axioms for such indexes and a proof that they are satisfied only by such indexes.

let L_i be the quantity of input of the lth labor service, measured in man-hours. The rate of growth of the index of total labor input, say L, is:

$$\frac{\dot{L}}{L} = \Sigma \nu_l \frac{\dot{L}}{L_l}$$

where ν_l is the relative share of the lth category of labor in the total value of labor input.[3] The number of man-hours for each labor service is the product of the number of men, say n_l, and hours per man, say h_l; using this notation the index of total labor input may be rewritten:

$$\frac{\dot{L}}{L} = \Sigma \nu_l \frac{\dot{n}_l}{n_l} + \Sigma \nu_l \frac{\dot{h}_l}{h_l}.$$

The index of labor input can be separated into three components—change in the total number of men, change in hours per man, and change in the average quality of labor input per man (or man-hour). Assuming that the relative change in the number of hours per man is the same for all categories of labor services, say $\dot{H}/H$,[4] and letting N represent the total number of men and e_l the proportion of the workers in the lth category of labor services, one may write the index of the total labor input in the form:

$$\frac{\dot{L}}{L} = \frac{\dot{H}}{H} + \frac{\dot{N}}{N} + \Sigma \nu_l \frac{\dot{e}_l}{e_l}.$$

Thus, to eliminate errors of aggregation one must correct the rate of growth of man-hours as conventionally measured by adding to it an index

[3] Where the $\dot{x}$ notation stands for dx/dt, and $\dot{x}/x$ represents the relative rate of growth of x per unit of time; and $\nu_j = p_j L_j / \Sigma_i p_i L_i$. In practice one never has continuous data and so the Laspeyres-Paasche problem is raised again, albeit in attenuated form. Substituting $\Delta L = L_t - L_{t-1}$ for L, one should also substitute $\nu_{jt} = \frac{1}{2} (\nu_{jt} + \nu_{jt-1})$ for ν_{jt} in these formulae. This is only approximated below by trying to choose the p_t's in the middle of the various periods defined by the respective Δe_t's.

[4] This assumption of proportionality in the change in the hours worked of different men, allows us to talk interchangeably about the "quality" of men and the quality of man-hours. If this assumption is too restrictive, one should add another "quality" term to the expression below, $\Sigma \nu_i \dot{m}_i / m_i$, where $m_i = h_i / H$ is the relative employment intensity (per year) of the ith category of labor.

TABLE 1

Civilian Labor Force, Males 18 – 64 Years Old, per cent Distribution by Years of School Completed

School year completed	1940	1948	1952		1957	1959	1959[a]	1962[a]	1965[a]	1967[a]
Elementary 0–4	10.2	7.9	7.6		6.3	5.5	5.9	5.1	4.3	3.6
5–6 or 5–7[b]	10.2	7.1	6.6	11.6	11.4	10.4	10.7	9.8	8.3	7.8
7–8 or 8[b]	33.7	26.9	25.1	16.8	16.8	15.6	15.8	13.9	12.7	11.6
High School 1–3	18.3	20.7	19.4		20.1	20.7	19.8	19.2	18.9	18.5
4	16.6	23.6	24.6		27.2	28.1	27.5	29.1	32.3	33.1
College 1–3	5.7	7.1	8.3		8.5	9.2	9.4	10.6	10.6	11.9
4+ or 4	5.4	6.7	8.3		9.6	10.5	6.3	7.3	7.5	8.0
5+	–	–	–		–	–	4.7	5.0	5.4	5.5

[a] Employed, 18 years and over.

[b] 5–6 and 7–8 for 1940, 1948 and the first part of 1952, 5–7 and 8 thereafter.

SOURCE: The basic data for columns 1, 3, 4, 5, and 6 are taken from U.S. Department of Labor, *Special Labor Force Report*, No. 1 "Educational Attainment of Workers, 1959." The 5–8 years class is broken down into the 5–7 and 8 (5–6 and 7–8 for 1940, 1948, and 1952) on the basis of data provided in *Current Population Report*, Series P–50, Nos. 14, 49, and 78. The 1940 data were broken down using the 1940 *Census of Population*, Vol. III, Part 1, Table 13. For 1952 the division of the 5–7 class into 5–6 and 7 was based on the educational attainment of all males by single years of school completed from the 1950 *Census of Population*. The 1962, 1965, and 1967 data are taken from Special Labor Force Reports Nos. 30, 65, and 92 respectively.

of the quality of labor input per man. The third term in the above expression for total input provides such a correction. Calling this quality index E, we have

$$\frac{\dot{E}}{E} = \Sigma \nu_l \frac{\dot{e}_l}{e_l}.$$

For computational purposes it is convenient to note that this index may be written as follows:

$$\frac{\dot{E}}{E} = \sum \frac{p_l}{\Sigma p_l e_l} \dot{e}_l = \Sigma p'_l \dot{e}_l,$$

where p_l is the price of the lth category of labor services and p'_l is its relative price. The relative price is the ratio of the price of the lth category of labor services to the average price of labor services, $\Sigma p_l e_l$.

In principle, it would be desirable to distinguish as many categories of labor as possible, cross-classified by sex, number of school years completed, type and quality of schooling, occupation, age, native ability (if one could measure it independently), and so on. In practice, this is a job of such magnitude that it hasn't yet been tackled in its full generality by anybody, as far as I know. Actually, it is only worthwhile to distinguish those categories in which the relative numbers have changed significantly.[5] Since our interest is centered on the contribution of "education," I shall present the necessary data and construct such an index of input quality labor for the United States, for the period 1940–67, based on a classification by years of school completed of the *male* labor force only. These numbers are taken from the Jorgenson-Griliches [37] paper, but have been extended to 1967.

Table 1 presents the basic data on the distribution of the male labor force by years of school completed. Note, for example, the sharp drop in the percentage of the labor force having no high school education (from 54 per cent in 1940 to 23 per cent in 1967) and the sharp rise in

---

[5] To adjust for changes in the age distribution, one would need to know more about the rate of "time depreciation" of human capital services and distinguish it from declines with age due to "obsolescence," which are not relevant for a "constant price" accounting. See Hall [29] for more details on this problem.

TABLE 2

Mean Annual Earnings of Males, Twenty-Five Years and Over by
School Years Completed, Selected Years

School year completed	1939	1949	1956	1958	1959	1963	1966
Elementary 0–4	$ 665	$1,724	$2,127	$2,046	$2,935	$2,465	$2,816
5–6 or 5–7	900	2,268	2,927	2,829	4,058	3,409	3,886
7–8 or 8	1,188	2,693 2,829	3,732	3,769	4,725	4,432	4,896
High School 1–3	1,379	3,226	4,480	4,618	5,379	5,370	6,315
4	1,661	3,784	5,439	5,567	6,132	6,588	7,626
College 1–3	1,931	4,423	6,363	6,966	7,401	7,693	9,058
4+ or 4	2,607	6,179	8,490	9,206	9,255	9,523	11,602
5+	—	—	—	—	11,136	10,487	13,221

NOTE: Earnings in 1939 and 1959; total income in 1949, 1958, 1963 and 1966.

SOURCE: Columns 1, 2, 3, 4, H.P. Miller [42, Table 1, p. 966]. Column 5 from 1960 *Census of Population*, PC(2)–7B, "Occupation by Earnings and Education." Columns 6 and 7 computed from *Current Population Reports*, Series P–60, No. 43 and 53, Table 22 and 4 respectively, using midpoints of class intervals and $44,000 for the over $25,000 class. The total elementary figure in 1940 broken down on the basis of data from the 1940 *Census of Population*. The "less than 8 years" figure in 1949 split on the basis of data given in H.S. Houthakker [34]. In 1956, 1958, 1959, 1963 and 1966, split on the basis of data on earnings of males 25–64 from the 1959 1-in-a-1000 Census sample. We are indebted to G. Hanoch [31] for providing us with this tabulation.

TABLE 3

Relative Prices,[a] Changes in Distribution of the Labor Force, and Indexes of Labor Input Per Man, U.S. Males, Civilian Labor Force, 1940–64

I. Relative Prices and Changes in the Distribution of the Labor Force

School Years Completed	p' 1939	$\dot{e}$ 1940–48	p' 1949	$\dot{e}$ 1948–52	p' 1956	$\dot{e}$ 1952–57	p' 1958	$\dot{e}$ 1957–59	p' 1958	$\dot{e}$ 1959–62	p' 1963	$\dot{e}$ 1962–65	p' 1966	$\dot{e}$ 1965–67
Elementary														
0–4	0.497	−2.3	0.521	−0.3	0.452	−1.3	0.409	−0.8	0.498	−0.8	0.407	−0.8	.380	−0.7
5–6 or 5–7	0.672	−3.1	0.685	−0.5	0.624	−0.2	0.565	−1.0	0.688	−0.9	0.562	−1.5	.525	−0.5
7–8 or 8	0.887	−6.8	0.813	−1.8	0.796	−3.3	0.753	−1.2	0.801	−1.9	0.731	−1.2	.661	−1.1
High School														
1–3	1.030	2.4	0.974	−1.3	0.955	0.7	0.923	0.6	0.912	−0.6	0.886	−0.3	.861	−0.4
4	1.241	7.0	1.143	1.0	1.159	2.6	1.113	0.9	1.039	1.6	1.087	3.2	1.030	+0.8
College														
1–3	1.442	1.4	1.336	1.2	1.356	0.2	1.392	0.7	1.255	1.3	1.269	0	1.223	+1.3
4+ or 4	1.947	1.3	1.866	1.6	1.810	1.3	1.840	0.9	1.569	1.0	1.571	0.2	1.566	+0.5
5+	—	—	—	—	—	—	—	—	1.888	0.3	1.730	0.4	1.785	+0.1

II. Labor Input Per Man: Percentage Change

	1940–48	1948–52	1952–57	1957–59	1959–62	1962–65	1965–67
Total	6.45	2.50	2.97	2.39	2.36	2.13	1.77
Annual	0.78	0.62	0.59	1.20	0.79	0.72	0.88

[a]The relative prices are computed using the appropriate beginning period distribution of the labor force as weights.

the percentage completing high school and more (from 28 in 1940 to 58 in 1967). Table 2 presents data on mean income of males by school years completed, and Table 3 uses these data together with Table 1 to derive an estimate of the implied rate of growth of labor input (quality) per worker.[6] The columns in Table 3 come in pairs (for example, the columns headed 1939 and 1940–48). The first column gives the estimated relative wage (income) of a particular class and is derived by expressing the corresponding numbers in Table 2 as ratios to their average (the average being computed using the corresponding entries of Table 1 weights). The second column of each pair is derived as the difference between two corresponding columns of Table 1. It gives the change in percentages of the labor force accounted for by different educational classes. The estimated rate of growth of labor quality during a particular period is then derived simply as the sum of the products of the two columns, and is converted to per annum units.[7]

For the period as a whole, the quality of the labor force so computed grew at approximately 0.8 per cent per year. Since the total share of labor compensation in GNP during this period was about 0.7, about 0.6 per cent per year of aggregate growth can be associated with this variable, accounting for about one-third of the measured "residual." A comparison and review of similar estimates for other countries can be found in Selowsky's [52] dissertation and Denison [18].

Note that in these computations no adjustment was made to the relative weights for the possible influence of "ability" on these differentials. Also, while a portion of observed growth can be attributed to the changing educational *composition* of the labor force, it should not be interpreted to imply that all of it has been produced by or can be attributed to the educational *system*. I shall elaborate on both of these points later on in this paper.

It is important to note that by using a Divisia type of index with shifting weights, one can to a large extent escape the criticism of using

[6] These income figures are deficient in several respects; among others: they are not standardized for age, and the use of a common $44,000 figure for the "over $25,000" class probably results in an underestimation of educational earnings differentials. I am indebted to E. F. Denison for pointing this out to me.

[7] The percentage change so calculated between any two dates, is the same as would be obtained by weighting the two educational distributions by the base (weight) period *i* earnings, aggregating and computing the percentage change.

"average" instead of "marginal" rates (or products) to weight the various education categories. If the return to a particular type of education is declining, such indexes will pick it up with not too great a lag and read-just its weights accordingly. Also, note that I have not elaborated on the alternative of using the growth in "human capital" to construct similar indexes. For productivity measurement purposes, we want indexes based on "rental" rather than "stock" values as weights. It can be shown (see Selowsky [52]), that if similar data are used consistently, there is no operational difference between the quality index described above and a "human capital times rate of return" approach, provided the capital valu-ation is made at "market prices" (i.e., based on observed rentals) rather than at production costs. For my purposes, the construction of "human capital" series would only add to the "round-aboutness" of the calcula-tions. Such calculations (or at least the calculation of the rates of return associated with them) are, of course, required for discussions of optimal investment in education programs.

III   EDUCATION AS A VARIABLE IN
AGGREGATE PRODUCTION FUNCTIONS

MUCH of the criticism of the use of such education per man indexes as measures of the quality of the labor force is summarized by two related questions: 1. Does education "really" affect productivity? 2. Is "educa-tion" and its contribution measured correctly for the purpose at hand? After all, the measures I have presented are not much more than account-ing conventions. Evidence (in some casual sense) has yet to be presented that "education" explains productivity differentials and that, moreover, the particular form of this variable suggested above does it best. There is, of course, a great deal of evidence that differences in schooling are a major determinant of differences in wages and income, even holding many other things constant.[8] Also, rational behavior on the part of employers would lead to the allocation of the labor force in such a way that the value of the marginal product of the different types of labor will

---

[8] See Blaug [6] and Schultz [55] for extensive bibliographies on this subject.

be roughly proportional to their relative wages. Still, a more satisfactory way of really nailing down this point, at least for me, is to examine the role of such variables in econometric aggregate production function studies. Such studies can provide us with a procedure for "validating" the various suggested quality adjustments, and possibly also a way of discriminating between alternative forms and measures of "education."

Consider a very simple Cobb-Douglas type of aggregate production function:

$$Y = AK^\alpha L^\beta,$$

where Y is output, K is a measure of capital services, and L is a measure of labor input in "constant quality units." Let the correct labor input measure be defined as

$$L = E \cdot N,$$

where N is the "unweighted" number of workers and E is an index of the quality of the labor force. Substituting EN for L in the production function, we have

$$Y = AK^\alpha E^\beta N^\beta,$$

providing us with a way of testing the relevance of any particular candidate for the role of E. At this level of approximation, if our index of quality is correct and relevant, when the aggregate production function is estimated using N and E as separate variables, the coefficient of quality (E) should both be "significant" in some statistical sense and of the same order of magnitude as the coefficient of the number of workers (N).[9] It is this type of reasoning which led me, among other things, to embark

---

[9] The E measure as used here is equivalent to the "labor-augmenting technical change" discussed in much of recent growth literature. I prefer, however, to interpret it as an approximation to a more general production function based on a number of different types of labor inputs. Allowing changing weights in the construction of such an E index implicitly allows for a very general production function (at least over the subset of different L types) and imposes very few restrictions on it. An interpretation of E as an index of embodied quality in different types and vintages of labor, fixed once and for all and independent of levels of K, would be very restrictive and is not necessary at this level of aggregation.

TABLE 4

*Education and Skill Variables in Aggregate
Production Function Studies*

Industry, Unit of Observation, Period and Sample Size		Labor Coefficient	Education or Skill Variable Coefficient	R^2
1. U.S. Agriculture, 68 Regions, 1949	a.	.45		.977
		(.07)		
	b.	.52	.43	.979
		(.08)	(.18)	
2. U.S. Agriculture, 39 "states," 1949–54–5 9	a.	.43		.980
		(.05)		
	b.	.51	.41	
		(.06)	(.16)	.981
3. U.S. Manufacturing, states and two–digit industries, N=417, 1958	a.	.67		.547
		(.01)		
	b.	.69	.95	.665
		(.01)	(.07)	
4. U.S. Manufacturing, states and two–digit industries, N=783, 1954–57–63	a.	.71		.623
		(.01)		
	b.	.75	.96	.757
		(.01)	(.06)	
	c.	.85	.56	.884
		(.01)	(.16)	

NOTE: All the variables (except for state industry, or time dummy variables) are in the form of logarithms of original values. The numbers in parentheses are the calculated standard errors of the respective coefficients.

SOURCES: 1. Griliches [23], Table 1. Dependent variable: sales, home consumption, inventory change, and government payments. Labor: full-time equivalent man-years. "Education" — average education of the rural farm population weighted by average income by education class-weights for the U.S. as a whole, per man. Other variables included in the regression: livestock inputs, machinery inputs, land, buildings, and other current inputs. All variables (except education) are averages per commercial farm in a region. 2. Griliches [24], Table 2. Dependent variable: same as in (1) but deflated for price change. Labor: total man—days, with downward adjustments for operators over 65 and unpaid family workers. Education: similar to (1). Other variables: Machinery inputs, Land and buildings, Fertilizer, "Other", and time dummies. All of the variables (except education and the time dummies) are per farm state averages. 3. Griliches [25], Table 5. Dependent variable: Value added per man-hour. Labor: total man-hours. Skill: Occupational mix-annual average income predicted for the particular labor force on the basis of its occupational mix and national average incomes by occupation. Other variable: Capital Services. All variables in per-establishment units. 4. Griliches [27], Table 3. Dependent, labor, and skill variables same as above. Other variables: a. and b. Capital based on estimated gross-book-value of fixed assets; c. also includes 18 Industry and 20 regional dummy variables.

on a series of econometric production function studies using regional data for U. S. agriculture and manufacturing industries. The results of these studies, as far as they relate to the quality of labor variables, are summarized in Table 4.[10]

In general they support the relevance of such "quality" variables fairly well. The education or skill variables are "significant" at conventional statistical levels and their coefficients are, in general, of the same order of magnitude (not "significantly" different from) as the coefficients of the conventional labor input measures. It is only fair to note that the inclusion of education variables in the agricultural studies does not

---

[10] The data sources and many caveats are described in detail in the original articles cited in Table 4 and will not be reproduced here. Note that for manufacturing, the quality variable is based on an occupation-by-industry rather than education-by-industry distribution, since the latter was not available at the state level. On the other hand, the first manufacturing study (Griliches [25]) also explored the influence of age, sex, and race differences on productivity, topics which will not be pursued further here.

increase greatly the explained variance of output per farm at the cross-sectional level, while the expected equality of the coefficients of E and N is only very approximate in the manufacturing studies. Nevertheless, this is about the only direct and reasonably strong evidence on the aggregate productivity of "education" known to me, and I interpret it as supporting both the relevance of labor quality so measured and the particular way of measuring it.[11]

There have been a few attempts to introduce education variables in a different way. Hildebrand and Liu [33] considered the possibility that an education variable may modify the exponent of a conventional measure of labor in a Cobb-Douglas type production function. Their empirical results, however, did not provide any support for such a hypothesis, partly because of lack of relevant data. They used the education of the total labor force in a state for the measurement of the quality of the labor force of individual industries within the same state. But the difficulty of estimating interaction terms of the form $E \log L$ implied by their hypothesis, arises mostly, I believe, because there is no good theoretical reason to expect this particular hypothesis (that education affects the share of labor in total production) to be true. Brown and Conrad [13] have proposed the more general (and hence to some extent emptier) hypothesis that education affects *all* the parameters of the production function. They did not, however, estimate a production function directly, including instead a measure of the median years of schooling in ACMS type of time series regressions of value added per worker on wage rates and other variables. Their results are hard to interpret, in part because their education variables are fundamentally trends (having been interpolated between the observed 1950 and 1960 values), and because the same final equation is implied by the very much simpler errors-in-the-measurement of labor model. Nelson and Phelps [46] have suggested that education may affect the rate of diffusion of new techniques more than their level. This would imply in cross-sectional data that education affects the over-all efficiency parameter instead of serving as a modifier of the labor variable. Nelson and Phelps do not present any empirical estimates of their model. Without further detailed specification of their hypothesis, it is not operationally different from the quality of labor view of educa-

[11] Somewhat similar results have also been reported by Besen [5].

tion in a Cobb-Douglas world, since any multiplicative variable can always be viewed as modifying the constant instead of one of the other variables.[12]

No studies, as far as I know, have used a human capital variable as an alternative to the labor-augmenting quality index in estimating production functions. While at the national accounting level it need not make any difference which variable is used, the two approaches used in a Cobb-Douglas framework would imply different elasticities of substitution between different types or components of labor. Consider two alternative aggregate production function models

$$Y = AK^{\alpha}L^{\beta} = AK^{\alpha}N^{\beta}E^{\beta}$$

where $E = \sum_i r_i N_i / N$ and the r_i's are some base period rentals (wages) for the different categories of labor, and

$$Y = BK^a N^b H^c$$

where H is a measure of "human capital." To be consistent with the E measure it would have to be based on a capitalization of the wage differentials over and above the returns to "raw," unskilled, or uneducated labor (r_0).[13] Thus, approximately

$$H = \delta \sum_i (r_i - r_0)N_i$$

where δ is a capitalization ratio on the order of one over the discount rate. Note, that given our definitions we can rewrite H as

$$H = \delta(EN - r_0 N) = \delta N(E - r_0)$$

---

[12] Data from the 1964 Census of Agriculture may allow a test of the Nelson-Phelps hypothesis. These data provide separate information on the education of the farm *operator* as distinct from that of the rest of the farm labor force. The Nelson-Phelps hypothesis implies that the education of entrepreneurs is a more crucial, in some sense, determinant of productivity than the education of the rest of the labor force.

[13] An H index based on costs (income forgone and the direct costs of schooling) would be similar to the one described in the text only if all rates of return to different levels of education were equal to each other and to the rate used in the construction of the human capital estimate.

TABLE 5

Various Education Measures in an Aggregate
Agricultural Production Function
(Sixty-Eight Regions, U.S. 1949)

| Education Variable | Coefficients of | | R^2 |
	X_6 (man-years)	Education Variable	
S	.539	.0165 (.0065)	.9789
log S	.536	.297 (.119)	.9789
E	.524	.431 (.181)	.9787
E_2	.520	.455 (.203)	.9785

S—Mean school years completed of the rural farm population (25 years old and over). E—Logarithm of the school years completed distribution of the rural farm population weighted by mean income of all U.S. males, 25 years and over in 1949. Mean incomes from H. Houthakker [34]. E_2—Same as E except that the weights are mean wage and salary income of native white males (over 25) in 1939. Mean incomes by school years completed computed from the 1940 *Census of Population, Education*, Washington, 1947, pp. 147 and 190. Other variables are the same as in row 1 of Table 4.

SOURCE: Unpublished mimeographed appendix to Griliches [23].

and substituting it into the human capital version of the production function we get

$$Y = CK^a N^{b+c} E^c \left(1 - \frac{r_0}{E}\right)^c.$$

Thus, the *H* version implies that the production function written in terms of *E* is not homothetic with respect to *E*. Moreover, it implies that the elasticity of substitution between *H* and *N* is unity, while the *E* version assumes (for fixed *r*'s) that the elasticity of substitution between different types of labor (the N_i) is infinite, at least in the neighborhood of the observed price ratios.

While such different assumptions are not operationally equivalent, it is probably impossible to discriminate between them on the basis of the type and amounts of data currently available to us. Consider the last equation; it differs from the straight E version by having a different coefficient on E than on N. If we estimate the E equation in an H world, we shall be leaving out the variable $\log(1 - r_0/E)$ with a c coefficient in front of it. But $\log(1 - r_0/E)$ is approximately equal to $-r_0/E$, since $r_0/E < 1$, and the regression coefficient of the left out variable, in the form of $1/E$ on the included variable $\log E$, will be on the order of one, for not too large variations in E. Hence, the estimated coefficient of E in an H world will be on the order of $2c$, which is not likely to be too different from the coefficient of N^{b+c}.

More generally, it is probably impossible to distinguish between various different but similar hypotheses about how the index E should be measured, at least on the basis of the kind of data I have had access to. Whether one uses "specific" or national income weights, or just simply the average number of school years completed, one has variables that are very highly correlated with each other. This is illustrated by the results reported in Table 5, based on an unpublished appendix to my 1963 study. Our data are just not good enough to discriminate between "fine" hypotheses about the form (curvature) of the relationship or the way in which such a variable is to be measured.

IV   AGGREGATION

OBVIOUSLY, in constructing such indexes of "quality" (or human capital) we are engaged in a great deal of aggregation. There are many different types and qualities of "education" and much of the richness and the mystery of the world is lost when all are lumped into one index or number. Nevertheless, as long as we are dealing with aggregate data and asking over-all questions, the relevant consideration is not whether the underlying world is really more complex than we are depicting it, but rather whether that matters for the purpose of our analysis. And even if we

TABLE 6

Ratios of Mean Incomes for U.S. Males
by Schooling Categories

Year	High School Graduates to Elementary School Grads		College Graduates to High School Graduates	
1939	1.40[a]		1.57[c]	
1949	1.41	1.34[b]	1.63	
1958		1.48	1.65	
1959		1.30		1.51[d]
1963		1.49		1.45
1966		1.56		1.52

[a]Elementary 7–8 years

[b]Elementary 8 years

[c]College 4 + years

[d]College 4 years

SOURCE: From Table 3

decide that one index of E hides more than it reveals, our response will surely not be "therefore let's look at 23 or 119 separate labor or education categories," but rather what kind of two-, three-, or four-way disaggregation of E will give us the most insight into the problem.

From a formal point of view, we can appeal either to the Hicks composite-good or to the Leontief separability theorems to guide us in the quest for correct aggregation. If relative prices (rentals or wages) of labor with different schooling or skill levels have remained constant, then we lose little in aggregating them into one composite input measure. A glance at the "relative prices" for different educational classes reported for the United States in Table 3 does not reveal any drastic changes in them. Thus, it is unlikely that at this level of aggregation much violence is done to the data by putting them further together into one L or E index. Similar results can be gleaned from a variety of occupational and skill differential data (see Tables 6 and 7). In general, they have remained remarkably stable in the face of very large changes in relative

TABLE 7

Ratios of Mean Incomes of U.S. Employed and Salaried Males: Professional and Technical Workers to Operatives and Kindred

Year	
1947	1.67
1950	1.58
1953	1.55
1959	1.67
1964	1.63

SOURCE: From U.S. Bureau of Census, *Trends in Income of Families and Persons in the U.S.: 1947 — 1964*, Technical Paper No. 17, Washington, 1967, Table 38.

numbers and other aspects of the economy.[14] In fact, the apparent constancy of such numbers constitutes a major economic puzzle to which I shall come back later.

When we abandon the notion of one aggregate labor input and are faced with a list of eight major occupations, eight schooling classes, several regions, two sexes, at least two races, and an even longer list of detailed occupations, there doesn't seem to be much point in trying to distinguish all these aspects of the labor force simultaneously. The next small step is obviously not in the direction of a very large number of types of labor but rather toward the question of whether there are a few underlying relevant "dimensions" of "labor" which could explain, satisfactorily, the observed diversity in the wages paid to different "kinds" of labor. The obvious analogy here is to the hedonic or characteristics approach to the analysis of quality change in consumer goods, where an attempt is made to reduce the observed diversity of "models" to a smaller set of relevant characteristics such as size, power, durability, and so forth.[15] One can identify the "human capital" approach as a one-dimen-

[14] The constancy of relative differentials implies a rise in absolute differential and a rise in the incentive to individuals to invest more in their education.

[15] See Griliches [26] and Lancaster [41] for a recent survey and exposition of such an approach.

sional version of such an approach.[16] Each person is thought of as consisting of one unit of raw labor and some particular level of embodied human capital. Hence, the wage received by such a person can be viewed as the combination of the market price of "bodies" and the rental value of units of human capital attached to (embodied in) that body:

$$w_i = w_o + rH_i + u_i$$

where u_i stands for all other relevant characteristics (either included explicitly as variables, controlled by selecting an appropriate sub-class, or assumed to be random and hence uncorrelated with H_i). If direct estimates of H are available, this type of framework can be used to estimate r. If proxy variables are used for H, such as years of schooling, age, or "experience," one can proceed to the estimation of income-generating functions as did Hanoch [31] and Thurow [59] which, in turn, can be interpreted as "hedonic" regressions for people. Alternatively, if one is willing to assume that the implicit prices (w_0 and r) are constant, and one has repeated observations for a given i, one can use such a framework to estimate the unobserved "latent" H_i variable. Consider, for example, a sample of wages by occupation for different industries: If one assumes that occupations differ only by the amount of human capital embodied per capita, and that the price of "bodies" and of "skill" is equalized across industries, then this is just a one-factor analysis model, and it can be used to estimate the implied relative levels of H_i for different occupations. Of course, having gone so far one need not stop at one factor, or only one underlying skill dimension. The question can be pushed further to how many latent factors or dimensions are necessary or adequate for an explanation of the observed differences in wages across occupations and schooling classes?

This is, in fact, the approach pursued by Mitchell [44] in analyzing the variation of the average wage in manufacturing industries by states. He concludes that one "quality" dimension is enough for his purposes. He does, however, make the very stringent assumption that the implied

---

[16] Actually, it could be thought of as a two-dimensional or factors model, body and skill, but since each person is taken to have only one unit of body (even a Marilyn Monroe), the B dimension becomes a numeraire and for practical purposes this reduces itself to a one-factor model.

relative price ratio of bodies to human capital, or of skilled and unskilled wages (w_0/r), is constant across states and countries. This is a very strong assumption, one that is unlikely to be true for data cross-classified by schooling. Studies of U. S. data (see, e.g., Welch, [62] and Schwartz [51] have in general found significantly more regional variation in the price of unskilled or uneducated labor than in the price of skilled or highly educated labor, implying the nonconstancy of skill differentials across regions (and presumably also countries).

In a recent paper, Welch [63] outlines a several dimensions model of the general form

$$w_{ij} = w_{0j} + r_{1j}S_{1i} + r_{2j}S_{2i}$$

where i is the index for the level of school years completed, j is the index for states, S_1 and S_2 are two unobserved underlying skill components associated with different educational levels. This is not strictly a factor-analysis model any longer, both because the r's are assumed to vary across states and because no orthogonality assumptions are made about the two latent skill levels. With a few additional assumptions, Welch shows that if the model is correct one should be able to explain the wage of a particular educational or skill level by a linear combination of wages for other skill levels and by no more than three such wages (since there are only three prices here: two "skills" and one "body"). The linearity arises from the implicit assumption that at given prices any unit of S_1 or S_2 (and "body") is a perfect substitute for another. Thus, even though different types of labor are made up of a smaller number of different qualities which may not be perfectly substitutable for each other, because the whole bundle is defined linearly, one can find linear combinations of several types of labor which will be perfectly substitutable for another type of labor. For example, while college and high school graduates may not be perfect substitutes, one college graduate plus one elementary school graduate may be perfect substitutes for two high school graduates. Welch analyzes incomes by education by states and concludes that in general one doesn't need more than three underlying dimensions to explain eight observed wage levels, and that often two are enough. It is not clear whether Welch is using the best possible and most parsimonious normalization, or whether a generalization of the factor-analytic approach with oblique factors could not be adapted to this problem, but clearly this is a very interesting and promising line of analysis.

The approximate constancy of relative labor prices by type, the implicit linearity of the Welch model, and some scattered estimates of rather high elasticities of substitution between different kinds of labor or education levels (e.g., Bowles [8]), all imply that we will lose little by aggregating all the different types of labor into one over-all index as long as our interest is not primarily in the behavior of these components and their relative prices.

V ABILITY

THIS is a very difficult topic with a large literature and very little data. What little relevant data there are have been recently surveyed by Becker [2] and Denison [17]. It has been widely suggested that the usual income-by-education figures overestimate the "pure" contribution of education because of the observed correlation between measured ability and years of school completed. On the basis of scattered evidence both Becker and Denison decide to adjust downward the observed income-by-education differentials, Denison suggesting that all differentials should be reduced by about one-third.

It is useful, at this point, to set up a little model to help clarify the issues. Assume that the true relation in cross-sectional data is

$$Y_i = \beta_0 + \beta_1 S_i + \beta_2 A_i + u$$

where Y is income, S is schooling and A is ability, however measured. The usual calculation of an income-schooling relation alone leads to an estimate of a schooling coefficient (b_{ys}) whose expected value is higher than the true "net" coefficient of schooling (β_1), as long as the correlation between schooling and the left out ability variable is positive. The exact bias is given by the following formula:

$$Eb_{ys} = \beta_1 + \beta_2 b_{As}$$

where b_{As} is the regression coefficient in the (auxiliary) regression of the left out variable A on S, the included one. Moving to time series now, and still assuming that the underlying parameters (β_1 and β_2) do not change, we have the relationship

$$\bar{Y} = \beta_0 + \beta_1 \bar{S} + \beta_2 \bar{A} + u$$

where the bars stand for averages in a particular year. Now if b_{YS} is derived from cross-sectional data and is used in conjunction with the change in the average schooling level to predict (or explain) changes in $\bar{Y}$ over time, it will overpredict them (give too high a weight to $\bar{S}$) unless $\bar{A}$ changes pari passu. But it is assumed that the distribution of A, innate ability, is fixed over time and hence, its mean $(\bar{A})$ does not change. This, therefore, is the rationale for considering the cross-sectional income-education weights with some suspicion and for adjusting them downward for the bias caused by the correlation of schooling with ability.

I should like to question these downward adjustments on three related grounds: 1. Much of measured ability is the product of "learning," even if it is not all a product of "schooling." Often what passes for "ability" is actually some measure of "achievement," and the argument could be made that it in turn is determined by a relation of the form

$$A = \alpha_0 + \alpha_1 S + \alpha_2 QS + \alpha_3 LH + \alpha_4 G + v$$

where S is the level of schooling, QS is the quality of schooling, LH are the learning inputs at "home," and G is the original genetic endowment. If one were to substitute this equation into the original relation for Y one would find that the "total" coefficient of the schooling variables is given by

$$\beta_1 + \beta_2 \alpha_1 + \beta_2 \alpha_2 b_{QS \cdot S}$$

where $b_{QS \cdot S}$ is the relation between the quality and quantity of schooling in the cross-sectional data, and the "total" coefficient associated with changes in total "reproducible" human capital (including that produced at home) by

$$\beta_1 + \beta_2 \mid \alpha_1 + \alpha_2 b_{QS \cdot S} + \alpha_3 b_{LH \cdot S} \mid$$

where $b_{LH \cdot S}$ summarizes the relation between learning at home and at school in cross-section. Now while the simple coefficient of income and schooling b_{YS} may overestimate the partial effect of schooling (β_1) holding achievement constant, it may not overestimate that much, if at all, the "total" effect of schooling. 2. The estimated downward adjustments for ability may be overdone particularly in the light of strong interaction of "ability" and schooling as they affect earnings. That is, since the relation between A and Y holding S constant is strong only at higher S levels, b_{AS} may be quite low, and the bias in the estimated b_{YS} may not be all that large. 3. Moreover, the whole issue hinges on whether or not $\bar{A}$ as measured has really remained constant over time. To the extent that proxies such as father's education are used in lieu of "ability," it can be shown that at least their levels did not remain constant.

It is probably best, at this point, to confess ignorance. "Ability," "intelligence," and "learning" are all very slippery concepts. Nor do we know much about the technology of schooling or education. What are the important inputs and outputs, what is the production function of education, how do the various inputs interact? Some work on this is in progress (see Bowles [9]) and perhaps we will know more about it in the future. We do know, however, the following things: 1. Intelligence is not a fixed datum independent of schooling and other environmental influences. 2. It can be affected by schooling.[17] 3. It in turn affects the amount of learning achieved in a given schooling situation. 4. Because the scale in which it is measured is arbitrary, it is not clear whether the relative distribution of "intelligence" or "learning abilities" has remained constant over time.

> The doctrine that intelligence is a unitary something that is established for each person by heredity and that stays fixed through life should be summarily banished. There is abundant proof that greater intelligence is associated with increased education. . . . On the basis of present information it would be best to regard each intellectual ability of a person as a somewhat generalized skill that has developed through the circumstances of experience, within a certain culture, and that can be further developed by means of the right kind of exercise. There may be limits to ability set by heredity, but it is probably safe to say that very rarely does an individual really test such limits.[18]

---

[17] See e.g., the studies of separated identical twins summarized in Bloom [7].
[18] Guilford [28], p. 619.

Actually, IQ and achievement tests are so intimately intertwined with education that we may never be successful in disentangling all their separate contributions. IQ tests were originally designed to determine which children could not learn at "normal" rates. Consequently, children with above average IQ are expected to learn at above normal rates. The effect of intelligence on learning is presumably twofold (or are these two sides of the same coin?): Higher IQ children know more to start with and this "knowing more" makes it easier to learn a given new subject (since knowing more implies that it is less "new" than it would otherwise be), and higher IQ children are "quicker." They absorb more for a similar length of exposure, and hence know more at the end of a given period. Since schools try, in a sense, to maximize the students' "achievement," and since achievement and IQ tests are highly enough correlated for us to treat them interchangeably, one might venture to define the gross output of the schooling system as ability. That is, schools use the time of teachers and students and their respective abilities to increase the abilities of the students. From this point of view, the student's ability is both the raw material that he brings to the schooling process, which will determine how much he will get out of it, and the final output that he takes away from it. Hence, at least part of the apparent returns to "ability" should be imputed to the schooling system.[19] How much depends on what is the bottleneck in the production of educated people—the educational system or the limited number of "able" people that can benefit from it. If, as I believe may be the case, ability constraints have not been really binding, very little, if any, of the gross return to education should be imputed to the not very scarce resource of innate ability.

---

[19] Consider two extreme worlds. In one, the only product of the school systems is "ability" or "achievement." In this world, school years completed are just a poor measure of the product of schools. If correct measures of "ability" were available, they would dominate any earnings-education-ability regressions and imply zero coefficients of the school years completed variable. Nevertheless, almost all of the observed "ability" differential would be the product of "education." A second world is one in which the educational system does nothing more than select people for "ability," by putting them through finer and finer sieves, without adding anything to their innate ability in the process. Again, an earnings-education-ability correlation would come out with zero coefficients to education net of ability. Still, in an uncertain world with significant costs of information, there is a significant social product even in the operation of grading and sorting schemes. Even in such a world there is a net value added produced by the educational system, though it may be very hard to measure it. See Zusman [66] for the beginning of an economic analysis of sorting phenomena.

Actually, the little data we have shows a surprisingly poor relation between earnings and "ability" measures when formal schooling is held constant. Wolfle summarized the conclusions of such studies as of 1960:

> High school grades, intelligence-test scores, and father's occupation were all correlated with the salaries being earned fifteen to twenty years after graduation from high school, but the amount of education beyond high school was more clearly, more distinctly related to the salaries being earned.
> There is another conclusion from the data, one of perhaps greater importance. It is this: the differences in income were greatest for those of highest ability. It is of some financial advantage for a mediocre student to attend college, but it is of greater financial advantage for a highly superior student to do so.[20]

Examining the tables from Wolfle's studies reproduced in Becker and Denison, one is struck both by the importance of interaction, and by the very limited effect of IQ on earnings except for those within the upper tail of the educational distribution.[21] In fact, the IQ adjustment constitutes only a very small portion of Denison's total "ability" adjustment. One of his major adjustments is based on a cross classification of earnings-by-education by father's occupation. It is not clear at all why this is an "ability" dimension.[22] Higher-income and -status fathers will provide both more schooling at home and *buy* better quality schooling in the market. To the extent that these differences reflect the latter rather than the former, it does not seem reasonable to adjust for them at all.

In most studies that use IQ or achievement tests, these tests are taken at the end of the secondary school period. As we have noted, such test scores are to some unknown degree themselves the product of the

[20] Wolfle [65], p. 178.

[21] This is also supported by the greater role of "ability" at the lower end of the educational distribution found by Hansen, Weisbrod, and Scanlon [32]. IQ tests, however, are not very good discriminators at the very extremes of the distribution. For a sample of Woodrow Wilson Fellowship holders, Ashenfelt and Mooney [1] found that: "The inclusion of an ability variable affected the estimate of the other education-related variables only in a very marginal fashion. . . . The misspecifications caused by the absence of an ability variable seem to be quite small indeed" (for samples of highly educated people).

[22] ". . . it is what the parents *do* in the home rather than their *status* characteristics which are the powerful determinants of home environment." Bloom [7], p. 124.

TABLE 8

Taxed Income at Thirty-Five by Number of Years of Formal Schooling and I.Q. at age Ten, Males, Malmo, Sweden

Number of Years of Formal Schooling

I.Q. at Age 10	Less than 8 yrs.			8–10 yrs.			11–14 yrs.			14 yrs. and more		
	M	S.D.	n	M	S.D.	n	M	S.D.	n	M	S.D.	n
115+	17,450	4260	20	21,943	7363	35	33,750	35238	32	43,158	19219	19
108–114	16,625	5165	32	19,538	7793	26	19,429	12893	14	41,000	18267	13
93–107	15,266	5270	109	18,176	8118	68	21,735	7477	34	31,400	26567	5
86–92	17,744	10306	39	17,462	5955	13	20,500	7527	10	—	—	—
–85	14,548	4041	73	14,929	4611	28	17,750	4763	4	35,533	6182	3

SOURCE: From Husén (35), Table 16.
NOTE: M = mean income in kroner; S.D. = standard deviation; n = number of cases.

educational system (at the high school and elementary level). To separate the "value added" component of schools one would like to have such scores at a much younger age, upon entry into the schooling system. I have come across only one set of data, for the city of Malmo in Sweden (from Husen, [35]), which provides a distribution of earnings at age thirty-five by formal schooling and by IQ at age *ten*.[23] They are reproduced in Table 8. One of the important aspects of this particular sample is that it does cover the whole range of both the schooling and IQ distribution. We can use these data to investigate how much change there is in the income-education coefficient when IQ is introduced as an explicit variable.

After some experimentation with scaling and the algebraic form of the relationship, the following weighted regressions were computed for these data (nineteen observations) with $n/(S.D.)^2$ as weights:[24]

$$\log Y = 9.317 + .053S \qquad\qquad R^2 = .589$$
$$(.011)$$

and

$$\log Y = 8.938 + .051S + .0042A \qquad R^2 = .836$$
$$(.007) \quad (.0009)$$

where Y is income, S is years of school completed and A is the IQ score. In these data "original" IQ is an important variable, "explaining" an additional 30 per cent of the variance in the logarithm of incomes, but its introduction does almost nothing to change the coefficient of schooling. There would have been little bias from ignoring it.[25]

Similar results, but based on much more tenuous evidence, can also be had for the United States. For the United States we do not have yet any data on earnings by education and ability on a large scale, but we do have a large body of income-by-education data from the 1960 census of population, and a distribution of "ability" (Armed Forces Qualifica-

---

[23] I am indebted to C. A. Anderson for drawing my attention to these data.

[24] The scaling chosen was 6, 9, 13, and 17 and 73, 89, 100, 111, 127 for the schooling and IQ categories respectively.

[25] The results were essentially the same for the linear and log-log forms. The semilog forms reported in the text fit the data best on the "standard error in comparable units" criterion. The results are also similar for unweighted regressions, except that the coefficient of schooling is significantly higher.

TABLE 9

Regression Coefficients of the Logarithm of Income on
Schooling and of "Ability" on Schooling by Regions

	$b_{(\log Y)S}$	b_{AS}
Northwest, total	.0663	.426
Northcentral, total	.0702	.470
South, total	.1011	.424
South, nonwhite	.0726	.343
West, total	.0760	.475

SOURCE: *Income by schooling,* data from 1960 Census of Population, median income for males age 35–44; schooling extimated as the midpoint of the class intervals and 18 for 5 + years of college category. *"Ability" by schooling,* based on the estimated distribution of the Army Forces Qualification Test for youths aged 19–21 in 1960; from Karpinos [38]. AFQT percentiles scaled by the approximate average score (probit) associated with the particular percentile range (−5, −2, 0, 2, 5 for less than 9, 10–35, 36–64, 65–92, and 93–100, respectively).

On the basis of the above numbers, the implied β and γ in the equation $\log Y_{ij} = \partial_j + \beta S_{ij} + \gamma A_{ij}$ are .112 and −.07, respectively.

tion Test) by school years completed based on tabulation of army induction tests of youths in 1964–65 (Karpinos, [38]).[26] Since the two bodies of data are not for the same population or time periods, what follows is very much an approximation, prompted by the desire to see whether these data could be of some use after all. Consider the equation

$$\log Y_{ij} = \alpha_j + \beta S_{ij} + \gamma A_{ij}$$

where the index i goes over schooling classes and j over regions. We cannot compute this relationship directly, since we do not have the covari-

---

[26] The AFQT is primarily an achievement rather than an innate ability test: "The examinee's score on the tests depends on several factors: on the level of his educational attainment; on the quality of his education (quality of the school facilities); and other knowledge he gained from his educational training or otherwise, in and outside of the school. These are interrelated factors, which obviously vary with the youth's socio-economic and cultural environment, in addition to his innate ability to learn—commonly understood as IQ, nor are they to be translated in terms of IQ." From Karpinos, [38]. Thus, it is probably inappropriate to use these data to get at a pure "net" schooling effect.

ances of A with log Y, but we do have information on the relationship of A to S. If we ignore A and estimate a truncated relationship of log Y on S for each region separately, we would get as our coefficient of S in each region (using the left-out-variable formula):

$$Eb_j = \beta + \gamma \cdot b_{ASj}$$

where the term b_{AS} is the regression coefficient in the auxiliary regression connecting the left-out variable A with the included variable S. Since we have such b_j's and b_{ASj} for several regions, we can compute the implied β and γ by another round of least squares. Table 9 summarizes such a computation based on data for five regions of the United States. Note that implicit in this computation is the assumption that regional differences in the observed slope of the income-education relationship must be due to regional differences in the association between schooling and ability.

The figures reported in Table 9 actually imply a negative γ. That is, if an adjustment were made for ability, it would *increase* the estimated influence of schooling on income. This is largely the result of the fact that the only major difference in the income-schooling slope is observed for the South (total, white and nonwhite), while the observed increase in ability with education in the South is only average or even lower.[27] Given the quality of these data, the inherent arbitrariness in the scaling of A, and the many tenuous assumptions required, these results should not be taken seriously. But they too do not come up with any strong evidence for the overwhelming importance of "ability" as distinct from "schooling."[28]

There are two more points to be made. First, to the extent that measured ability is an important determinant of earnings *only* at the higher education levels, it is not correct to "reduce" the education coefficient, or the weights attached to the higher education classes in the con-

---

[27] A more detailed analysis using the AFQT-schooling distribution for ten rather than five regions and mean income by schooling data for males aged forty-five–fifty-four, yielded very similar results and will not be reported here. I am indebted to F. Welch for providing me with the adjusted state data on mean income by schooling.

[28] The Carroll and Ihnnen [15] study of a group of North Carolina technical school graduates can also be interpreted to support this view.

struction of quality indexes, unless there is evidence that the observed increases in educational attainment have been associated with a lowering in the average ability of the educated. I know of no evidence which points in this direction. There is no evidence that the growth in educational attainment has been restricted by the drawing down of the "pool of ability."[29] There is a large body of evidence pointing to the existence of many high-ability lower-class children who do not go on to college or finish high school for a variety of economic and social reasons.[30] In spite of the tremendous increase in the number of college graduates in this country, the distribution of college students by social origin (father's occupation) has not changed significantly or adversely in the last thirty years.[31] Also, if ability were a major constraint one might have expected that the observed income differentials would narrow, as poorer-quality

[29] See Halsey [30] for a discussion and criticism of this metaphor.
[30] See, e.g., Telser [58], and Folger and Nam [21].
[31] The following table adapted from the U.S. Bureau of the Census (*Current Population Reports,* Census P-20, No. 132, 1964, "Educational Changes in a Generation," Table 1) sheds some light on this question:

DISTRIBUTION OF MALES BY YEARS OF SCHOOL COMPLETED, BY AGE, AND BY FATHER'S OCCUPATION AND EDUCATION, U.S., MARCH, 1962
(in per cent)

Age and Cohort	College Graduates		Some College	
	Father White Collar	Father White Collar, Some College Education	Father White Collar	Father White Collar, Some College Education
20–24 1938–42	—	—	88	31
25–34 1928–37	64	27	60	23
35–44 1918–27	62	26	55	19
45–54 1908–17	62	25	55	19
55–64 1898–1907	60	14	56	15

Similar implications can also be read into the British data reported by Floud and Halsey [20].

people were getting more education.[32] This does not appear to have happened, however. One might even conjecture that as education spread, the selection processes were actually improved, and hence that there may be a higher correlation of ability with education today than was true thirty years ago.[33] It is also possible that our children being taller and healthier than the previous generations may also be more intelligent.[34]

The second point to be made is that much of what is used as a proxy for "ability" is not really an innate ability and need not and has not remained constant over time. Denison in examining the Wolfle-Smith data concludes that about 6 per cent of the observed college-high school income differential can be attributed to the "rank in high school" and about 3 per cent to IQ. These, of course, are not independent, but in any case, at most 10 per cent of the differential can be ascribed on the basis of the internal evidence of the Wolfle-Smith data to something that could be a reflection of innate ability. An additional 7 per cent of the differential is ascribed to differences in father's occupation. The rest, about *half*

[32] Unless, of course, the quality of high school graduates deteriorated more than that of college graduates. Given the relative size of the two groups and the observed minor effect of "ability" on earnings for high school graduates, this is an unlikely event, at least as measured by conventional IQ scores. But the widening of the differential between elementary and high school graduates may indicate that those who do not get past elementary education may today be much more affected by ability constraints and other handicaps than used to be the case in the past.

[33] Something like this is implied in the slightly higher regression and correlation coefficient for the relationship of ability to schooling in the North Central States than in the South, reported in Table 8. This is also supported by the following table taken from a recent article by Turnbull [60], p. 1426; the data are derived from Wolfle's study and from the Project TALENT survey:

PERCENTAGES OF HIGH SCHOOL GRADUATES GOING ON TO COLLEGE,
BY ABILITY GROUP

Ability group	Wolfle 1953	TALENT 1960
Lowest (fourth) quarter	20	19
Third quarter	32	32
Second quarter	38	54
Top (first) quarter	48	80

[34] The Educational Testing Service recently notified a large number of students who took the Graduate Record Examination that instead of having scored in the, say, ninety-eighth percentile, as previously announced, upon restandardization for the more recent experience, their scores were more accurately described as being in the ninety-fourth percentile. The mean score of men in the 1964–67 norm group was 5.5 per cent higher on the verbal ability test and 10.7 per cent higher on the quantitative ability test than that of the 1952 basic reference group. (See Educational Testing Service, [19].)

of the one-third adjustment, is based on the difference between the size of the over-all differential as reported in these data (for Illinois, Minnesota, and Rochester men) and the national average differential. At best, therefore, this is not an adjustment for "ability" but for *regional* differences in income and the regional correlation between average incomes and levels of education.[35] Thus, less than one-third of the "one-third" adjustment is related conceptually to ability per se.

Even if one allows that the underlying IQ distribution has not changed over time, the other proxy variables, such as father's occupation and regional distribution have changed. Consider, for example, the simple model where father's education is used as a control variable. Then in cross section we have

$$Y_s = \beta_0 + \beta_1 S_s + \beta_2 S_F$$

where the subscripts s and F stand for sons and fathers respectively. If one ignored the education of fathers variable, one would estimate

$$Eb_{YS} = \beta_1 + \beta_2 b_{S_F S_s}$$

where $b_{S_F S_s}$ is probably less than one (the slope of the relationship between the schooling of fathers and sons). In time series, however, we would have

$$\overline{Y}_s = \beta_0 + \beta_1 \overline{S}_s + \beta_2 \overline{S}_F.$$

But the average schooling of fathers has been growing at approximately the same rate as that of sons! Hence, the total effect of schooling should be measured by $\beta_1 + \beta_2$, and the unadjusted b_{YS} is closer to that than the "net" β_1!

Similarly, the average level of education in the North grew at about the same rate as that in the South. Since the North had more education to start with and a higher average wage associated with it, this would lead to a growth in the *share* of the North in "total" labor quality. Hence, if one holds region constant in deriving the educational weights, one should, on the other hand, also adjust the labor input upward for the

---

[35] This adjustment is also probably overdone, since we know that education differentials in the North Central States were lower than in most of the rest of the U.S. In that sense, the Wolfle-Smith figures are not representative.

fact that the share of the higher quality regions grew at the same time. Thus, the one-third downward adjustment suggested by Denison may be a serious overadjustment if what we are interested in is an estimate of the rate of growth in the *total* quality of the labor force. One should recognize, however, that not all of the growth attributed to changing educational attainment is the *net* product of the education system per se.

VI THE PUZZLE OF THE CONSTANCY OF DIFFERENTIALS

THE main evidence on the relative constancy of educational and skill differentials in the post-World War II period in the U. S. is summarized in Tables 3, 6, and 7 and has been alluded to before. Becker [2] (Table 14, p. 128) reaches similar conclusions about the behavior of rates of return to higher education over time. The puzzling thing is that these differentials and rates of return should change so little in the face of very large shifts in the relative numbers of educated workers. Between 1952 and 1966 the ratio of males between the ages of eighteen and sixty-four in the U. S. civilian labor force with high school education and more to those with elementary education and less changed from about 1 to 1 to about 2.5 to 1, and still their relative incomes did not change greatly.

There appear to be four possible explanations of the phenomenon, three on the demand side and one on the supply side.[36] On the demand side we can conceive three sources of increased demand for skilled workers which could have counterbalanced the depressing effect of the increase in their supply: 1. It may just happen that goods that have an income elasticity higher than one have on average a higher skill content embedded in them than do goods whose income elasticity is less than one. 2. It may be that for some reason not yet clear technical change has been on the average "skill using" and "unskilled labor saving." 3. It is possible, and plausible, that physical capital is more complementary with skilled than with unskilled labor. Since physical capital has been growing

---

[36] This section and also parts of Section 4 have been inspired and owe a great deal to my reading of Welch's [64] unpublished paper on this topic.

at a higher rate than the labor force, this would imply also a growth in the relative demand for educated labor. 4. Finally, it may be that all of this is essentially a reflection of the nature of the supply of skills. The most important factor in the production of skill is the labor of students and teachers. If the production function (time requirements) of skills does not change much over time, the prices of skilled and unskilled labor must move roughly in proportion to each other, since skilled labor can be "manufactured" from unskilled labor in a roughly unchanging way, using resources whose price is proportional both to the input and output price of this process. The existence of such a relation does not, of course, contradict the various demand hypotheses, but makes it very much harder to distinguish among them.

There is very little empirical evidence on any of these points. Nor is it obvious that a priori they are all plausible. It is easy, for example, to think of some commodities such as "food away from home" that have a high income elasticity and a rather low skill content. A crude check on the over-all demand hypothesis can be made by investigating whether changes in employment between 1950 and 1960 by industries have any association with the average educational attainment of the labor force in each of the industries. Using data from the 1960 Census of Population for 149 industries we get a correlation coefficient of about .33 for the relationship between the percentage change in the employment of males between 1950 and 1960 and the logarithm of mean school years completed by industry in 1960.[37] This is a statistically significant but not very strong relationship. A similar calculation for females yields no relationship at all ($r^2 = -.07$). While such a relation could be due to several causes, there does appear to be something in the demand hypothesis which may warrant further exploration.

Since we do not know how to measure neutral technical change very well, the probability of measuring the "skill-bias" of technical change in a nontautological fashion is even lower, and I shall not pursue this further here. There remains yet the possibility of capital-skill complementarity which will be explored in the next section.

[37] The figures were taken from the 1960 Census of Population, Vol. I, Part 1, Table 211 and Vol. II, Part 7F, "Industrial Characteristics," Table 21. The results of using median years of school completed, a weighted E index, and the logarithm of the E index were almost identical.

VII ARE PHYSICAL AND HUMAN CAPITAL COMPLEMENTS?

TO investigate this question we have to start with a three-input production-function output depending on capital and two types of labor (or "bodies" and "skill"). We shall write it in the form

$$Y = F(K, L, S)$$

with the hypothesis to be investigated being that (in the Allen sense):

$$0 < \sigma_{LK} > \sigma_{SK} \lessgtr 0$$

where the σ_{ij}'s are the respective partial elasticities of substitution. It is not clear where one could get some evidence on this. At the aggregate level things are much too collinear to be of much help (moreover, we can't really measure anything more than the trends in K, L, and S with any degree of accuracy). At the micro level, one usually does not have data on S and K at the same time or place, and what is even worse, one rarely has any relevant input price data and the price data one has (such as wages) are subject to significant biases precisely because of the existence of the third variable S, significant differences in the quality of the labor force. The following model may, however, give some hope of success:[38] If one starts with inputs defined per unit of output (assuming for this purpose constant returns to scale), and measures everything in logarithms of the variables, one can write (as an approximation), the demand functions for inputs as

$$x_i = a_i + \Sigma \eta_{ij} p_j = a_i + \Sigma v_j \sigma_{ij} p_j$$

where x_i is the logarithm of the ith input per unit of output, p_j is the logarithm of the "real" price of the jth input, η_{ij}'s are the respective price elasticities ($\Sigma_i \eta_{ij} = 0$), v_j is the share of the jth factor in total cost, and the σ_{ij}'s are the Allen-Uzawa partial elasticities of substitution ($\sigma_{ij} = \sigma_{ji}$, and $\sigma_{ii} < 0$). Consider now the special case of three inputs: L–labor, K–capital, and S–skill or schooling, with the corresponding (rental) prices W, R, and Z. Then, using the homogeneity condition, we can write (using lower case letters to denote the logarithms of the corresponding variables)

---

[38] This model is based on unpublished notes by H. G. Lewis. See also Mundlak [45].

$$l = \eta_{ll}(w - z) + \eta_{lk}(r - z) + a_l$$
$$k = \eta_{kl}(w - z) + \eta_{kk}(r - z) + a_k$$
$$s = \eta_{sl}(w - z) + \eta_{sk}(r - z) + a_s$$

and subtracting the first two equations from the third

$$s - l = (\eta_{sl} - \eta_{ll})(w - z) + (\eta_{sk} - \eta_{lk})(r - z) + (a_s - a_l)$$
$$s - k = (\eta_{sl} - \eta_{kl})(w - z) + (\eta_{sk} - \eta_{kk})(r - z) + (a_s - a_k)$$

or

$$(s - l) = v_l(\sigma_{sl} - \sigma_{ll})(w - z) + v_k(\sigma_{sk} - \sigma_{lk})(r - z) + c_1$$
$$(s - k) = v_l(\sigma_{sl} - \sigma_{kl})(w - z) + v_k(\sigma_{sk} - \sigma_{kk})(r - z) + c_2$$

The hypothesis that skill or education is more complementary with physical capital than is physical (or unskilled, or unschooled) labor would imply that the coefficient of $(r - z)$ in the first equation is negative $(\sigma_{lk} > \sigma_{sk})$ and that the coefficient of $(w - z)$ in the second equation is also negative $(\sigma_{kl} > \sigma_{sl})$. At the same time, one would expect the other two coefficients to be positive.[39]

If data were available on the relevant prices, one could estimate either version, in one case assuming that the approximation is better when one assumes the demand elasticities to be constant over the observed range, or alternatively, making the same assumption about the elasticities of substitution.

There is an additional set of assumptions that may allow us to estimate these questions almost without any price data. If one has data by state and industry for the two-digit manufacturing industries in the United States (and assumes that σ's are approximately the same for all these industries, though not the v's), one may hypothesize (a) that the true rental price of capital r does not differ among states but may differ as between industries (because of different depreciation, obsolescence, and risk rates), (b) that the real price of skilled labor has been effectively equalized by migration and the unions, and hence that z is a constant at a point of time, and (c) that the price of pure physical labor does differ between states (not having been equalized by migration) but

---

[39] This model could be "simplified" further by noting the relationship between input and output prices and using it to solve one of the input prices, substituting the output price throughout. But unless one has good data on output prices by states and industries, or is willing to assume that they are constant, there is little to be gained from such a substitution.

is essentially the same for all industries within the same state. The coefficients of $(w - z)$ could then be effectively estimated by state dummy variables (or more correctly cross-dummies, if we allow also the v's to vary, which we'll have to, to achieve identification) and the coefficients of $(r - z)$ by industry dummies. The expected sign relations could then be checked by computing the ratio of the respective coefficients in the two equations (e.g., $\overline{v_l(\sigma_{sl} - \sigma_{kl})}(w - z)/\overline{v_l(\sigma_{sl} - \sigma_{ll})}(w - z)$ should be negative).

Alternatively, at a more aggregate time-series level, one may assume that factor prices are changing in the same way for all industries. Then, using an alternative but equivalent set of two equations, we have

$$(s - l) = v_l(\sigma_{sl} - \sigma_{ll})(w - z) + v_k(\sigma_{sk} - \sigma_{lk})(r - z)$$
$$(k - l) = v_l(\sigma_{kl} - \sigma_{ll})(w - z) + v_k(\sigma_{kk} - \sigma_{lk})(r - z)$$

In time series we expect that the rate growth of $r - z$ will be negative, that the rate of growth of $(w - z)$ may be positive (due to the larger increase in S over time) but close to zero, which should lead to a positive correlation between the change in $(s - l)$ and $(k - l)$ under our hypotheses, with the regression coefficient of $(s - l)$ on $(k - l)$ being less than one. This is implied by our hunch that $\sigma_{sl} < \sigma_{kl} > 0$ and $\sigma_{kk} < \sigma_{sk} < \sigma_{lk} > 0$.

A preliminary and crude foray into data for twenty-eight "two-digit" industries in the United States in 1949 and 1963 yielded some not very strong support for the hypothesis outlined here.[40] There is a positive

[40] The limits of this set of data are based on the availability of time series on gross capital stocks in constant prices at the two-digit level. These are derived from a forthcoming book by M. Gort. (I am indebted to Michael Gort for making these yet unpublished data available to me.) The list of industries runs through ten manufacturing industries from "food" to "other transportation equipment," and nine other large industries: mining, railroads, electric utilities, gas utilities, telephone, contract construction, wholesale trade, and retail trade. The capital stocks are as of beginning of 1949 and 1963. Total employment for these industries for 1948 and 1963 is taken from BLS Bulletin 1312-5; the percentage of the male labor force that consists of professional and technical workers is taken from the "Occupation by Industry" volumes of the 1950 and 1960 Census of Population; and the wage of unskilled labor is identified with the median earnings of laborers who worked 50–52 weeks in these industries and is taken from the respective 1950 and 1960 Census volumes on occupational characteristics. Denoting total employment by N and professionals as a fraction of the labor force by P, S is given by $N \cdot P$ and L, the level of the "unskilled" labor force by $N(1-P)$. All the regressions and correlations were computed using total employment in 1963 as weights.

relation between *capital* per unskilled worker and *skilled worker* per unskilled worker across these industries. The simple weighted correlation coefficient between the logarithms of these variables is .48 in 1949, .50 in 1963, and .47 for the change in these variables between these two years.[41] Assuming that the omission of the capital-rental variable does not significantly bias the other results (this is equivalent to assuming that it is uncorrelated with the unskilled labor wage rate across industries), we get the "right" signs in the regressions $s - l$ and $s - k$ on w. The estimated coefficients in the two equations are respectively 4.4(.9) and $-2.0(1.8)$ for 1949 and 2.6(.5) and $-.8(.8)$ for 1963. The second of the four coefficients is the one we are most interested in, as it is proportional to $\sigma_{sl} - \sigma_{kl}$ and is negative, as expected, but this finding, however, is not statistically "significant" at conventional levels. Similarly, the regression coefficient of $\Delta(s - l)$ on $\Delta(k - l)$ is positive and less than one (.47 with an estimated standard error of .17), but again this result should not be taken too seriously. It could be due to common errors in the measurement of l and the spuriousness arising out of the appearance of L in the denominator of both variables. Better and more extensive data for testing such hypotheses is being assembled, but their analysis is only in its earliest stages.

VIII   TENTATIVE SUMMARY

THERE are a large number of important topics which have not been even touched upon in this survey. I have neglected the very important one of the interaction of on-the-job training, schooling, experience, obsolescence, and aging. I have also said nothing about different types of education

---

[41] While such correlation coefficients are "significant" at conventional levels, the over-all fit is quite poor and there are a number of notable outliers. The chemical industry has a high capital-labor and a high skill ratio, but the electric machinery industry has a high skill ratio and a relatively low capital-labor ratio, while the utility industries have very high capital-labor ratios but only average skill ratios. Similarly, the highest rates of growth in capital-per-man occurred in this period in mining and construction. Mining had also probably the highest rate of growth in the relative number of highly skilled workers, while construction had one of the lowest. There are no easy answers.

and the measurement of the quality of education. Nor have I discussed models of optimal investment in human capital or the correct treatment of the educational sector and the investment in human capital in a more comprehensive set of national accounts. Hopefully, many of these topics will be dealt with by other participants in this conference.[42]

It would seem to me that the over-all state of the measurement of the contribution of education is in reasonably good shape and has been validated by econometric studies. What needs more work is the elucidation of the processes of production of human capital and the determinants of the rates of return to different types of educational investment.

REFERENCES

[Note: This list includes several important works not referred to explicitly in the text.]

1. Ashenfelter, O., and J. D. Mooney, "Graduate Education, Ability, and Earnings," *Review of Economics and Statistics,* XLX (1), 1968, 78–86.
2. Becker, G. S., *Human Capital,* New York, NBER, 1964.
3. ————, *Human Capital and the Personal Distribution of Income,* Woytinsky Lecture No. 1, University of Michigan, 1967.
4. Ben-Porath, Y., "The Production of Human Capital and the Life Cycle of Earnings," *Journal of Political Economy,* 75 (4), 1967, 352–65.
5. Besen, S. M., "Education and Productivity in U. S. Manufacturing: Some Cross-Section Evidence," *Journal of Political Economy,* 76 (3), 1968.
6. Blaug, M., *Economics of Education,* A Selected Annotated Bibliography, Oxford, 1966.
7. Bloom, B. S., *Stability and Change in Human Characteristics,* New York, 1964.

---

[42] On the issue of training and experience see Mincer [43] and Thurow [59] among others; see Denison [16], Welch [62], and the Coleman report [14] for very different ways of estimating the relative quality of schooling; see Ben-Porath [4] for a model of human capital investment and Bowman [12] and Kendrick [40] for discussions of the treatment of education in national accounts.

8. Bowles, S., "Aggregation of Labor Inputs in Economics of Growth and Planning," *Journal of Political Economy,* January–February, 1970.

9. ————, "Towards an Educational Production Function," this volume.

10. Bowman, M. J., "Schultz, Denison, and the Contribution of 'Eds' to National Income Growth," *Journal of Political Economy,* 72 (5), 1964, 450–64.

11. Bowman, M. J., and C. A. Anderson, "Distributed Effects of Educational Programs," in *Income Distribution Analysis,* North Carolina State University, 1966.

12. Bowman, M. J., "Principles in the Valuation of Human Capital," *Review of Income and Wealth,* 14 (3), 1964, 217–46.

13. Brown, M., and A. Conrad, "The Influence of Research and Education on CES Production Relations," in M. Brown, ed., *The Theory and Empirical Analysis of Production,* New York, NBER, 1967, 341–71.

14. Coleman, J. S., *et al., Equality of Educational Opportunity,* U. S. Dept. of Health, Education and Welfare, Washington, D. C., 1966.

15. Carroll, A. B., and L. A. Ihnnen, "Costs and Returns for Two Years of Post Secondary Technical Schooling: A Pilot Study," *Journal of Political Economy,* 75 (6), 1967, 862–73.

16. Denison, E. F., *The Sources of Economic Growth in the United States and the Alternatives Before Us,* Supplementary Paper No. 13, New York, Committee for Economic Development, 1962.

17. ————, "Measuring the Contribution of Education," in *The Residual Factor and Economic Growth,* OECD, 1964, 13–55, 77–102.

18. ————, *Why Growth Rates Differ,* Brookings Institution, 1967.

19. Educational Testing Service, *Handbook for the Interpretation of GRE Scores, 1967–68,* Princeton, 1967.

20. Floud, J., and A. H. Halsey, "Social Class, Intelligence Tests, and Selection for Secondary Schools," in Halsey, Floud, and Anderson, eds., *Education, Economy and Society,* Glencoe, Ill., 1961, 209–15.

21. Folger, J. K., and C. B. Nam, *Education of the American Population,* A 1960 Census Monograph, Washington, D. C., 1967.

22. Griliches, Z., "Measuring Inputs in Agriculture: A Critical Survey," *Journal of Farm Economics,* XLII (5), 1960, 1411–27.

23. ————, "Estimates of the Aggregate Agricultural Production Function from Cross-Sectional Data," *Journal of Farm Economics,* XLV (2), 1963.

24. ————, "Research Expenditures, Education, and the Aggregate Agricultural Production Function," *The American Economic Review,* LIV (6), 1964, 961–74.

25. ————, "Production Functions in Manufacturing: Some Preliminary Results," in M. Brown, ed., *The Theory and Empirical Analysis of Production,* Studies in Income and Wealth, Vol. 31, New York, NBER, 1967.

26. ————, "Hedonic Price Indexes Revisited: Some Notes on the State of the Art," in Amer. Stat. Assoc., *1967 Proceedings of the Business and Economics Section,* 1967b.

27. ————, "Production Functions in Manufacturing: Some Additional Results," *Southern Economic Journal,* 35 (2), 1968, 151–56.

28. Guilford, J. P., "Intelligence Has Three Facets," *Science,* 160 (3828), 1968, 615–20.

29. Hall, R. E., "Technical Change and Capital from the Point of View of the Dual," *Review of Economic Studies,* 1968.

30. Halsey, A. H. (ed.), *Ability and Educational Opportunity,* OECD, 1961.

31. Hanoch, G., "An Economic Analysis of Earnings and Schooling," *Journal of Human Resources,* II (3), 1967, 310–29. Also, unpublished Ph.D. dissertation, "Personal Earnings and Investment in Schooling," Chicago, 1965.

32. Hansen, W. L., B. A. Weisbrod and W. J. Scanlon, "Schooling and Earnings of Low Achievers, *American Economic Review,* vol. 60, no. 3, (June 1970).

33. Hildebrand, G. H., and T. C. Liu, *Manufacturing Production Functions in the U. S., 1957,* Cornell University Studies in Industrial and Labor Relations, Vol. XV, 1965.

34. Houthakker, H. S., "Education and Income," *Review of Economics and Statistics,* 41 (1), February 1959, 24–28.

35. Husen, T., "Talent, Opportunity, and Career: A 26 Year Follow-up," *School Review,* 76 (4), December, 1968, University of Chicago.

36. Johnson, H. G., "Comment," in *The Residual Factor and Economic Growth,* OECD, 1964, 219–27.

37. Jorgenson, D. W., and Z. Griliches, "The Explanation of Productivity Change," *Review of Economic Studies,* XXXIV (3), No. 99, 1967.

38. Karpinos, B. D., "The Mental Qualifications of American Youths for Military Service and Its Relationship to Educational Attainment," *1966 Proceedings of the Social Statistics Section of the American Statistical Association,* 1966, 92–111.

39. Kendrick, J. W., *Productivity Trends in the United States,* Princeton, 1961.

40. ————, "Investment Expenditure and Imputed Income in Gross National Product," in *47th Annual Report of the NBER,* New York, 1967.

41. Lancaster, K., "A New Approach to Consumer Theory," *Journal of Political Economy,* 74 (2), 1966, 132–57.

42. Miller, H. P., "Annual and Lifetime Income in Relation to Education," *The American Economic Review,* (5), December, 1960, 962–86.

43. Mincer, J., "On-the-Job Training: Costs, Returns, and Some Implications," *Journal of Political Economy,* 70 (5), 1962, Part 2, Supplement: *Investment in Human Beings.*

44. Mitchell, E. J., "Explaining the International Pattern of Labor Productivity and Wages: A Production Model with Two Labor Inputs," *Review of Economics and Statistics,* L (4), 1968, 461–69.

45. Mundlak, Y., "Elasticities of Substitution and the Theory of Derived Demand," *Review of Economic Studies,* 1968.

46. Nelson, R. R., and E. S. Phelps, "Investment in Humans, Technological Diffusion, and Economic Growth," *The American Economic Review,* LVI (2), 1966.

47. Nerlove, M., "Embodiment and All That: A Note," unpublished mimeographed paper, 1965.

48. Richter, M. K., "Invariance Axioms and Economic Indexes," *Econometrica,* October 1966.

49. Rosen, S., "Short-Run Employment Variation on Class-I Railroads in the U. S., 1947–1963," *Econometrica,* 36 (3–4), 1968, 511–29.

50. Schmookler, J., "The Changing Efficiency of the American Economy, 1869–1938," *Review of Economics and Statistics,* 34 (3), August 1952, 214–31.

51. Schwartz, A., "Migration and Life Span Earnings in the U. S.," unpublished Ph.D. dissertation, University of Chicago, 1968.

52. Selowsky, M., "Education and Economic Growth: Some International Comparisons," unpublished Ph.D. dissertation, University of Chicago, 1967.

53. Schultz, T. W., "Capital Formation by Education," *Journal of Political Economy,* 1960, 571–83.

54. ————, "Education and Economic Growth," in N. B. Henry, ed., *Social Forces Influencing American Education,* Chicago, 1961.

55. ————, *The Economic Value of Education,* New York, 1963.

56. Solow, R. M., "Technical Change and the Aggregate Production Function," *Review of Economics and Statistics,* 39 (3), August 1957, 312–20.

57. Strumlin, S. G., "The Economic Significance of National Education," 1925, translated from Russian and reprinted in Robinson and Vaizey (eds.), *The Economics of Education,* New York, 1966, 276–323.

58. Telser, L. G., "Some Economic Aspects of College Education," Economics of Education Research Paper No. 59–5, University of Chicago, unpublished dittoed paper, 1959.

59. Thurow, L. C., *Poverty and Discrimination,* Brookings Institution, Washington, D. C., 1969, Chapter V.

60. Turnbull, W. W., "Relevance in Testing," *Science,* 160, 1968, 1424–29.

61. U. S. Bureau of the Census, *Trends in the Income of Families and Persons in the U. S.: 1947–1964,* Technical Paper No. 17, Washington, D. C., 1967.

62. Welch, F., "The Measurement of the Quality of Schooling," *The American Economic Review,* XLVI (2), 1966, 379–92.

63. ————, "Linear Synthesis of Skill Distributions," *Journal of Human Resources,* IV (3), Summer 1969, 311–27.

64. ————, "Education in Production," *Journal of Political Economy,* January-February, 1970

65. Wolfle, D., "Economies and Educational Values," in S. E. Harris (ed.), *Higher Education in the U. S.: The Economic Problems,* Cambridge, Mass., 1960.

66. Zusman, P., "A Theoretical Basis for Determination of Grading and Sorting Schemes," *Journal of Farm Economics,* 49 (1), 1967, 89–106.
67. Griliches, Z., "Capital-Skill Complementarity," *Review of Economics and Statistics,* 51 (40), November 1969, 465–68.
68. Jensen, Arthur R., "How Much Can We Boost IQ and Scholastic Achievement?" *Harvard Educational Review,* 39 (1), Winter 1969, 1–123.
69. Schrader, W. B., "Test Data as Social Indicators," Educational Testing Service, SR-68-77, Princeton, N. J., September 1968.
70. Taubman, P., and Wales, T. J., "Mental Ability and Higher Educational Attainment Since 1910," University of Pennsylvania Discussion Paper No. 139, October 1969.

COMMENTS

JOHN CONLISK
UNIVERSITY OF CALIFORNIA, SAN DIEGO

Most of this comment concerns the role of education in aggregate production functions and in growth analysis. Some brief remarks on the income-education-ability interrelation conclude the comment.

I. THE ROLE OF EDUCATION IN AGGREGATE PRODUCTION FUNCTIONS AND IN GROWTH ANALYSIS

For a long time, a major puzzle in the growth literature was that the total measured growth in inputs did not add up to measured growth in output. Consider this puzzle in the context of an aggregate production function $Y = F(X_1, \ldots, X_m)$ which gives output Y as a constant returns function F of m inputs $X_1, \ldots, X_m$. Taking the growth rate of both sides:

$$\dot{Y}/Y = v_1 \dot{X}_1/X_1 + \ldots + v_m \dot{X}_m/X_m \tag{1}$$

where v_i is the relative marginal product share of X_i $[v_i = (\partial F/\partial X_i)X_i/Y]$.

The puzzle in the literature was that, when observed values of the magnitudes on the right were plugged in, they did not add up to the observed value of $\dot{Y}/Y$. The difference, or residual, was often vaguely referred to as "technical change." It was not (to my knowledge) until the important paper by Griliches and Jorgensen [4] that the terms on the right of (1) were measured carefully and completely enough to add up to $\dot{Y}/Y$. They accomplished this full "explanation" of growth in substantial part by their quality correction to observed labor growth (reviewed in Section II of the current Griliches paper).

However, this "explanation" of growth of output in terms of growth of inputs may be viewed as only the first of two prinicipal levels of growth explanation. At the second level, one may ask why the inputs grew as they did, particularly inputs like physical and human capital, which are endogenous to the economic system. In an aggregate modeling context, the first level of explanation requires only the specification of an aggregate production relation; the second level of explanation requires enough additional relations to form a complete growth system. There is a large neoclassical growth literature devoted to such complete aggregate growth systems; but, unfortunately, this literature has not come to grips with the problem of how to treat education. While under the influence of Griliches' stimulating paper, I have had some thoughts on this problem which I would like to relate here.

Griliches suggests two ways in which an aggregate production function might include education (defined in a broad sense):

$$Y = F(K,H,N) \quad \text{and} \quad Y = F(K,EN) \tag{2}$$

In the first case, output Y is given as a constant returns function of physical capital K, human capital H, and the number of workers N. In the second case, output is given as a constant returns function of physical capital K and quality-corrected labor EN, where N is the number of workers and E is a labor-augmenting quality multiplier. The two hypotheses are not observationally equivalent (nor exclusive for that matter); but, as Griliches points out, it is doubtful that available data can distinguish them by ordinary production-function estimation methods. However, if the two versions of (2) are built into complete growth models in what appear to be "natural" ways, they yield quite different implications about long-run growth behavior. Perhaps these implications can be used to distinguish the two functions empirically.

First, consider very briefly the standard neoclassical growth model without education; we will call it Model A:

$$Y = F(K,N)$$
$$\dot{K} = sY - \delta K$$
$$\dot{N}/N = n$$

Here $\dot{K} \equiv dK/dt$; s is a constant gross savings rate; δ is a constant depreciation rate; and n is a constant population growth rate. F, like all production functions used here, is assumed to exhibit constant returns to scale. Given some very weak additional restrictions of F and the parameters, Model A has a unique, stable, equilibrium growth path on which $\dot{Y}/Y = \dot{K}/K = n$. (For a reference to a derivation of this standard result, see footnote 1.) Heuristically, the reason K, and thus Y, are limited to growth rate n in equilibrium is that diminishing average returns to K as K/N rises prevent K/N from rising indefinitely. Put another way, K cannot grow indefinitely faster than N because N will ultimately become scarce enough relative to K to bottleneck further growth in K/N. The observed output growth rate in real life is of course larger than the population growth rate n. So there is here an unexplained difference, or residual, between the observed output growth rate and the rate $\dot{Y}/Y = n$ predicted by Model A. Thus, at both the first level of growth explanation of equation 1 and at the second level of growth explanation of Model A, the literature has been puzzled by an unexplained residual. (To invoke an exogenously given rate of Harrod neutral factor augmentation in Model A is of course no more of a real explanation of the second level residual than invoking the catch phrase "technical change" is an explanation of the first level residual.)

Now introduce education into Model A via the first of functions (2) and we have Model B:

$$Y = F(K,H,N)$$
$$\dot{K} = sY - \delta K$$
$$\dot{H} = s'Y - \delta'H$$
$$\dot{N}/N = n$$

where s' and δ' are savings and depreciation parameters for human capital. If human capital is treated in parallel to physical capital, then these equations seem a natural extension of Model A. Under some weak restrictions on F and the parameters, Model B has a unique, stable, equilibrium path on which $\dot{Y}/Y = \dot{K}/K = \dot{H}/H = n$.[1] This is the same result as for Model A, and for the same reason. K and H cannot grow indefinitely faster than N because N will ultimately become scarce enough relative to K and H to bottleneck growth to rate n. Thus, the residual between the observed level of $\dot{Y}/Y$ in real life and the predicted rate $\dot{Y}/Y = n$ is the same in Model B as in Model A, despite the inclusion of human capital in Model B.

Now introduce education into Model A via the second of function (2) and we get Model C:

$$Y = F(K,EN)$$
$$\dot{K} = sY - \delta K$$
$$\dot{E} = s'Y/N - \delta'E$$
$$\dot{N}/N = n$$

where s' and δ' are a savings and a depreciation parameter regulating growth in E. Since E is a productivity multiplier with an implicit "per worker" dimension (in contrast to H which does not have a per worker dimension), it is appropriate that the first term on the right of the $\dot{E}$ equation is in per worker units (that is, divided by N). Let $L = EN =$ the quality-corrected labor force. Then Model C may be written more compactly:

$$Y = F(K,L)$$
$$\dot{K} = sY - \delta K \tag{3}$$
$$\dot{L} = s'Y - (\delta' - n)L$$

Displayed in this form, Model C shows a symmetric treatment of the two inputs K and L. That is, neither input grows at an exogenously given rate, as the labor input does in both Models A and B. Hence the equilibrium behavior of Model C is different. Under some weak restrictions on F and the parameters, Model C has a unique, stable, equilibrium path on which:

---

[1] References to derivations are needed for Models A, B, and C. For Model A, the path-breaking article by Solow [5] will still do as well as any. For Model B, I do not know of a reference which is right to the point, but the results will be grasped immediately by anyone who understands Model A. For Model C, see Conlisk [2].

$$\dot{Y}/Y = \dot{K}/K = \dot{L}/L = g(s,s',\delta,\delta',n) > n \qquad (4)$$
$$(+,+,-,-,+)$$

where g is a function which is related to F and which has partials of the indicated signs. (For reference to derivations, see footnote 1.) Note especially that $\dot{Y}/Y > n$ in equilibrium. That is, in strong contrast to Models A and B, Model C *can* explain the difference, or residual, between the observed level of $\dot{Y}/Y$ in real life and the population growth rate n. The sensitivity of $\dot{Y}/Y$ to all the parameters of Model C is another strong contrast with Models A and B (where $\dot{Y}/Y = n$, regardless of other parameters).

These results suggest that Model C, which centers around Griliches' function $Y = F(K,EN)$, is more relevant to real life than Model B, which centers around Griliches' function $Y = F(K,H,N)$. The victory of the $Y = F(K,EN)$ function over the $Y = F(K,H,N)$ function, of course, depends on the other relations in Models B and C also. However, I think I have rounded out Models B and C in a "natural" fashion, given the conventional ways of doing things in the growth literature.

If we now make the distinction between equilibrium and disequilibrium behavior in Models B and C, we can go considerably further in discussing their contrasting relevance to real life. Start with the question of whether it is Model B's equilibrium or disequilibrium behavior which should be tested against real economies. As discussed above, equilibrium is reached in Model B when the ratios K/N and H/N get so large that the relative scarcity of N bottlenecks further growth in K/N and H/N. It would seem that even a rich country like the United States is nowhere near this situation. Surely the amounts of physical and human capital per worker in the United States are not so large that workers cannot sustain any further increases. (In part, this is what Griliches is saying when he argues in Section V of his current paper that further educational attainment is not restricted by past "drawing down of the 'pool of ability'.") This suggests that the relevant part of Model B's behavior is its disequilibrium behavior when K/N and H/N are far below their equilibrium levels.

If the last paragraph is correct, it might be asked why numerical studies of the speed of adjustment of neoclassical growth models do not show more clearly that such models cannot reach equilibrium in anything like relevant time periods. There is a simple answer. Suppose a speed of adjustment study uses a Cobb-Douglas function of the form $Y = AK^{1-\alpha}N^\alpha$ (as several studies have). It would be conventional to use an α-value of about $\alpha = .7$, on the grounds that .7 is about labor's relative share of output. However, labor's relative share is in large part due to the human capital embodied in labor. So, in the expanded function $Y = AK^{1-\alpha-\beta}H^\beta N^\alpha$, an appropriate value for α is probably very much less than .7. But it can be shown (see Conlisk [1], for example) that the speed of adjustment of a model like Model B is very much faster for larger values of α than for smaller values of α. (α is the crucial exponent because N is the bottle-necking input.) Thus, the available numerical studies tend to underestimate the time it takes for neoclassical models to approach equilibrium, because these studies give much too high a value to α (or the corresponding magnitude in non-Cobb-Douglas models).

Once a case is made that real life growth corresponds to the disequilibrium behavior of Model B, economists are likely to look for a new model which describes real life growth as equilibrium behavior. Equilibrium analysis is easier to work with than disequilibrium analysis. (A good example of this is unemployment theory. Unemployment is a disequilibrium state with respect to the classical macro-model; so economists have naturally gravitated to Keynesian models which describe unemployment as an equilibrium state.) Starting from Model B in search of a model with a shorter run equilibrium, an obvious question is—will Model C do?

In Model C, equilibrium is reached when K/L reaches its equilibrium value. But equilibrium constancy of $K/L = (K/N)/E$ is possible both for very high values of K/N and E (such as for a rich country) and for very low values of K/N and E (such as for a poor country). Thus, Model C's equilibrium behavior applies to both rich and poor countries. This indicates that the equilibrium behavior of Model C is much shorter run in nature than that of Model B (which applies only to economies so rich that they can sustain no more physical and human capital per worker). Putting this argument another way: there is no mechanism in Model C by which increases in K/N and E can result in a bottlenecking scarcity of N. Workers are able to handle effectively unlimited amounts of capital and education per worker. That is the situation that real economies are now in—able to handle more capital and education per worker.

The discussion thus far may be summarized in the following points:

1. Growth explanation may be viewed from two levels—a first level, centering on an aggregate production function, in which growth in output is explained in terms of growth of inputs; and a second level, requiring a complete system of equations, in which the growth of both output and inputs is explained.

2. At both levels of explanation, the literature reflects puzzlement at the difference, or residual, between the amount of output growth observed in real life and the amount of output growth explained by the economic models.

3. Griliches suggests two ways of including education in an aggregate production function—the $Y = F(K,H,N)$ form and the $Y = F(K,EN)$ form. If one uses the measurement techniques of the Griliches-Jorgensen work, the puzzle of the residual at the first level of explanation can apparently be solved with either production function form (though they in fact concentrate on the $Y = F(K,EN)$ form).

4. If one straightforwardly expands Griliches' two production functions to complete models, and if one sticks to equilibrium analysis, the puzzle of the residual at the second level of growth explanation can apparently be solved only with the $Y = F(K,EN)$ function.

5. More specifically, the equilibrium state of Model B, which is built around the $Y = F(K,H,N)$ function, is a state in which the amount of physical and human capital per worker are so great that a relative scarcity of workers bottlenecks further growth in K/N and H/N. The real world seems nowhere near such a state, though it seems impossible to rule out the possibility of such a state in the distant future. Thus, if Model B is currently relevant at all, it would seem that its disequilibrium behavior is what is relevant.

6. On the other hand, the equilibrium state of Model C, which is built around the $Y = F(K,EN)$ function, appears to be much shorter run in nature. As in real life, the workers in Model C are always ready to handle effectively greater amounts of physical capital and education per worker.

7. All this adds up to a tentative preference for Griliches' $Y = F(K,EN)$ function over his $Y = F(K,H,N)$ function, at least in currently popular growth modelling contexts.

In my opinion, the growth model literature is far too little concerned with questions of interpretation and practical relevance; so I am grateful to Griliches for stimulating a helpful viewpoint on the Model B versus Model C issue. One can hope that Griliches and other education experts will in the future delve further into what I have here called the second level of growth explanation. Growth model theorists and education experts would seem to be more natural allies than their past cooperation indicates.

II. THE INCOME-EDUCATION-ABILITY INTERRELATION

Four brief remarks on the ability issue will conclude my comment.

1. The determination of a person's income involves a number of jointly dependent variables and a number of independent variables. Variables like wealth and debt would ordinarily be included along with income in the dependent variable list, while variables like parents' education and age would be included in the independent variable list. Variables like education and ability might fall in either list, depending on the time period involved and the exact way the variables are defined. In any case, a simultaneous-equations model seems needed to handle the situation. Yet individual income determination analysis more often than not centers on a single equation with income the dependent variable. In studying macroeconomic income determination, economists would typically reject this single-equation approach outright, even though the macro problem is probably a conceptually easier one (since an economy does not have a life cycle in any sense relevant here, and since the law of large numbers operates strongly to simplify aggregate behavior). Thus, I think Griliches is taking a useful line when (in the third paragraph of his Section V) he starts taking a simultaneous-equations view of things.

2. I sometimes worry that economists will no sooner get the ability issue apparently nailed down than the whole bias problem will arise again with respect to another type of excluded variable, which I shall call motivation. Consider two men of junior college education who are apparently similar in every way except that one has a very high IQ (measured at age ten, say) and the other a very low IQ. The usual hypothesis in the literature is that the high-IQ man may be expected to earn more. However, one might ask why the high-IQ man never finished college and how the low-IQ man got that far. A plausible suggestion is that the high-IQ

man has considerably less motivation. If this suggestion is correct and applies across human beings in general, then we have another explanatory variable, collinear with education and ability, which needs to be included if the quantitative effects of various determinants of income are to be sorted out.

3. The matched data on income, education, and age ten IQ which Griliches presents for Malmo, Sweden, are of great interest, since they are just the sort of data which are often asked for. However, I'm not sure the data show what Griliches says they show. In Griliches' regression of income on education and IQ, using this data, education and IQ are both highly significant and quantitatively important. Nonetheless, excluding the IQ variable from the regression has virtually no effect on the estimated coefficient of education. This must mean that education and IQ are not very collinear. If such is the case, then this data set cannot contain much information on excluded-variable bias for data sets where education and IQ are considerably more collinear.

4. Finally, I might review here some small bits of evidence I have recently collected on the income-education-ability interrelation. In Conlisk [3] I suggested two approaches for getting around the lack of matched data on a person's earnings, education, and ability. The first approach was to substitute occupation as a proxy for earnings, and then to use data from psychologists' and educators' studies of intelligence (in which matched data on occupation, education, and other variables are routinely recorded). This approach was illustrated with a human development sample of about seventy men. Occupation at age thirty was used to construct a proxy for income; education was measured as years of schooling; IQ measures were available for a number of age levels from infancy to eighteen years; and various background variables were also available. In a series of regressions with the earnings proxy the dependent variable, education was highly significant and IQ highly insignificant in every regression run. The second approach for getting around the lack of matched income-education-ability data involves aggregate observational units. Data from separate samples, which are unmatched on individuals, may be matched on the aggregate units. Two illustrations of this approach were presented—the first a cross-state analysis using World War I army intelligence test data and income-education data from other

sources, and the second a cross-occupation analysis using World War II army intelligence test data and census income-education data. In the cross-state analysis, the education variable dominated the ability variable. In the cross-occupation analysis, however, the ability variable displaced about half of education's explanatory importance.

REFERENCES

1. John Conlisk, "Unemployment in a Neoclassical Growth Model—the Effect on Speed of Adjustment," *Economic Journal*, September 1966, 550–66.
2. ———, "A Modified Neoclassical Growth Model with Endogenous Technical Change," *Southern Economic Journal*, October 1967, 199–208.
3. ———, "A Bit of Evidence on the Income-Education-Ability Interrelation," 1968, unpublished.
4. Zvi Griliches, and D. W. Jorgensen, "The Explanation of Productivity Change," *Review of Economic Studies,* July 1967, 249–83.
5. Robert Solow, "A Contribution to the Theory of Economic Growth," *Quarterly Journal of Economics,* February 1956, 65–94.

RICHARD R. NELSON
YALE UNIVERSITY AND THE RAND CORPORATION

One of the characteristics of a superb craftsman, like Zvi Griliches, is that he leaves a discussant very little room for examining problems of commission. Even were this not so, I still would feel compelled to focus my remarks on a set of issues with which Griliches dealt hardly at all; namely, the conceptual problems of education as an input to a production function.

I am quite uneasy about the way we economists, theorists, and econometricians are thinking about our dynamic production functions these days. I am concerned that somehow we think the "production function" of growth economics is the same as the "production function" in the old theory of the firm. I think they are quite different animals.

Not so many years ago, before the focus of interest turned to growth and related topics, the production function, in its setting of the neoclassical theory of the firm, was a reasonably clear and solid concept. To produce a given quantity of output certain minimal (alternative sets of) inputs were required. Some of these inputs were needed because they went into the product, like the eggs and milk that go into cake. Others were required because certain operations needed to be performed on the former; an egg beater, a stove, electricity to power both, and man time to operate and control. This notion of a production function one can almost "feel." While, of course, the kinds of production functions we played with in the theory of the firm were much more aggregate than this, beneath the aggregate we could think of a set of more solid production functions.

Underlying (or related to) this concept of the production function there are a *number of related notions.* Behind the scenes is the notion of a well-defined production set, with certain possibilities known, and others unknown, and nothing blurry about the distinction between the two. With all possibilities perfectly known, there really is no problem of technological efficiency. Neither are there problems with making optimizing choices of factor mix.

As we economists have broadened our concerns beyond the relatively uninteresting questions of the comparative statics of a very statical firm, our concept of a production function has also broadened and, I maintain, become very different, although we often write and crank turn as if they were the same. Surely, variables like accumulated research and development expenditure, or investment in extension, have no place in the earlier concept of the production function. Common use is evolving a new definition of the production function, which includes anything and everything that explains output differences (including overtime). Pragmatically this may be convenient. But certainly the older, more solid, concept has fallen by the wayside and there is no reason why concepts associated with it, such as perfect knowledge and optimal choice, should be associated with the new. But sometimes we seem to carry them over mechanically.

Which brings me to education and the production function. In the old concept of the production function, labor simply operated (cooperatively with machines) on the used-up inputs. With this concept it certainly makes sense to think of some minimal body of experience that the worker has to have in order to make a cake. (Some investment is needed in order to obtain the relevant knowledge.) And beyond that level it is easy to think of how, at least up to a point, more experience could make the worker more effective. At the simplest level, less time might be spent looking at the recipe, the set-up operations (getting out all the ingredients) might take less time, etc. In this case experience would be "labor augmenting." It also is possible that a more experienced worker would use less materials per cake (no wastage) and by working faster would require less reserved machine time. In this case experience would be "total-factor-productivity" increasing. And there are other forms one can think of. If one associates education (a chefs' school?) with experience, one can, within this concept of the production function, think meaningfully about how education enters.

However, I maintain that more experienced chefs making a constant cake is not what the observed high returns to education are all about. It is well known that the educated élite do not have dirty (or doughy) hands. I have not taken the trouble to look up what our college-educated members of the work force do, as compared to those with less education. I am confident that most of them are in positions requiring them to make decisions of one kind or another on the basis of information, which it would be difficult or impossible for them to interpret without their educational background, or a lot of special training or experience. And the decisions are real ones, it is not a matter of simply following a static decision rule, or recipe, more efficiently. This certainly is a reasonable characterization for doctors, scientists, lawyers, business executives, and government officials. Generally they are in an environment of considerable flux so that the decision problems they face do not follow a regular routine, not because someone neglected to draw one up but because such problems cannot be made fully formal and routine. Periodically or continuously persons in these professions face the problem of having to learn about something new.

The notion that our better educated people are more adequately equipped to make, or learn to make, decisions, is at once obvious, and very difficult to fit into our traditional production function concept. The reason, of course, is that in our theory of the firm—the unit that operates the production function—no one makes decisions. There is no process of decision making. Decisions (or actions) simply occur and are optimal. And there is nothing to "learn." Everything relevant to decision making simply is known.

I think these are serious problems in the theory of the firm and in the concept of the production function in the theory of the firm, but that is not my concern here. For certainly within the concept of a production function that is evolving for analysis of economic growth we are not stuck with the traditional formulation. How should we proceed to model?

Edmund Phelps and I made a left-handed try, a few years ago, to build a simple model in the spirit of my discussion here. Making decisions regarding new technological options certainly is an archetype of the kind of situation where, I argued here, education should have payoff. Thus, we developed a little model of education as a variable influencing the rate of diffusion. One predictive implication is that the returns to education would be greater, the faster the pace of technological change. Finis Welch, in a recent paper, appears to have found just that. One policy implication is that the returns to an R & D project should be lower the lower the educational attainments of the people who could use the results. If right, this has some significance.

Another model, in this spirit, that I have recently developed, relates education to a head start on learning a specific set of tasks. Education on the part of the new worker is a substitute for experience. One implication of this is that the cost level of an industry will be related to its pace of expansion, but that the penalties of rapid growth will be less when the young work force is well educated than when it is not. This model seems to explain the high costs of rapidly expanding industries in certain less developed countries, and also why countries like Taiwan seem to have less trouble with the worker inexperience problem. The model has some implications for both educational and manufacturing policy in the less developed countries.

I give these examples not to push my own work but rather to suggest that there may be real payoffs from modeling education in quite different ways than those on which Griliches focuses and which seem to have drawn the lion's share of the attention up to now. Predictive and policy implications are not insensitive to specification. Clearly a lot more thinking needs to be done about education in dynamic production functions.

THE PRODUCTION OF HUMAN CAPITAL OVER TIME • YORAM BEN-PORATH
• THE HEBREW UNIVERSITY OF JERUSALEM

THIS paper is a continuation of an earlier study[1] of the time path of investment in human capital over the life cycle. The theoretical model draws on, and was stimulated by, the earlier work of Becker and Mincer on investment in man,[2] and by the view of the household as a unit engaged in production.[3,4]

NOTE: I thank my colleagues, Michael Bruno, Reuben Gronau, and Gur Ofer for making valuable comments on an earlier draft. In rewriting the paper I benefited from comments by Mary Jean Bowman, Ruth Klinov, and Zvi Griliches and particularly from the valuable discussions of the paper by Jacob Mincer in the conference.

[1] Yoram Ben-Porath, "The Production of Human Capital and the Life Cycle of Earnings," *Journal of Political Economy,* August 1967, as well as other parts of "Some Aspects of the Life Cycle of Earnings" (unpublished Ph.D. dissertation, Harvard University, February 1967).

[2] Gary S. Becker, "Investment in Human Capital: A Theoretical Analysis," Jacob Mincer, "On-the-Job Training: Costs, Returns, and Some Implications," *Journal of Political Economy,* Supplement, October 1962, as well as the earlier work by Mincer, "A Study of Personal Income Distribution" (unpublished Ph.D. dissertation, Columbia University, 1957) which is being currently revised.

[3] See in particular Gary S. Becker, "A Theory of the Allocation of Time," *Economic Journal,* September 1965, and Kelvin Lancaster, "A New Approach to Consumer Theory," *Journal of Political Economy,* April 1966, as well as the applications by Jacob Mincer and others. In particular, there is much in common between our model and Gary S. Becker, "Human Capital and the Personal Distribution of Income: An Analytical Approach," New York, NBER, October 1966 (mimeo.).

[4] The problem of the time path of investment in human capital was tackled from a different angle in Giora Hanoch, "Personal Earnings and Investment in Schooling" (unpublished Ph.D. dissertation, University of Chicago, August 1965), chapter II. An approach similar to ours was recently utilized in a more general model, systematically analyzed by Hajime Oniki in his doctoral dissertation entitled "A Theoretical Study on the Demand for Education," 1968 (mimeo). See also C. C. Weizsäcker, "Training Policy under Conditions of Technical Progress: A Theoretical Treatment," in *Mathematical Models in Educational Planning,* Paris, Office of Economic Cooperation and Development, 1967.

The purpose of our model is to introduce explicitly considerations related to the production side of human capital into the analysis of investment in man. This is done by writing down a production function of human capital of the individual. By letting this function generate rising marginal costs of human capital production a mechanism is provided for regulating investment over life.

The main purpose of this paper, aside from a slightly more general formulation of the model, is to use this model as a basis for dealing with a specific question concerning the nature of human capital, namely—to what extent can the accumulation of human capital be described as a neutral augmentation of human productive capacity, where neutrality is considered in reference to two types of activity: market activity, i.e., providing the labor input into the general economy; and the production of human capital, the building up of human productive capacity. While it is customary to emphasize the former role, there is no doubt about the existence of the latter. The question is examined by incorporating the "neutrality hypothesis" into the model. On the basis of estimates of investment in human capital prepared by Jacob Mincer, the hypothesis is tested and tentatively rejected. It is also shown that where the hypothesis is accepted, the key parameter in the production function of human capital can be estimated.

I

CONSIDER an individual, who expects with complete certainty to live for T years, and is faced with a given interest rate r, at which he can borrow and lend indefinitely, and a rental per unit of time of the services of a unit of human capital, w, both of which he expects to remain constant through life. In a classical fashion, define $K(t)$ to be an index of the homogeneous stock of human capital of the individual. It is a measure of labor in standard units and its size, together with the market-determined rental, defines earning capacity, $Y(t)$.

$$Y(t) = wK(t). \tag{1}$$

There are opportunities for increasing the stock of human capital by allocating some services of human capital and purchased inputs D into producing human capital at the rate Q. These opportunities are summarized in a production function:

$$Q(t) = F[s(t) K(t), D(t)]. \tag{2}$$

The volume of services of human capital depends on the size of the available stock K, which is given at any period but can be changed over time, and the fraction of time devoted to human capital production, s, which can be varied between the limits 0 and 1. (We proceed as if the length of each period is 1, yet still use continuous time for convenience.) Time is assumed to be allocated only between the labor market and the production of human capital, and other uses of time are ignored. Thus, the allocation of time between leisure and the two types of production activities is ignored here, a complete separation between consumption and production decisions is maintained, and hence, some potentially interesting implications for the problem at hand are excluded.

Let the cost-minimizing factor combination of producing one unit of human capital be $(s\widetilde{K}, \widetilde{D})$, where we assume that K is large enough for $s < 1$; unit cost is:

$$\widetilde{I} = w \, s\widetilde{K} + P_d\widetilde{D}. \tag{3}$$

$\widetilde{I}$ is composed of a "foregone earnings" element $(w \, s\widetilde{K})$ and a direct costs element $(P_d\widetilde{D})$, where P_d is the unit price of the composite purchased input.

Although in reality the production function may be shifting with age, probably first upward and later downward, the desire to focus on specific aspects of the problem leads us to assume F independent of age.

Assume that F is homogeneous of degree μ in sK and D, with $\mu < 1$. Total costs of producing Q at any period are thus given by:

$$I(Q) = \widetilde{I}Q^{\frac{1}{\mu}} \tag{4}$$

and marginal costs are given by:

$$MC(Q) = \frac{1}{\mu} \widetilde{I}Q^{\frac{1}{\mu} - 1}. \tag{5}$$

By the assumption $\mu < 1$, $MC'' > 0$, i.e., marginal costs rise with the rate of production.

If the individual is assumed to behave as if maximizing the discounted value of his net earnings (earning capacity minus all investment costs), then:

$$W(t) = \int_t^T e^{-r(z-t)}[Y(z) - I(z)]\, dz = \int_t^T e^{-r(z-t)}E(z)\, dz. \tag{6}$$

Thus, the services of human capital as a durable consumption good are ignored, and so is the utility or disutility that may be associated with its production.

The discounted value to the individual of an additional unit of human capacity that earns w, at each point in time from time t to T, is given by:

$$P(t) = \frac{w}{r}[1 - e^{-r(T-t)}]. \tag{7}$$

The quantity produced, Q^*, will be that quantity for which $MC(Q)^*$ equals $P(t)$. Alternatively, the *marginal* rate of return, i.e., the return $w(1 - e^{-r(T-t)})$ on the marginal dollar $\dfrac{1}{MC}$ will be equated to the rate of interest r. Thus, the optimum rate of production is given by:

$$Q^*(t) = \left[\frac{\mu}{r}\frac{w}{\tilde{I}}(1 - e^{-r(T-t)})\right]^{\frac{\mu}{1-\mu}} =$$

$$\left[\frac{\mu}{r}\frac{1}{\left(s\tilde{K} + \dfrac{\tilde{P}_d\tilde{D}}{w}\right)}(1 - e^{-r(T-t)})\right]^{\frac{\mu}{1-\mu}}. \tag{8}$$

Substitution of (8) into (4) gives the time profile of investment outlays:

$$I(t) = \hat{I}\left[\frac{\mu}{r}\frac{w}{\tilde{I}}(1 - e^{-r(T-t)})\right]^{\frac{1}{1-\mu}} \tag{9}$$

Both Q and I decline with t. The relative rate of decline of investment is given by:

$$\frac{\dot{I}}{I} = \frac{-r}{1 - \mu}\frac{e^{-r(T-t)}}{(1 - e^{-r(T-t)})} < 0. \tag{10}$$

The reason for spreading investment over many periods is that at any particular period opportunities are limited and one has to forgo more and more in the present in order to acquire additional future streams of earnings. Postponement of investment entails greater savings in the production costs of human capital, the smaller is μ; the postponement of associated benefits is less costly, the smaller is the rate of interest. It is therefore, reasonable to expect, as in (10), that the smaller are r and μ, the more evenly spread and more moderately declining is investment. Because of the assumption of homogeneity, direct costs (P_dD) and forgone earnings $(w\ sK)$ remain in fixed proportion, both decreasing at the rate $\frac{\dot{I}}{I}$ (10). Time input into the production of human capital declines at a quicker rate—the human capital input is sK and if it changes at the same rate as I does, then it follows:

$$\frac{\dot{s}}{s} = \frac{\dot{I}}{I} - \frac{\dot{K}}{K} \tag{11}$$

It is easy to derive from this behavior the implied pattern of change of earnings over life. Net earnings as defined in (12) rise with age (13):

$$E(t) = Y(t) - I(t) = wK(t) - I(t) \tag{12}$$

$$\dot{E}(t) = wQ(t) - \dot{I}(t) > 0 \tag{13}$$

owing both to the increase in the stock of human capital and the decline in investment.

We spare the reader the laborious derivation of differentiating $\dot{E}(t)$ with respect to time (14). The result means that earnings rise at a declining rate:

$$\ddot{E}(t) = \dot{I}\left(\frac{w}{MC} + \frac{\mu - r}{1 - \mu}\right) < 0. \tag{14}$$

Forgone earnings are a constant fraction of investment outlays, so that a pattern like the one described by (13) and (14) holds for observed earnings, i.e., earnings realized in the labor market before deduction of direct costs. If a depreciation factor is introduced for the stock of human capital, the earnings profile will have a declining portion toward the end of life.

All the preceding analysis is confined to the phase where $s < 1$.

This is a situation where only part of the available stock of human capital is allocated to the production of human capital, the implication being that at the ruling prices, factors can be obtained without effective limitation and Q is produced at minimum cost. It is possible for K to be small enough relative to the desired Q so that the quantity demanded of services of human capital for the production of Q will exceed K, so that there is no labor force participation, $s = 1$, and the size of the available stock K is an effective constraint forcing the production of human capital at less than optimum factor combination. It is possible, and likely, to have in this phase periods in which investment rises over time. This is a description fitting early life, when the stock of human capital is still small, and the desired rate of adding to it is very high, so that all time is allocated to the formation of human capital.

II

THE model can be used for analyzing qualitatively the effects on behavior of two kinds of parametric disturbances: changes in market prices and variations in the technical parameters.

To the first group belong changes in r, P_d, and w. There are no surprises here—a rise in the rate of interest reduces the production of human capital and investment outlays and increases the rate at which investment declines. An equiproportionate rise in w and P_d leaves the quantity of human capital produced, Q, unaffected, but causes a rise of the same proportion in earning capacity, in investment outlays, and in net earnings of every period, leaving unchanged the (log) earning profile. If w rises more than P_d, Q will rise (see equation 8). The use of time for the production of human capital per unit produced will decrease, but the proportion of forgone earnings in investment costs will rise or fall depending on the elasticity of substitution between the two inputs.

The length of life T is treated as given and affects behavior through the demand price. The higher T is, the larger the quantity of human capital produced, approaching a constant rate

$$\left[\frac{\mu}{r}\Big/\left(s\widetilde{K} + \frac{P_d}{w}\widetilde{D}\right)\right]^{\frac{\mu}{1-\mu}} \text{ as } T \to \infty. \tag{15}$$

The other group of parameters consists of those appearing in the production function. The production function is a summary expression for the opportunities for increasing human capital, opportunities that depend both on the abilities of the individual and the structure of the market. Together with the market prices w and P_d, the technical parameters determine unit costs and structure of costs of human capital. The higher $\widetilde{I}$, the less investment will be undertaken. For a given pair of prices (w, P_d), $\widetilde{I}$ will be an index for ranking one dimension of the ability to produce human capital; ranking may be different with other sets of prices. An important technical parameter already discussed is μ; the smaller μ is, the quicker the ability of producing human capital declines with the rate of production—the faster the decline in the slope of the "learning curve."

In addition to the abilities associated with the production of human capital there is an initial endowment of human capital $K(0)$. The larger $K(0)$, the earlier will be the date of entry into the labor force and the longer the time spent in it.

III

THE model incorporates many assumptions that have become standard in human capital literature and their limitations are fairly well known. It contains, however, further restrictions, incorporated in the production function. One is the assumption of homogeneity, which is technical; the other, to which we refer as the "neutrality hypothesis," is substantive.

In what we called the production function of human capital (2), one of the inputs is $[sK(t)]$, which represents the services of human capital. At any period t, $K(t)$ is given so that variation in the input of human capital comes from varying the time allocated to the production of human capital. When K increases, as a result of engaging in an investment activity, the services of human capital carried by a unit of time likewise increase regardless of whether time is allocated to the market or to the production of human capital. Investment in human capital is thus treated as an augmentation of the human factor, neutral with respect to its use.

Because Q depends on (sK) the investment cost function (4) is

TABLE 1

On-the-Job Training by Age and Level of Education—Estimated Costs and Annual Rates of Decline, U.S. Males, 1958

Age (1)	Total Costs ($)			Percentage Annual Rate of Decline of Investment[a]				Percentage Change in the Relative Decline of Investment[b]			
	Elementary School (2)	High School (3)	College (4)	Elementary School (5)	High School (6)	College Original	College Smoothed[c] (7)	Elementary School (8)	High School (9)	College Original	College Smoothed (10)
14	296										
15	314			+5.9							
16	303			−3.6							
17	300			−1.0				112.5			
18	297	522		−1.0				0.9			
19	293	517		−1.4	−1.0			29.5			
20	289	512		−1.4	−1.0			0.7	1.0		
21	284	506		−1.8	−1.2			24.4	18.7		
22	278	498	2,588	−2.1	−1.6			20.1	30.4		
23	271	488	2,489	−2.5	−2.0	−3.9	−1.6	17.5	23.8	16.5	7.0
24	262	476	2,378	−3.4	−2.5	−4.6	−1.8	28.0	20.4	−122.8	9.8
25	251	462	2,353	−4.3	−3.0	−1.1	−2.0	24.0	18.3	0.9	12.0
26	237	445	2,325	−5.7	−3.7	−1.2	−2.2	28.7	22.6	160.7	12.0
27	221	425	2,085	−7.0	−4.6	−10.9	−2.5	19.8	20.4	160.7	11.9
28	202	402	1,930	−9.0	−5.6	−7.7	−2.6	25.0	19.1	−34.4	6.6

29	180	375	1,752	-11.5	-6.9	-9.7	-3.0	24.8	22.1	23.0	12.4
30	161	350	1,547	-11.1	-6.9	-13.2	-3.5	-3.3	-0.7	30.6	15.4
31	153	336	1,485	-5.0	-4.1	-4.1	-4.1	-75.9	-51.2	-111.9	15.5
32	144	319	1,415	-6.1	-5.2	-4.8	-4.8	18.8	23.9	16.1	16.1
33	133	298	1,335	-7.9	-6.8	-5.8	-5.8	26.8	26.8	18.6	18.6
34	120	274	1,245	-10.3	-8.4	-7.0	-7.0	25.6	20.9	18.2	18.2
35	104	245	1,143	-14.3	-11.2	-8.5	-8.5	32.7	28.4	20.2	20.3
36	85	211	1,026	-20.1	-14.9	-10.8	-10.8	33.8	28.7	23.2	23.2
37	63	172	991	-29.7	-20.4	-3.5	-12.0	38.6	30.9	-102.0	10.7
38	37	126	742	-52.0	-30.9	-12.9	-14.6	90.0	41.0	114.7	19.5
39	6	73	574	-144.2	-53.3	-25.5	-17.1	94.0	53.2	65.6	15.8
40		43*	466		-51.7	-20.8	-20.8		-2.9	-20.4	19.3
41		16	355		-91.5	-27.0	-27.0		55.5	25.9	26.3
42			246			-36.3	-36.3			29.4	29.2
43			144			-52.3					

Source: Columns 2–4, J. Mincer "On the Job Training: Costs, Returns, and Some Implications," *Journal of Political Economy*, Supp., October 1962, Table A7, (cols. 4–6).

[a]Calculated from columns 2–4 respectively by dividing differences of adjacent years by this average.

[b]Calculated from columns 5–7 by same method as columns 2–4.

[c]Figures obtained by reading from a curve fitted with a free hand to the original data (see Figure 1).

independent of the stock of human capital K, provided s is smaller than 1. If investment in human capital is biased towards the market, i.e., if people become comparatively more productive in the market than in the production of human capital, then any hour taken away from the market becomes more expensive and this makes the nonmarket good—in this case human capital—more costly. This provides another reason for the decline of investment over time.

The neutrality hypothesis is a strong one, and cannot be expected to hold strictly. It is strong enough to impart testability, and it is probably useful to know whether it is roughly consistent or grossly inconsistent with reality.

Several implications of the model can be tested in principle, but not in practice. Thus, there are implications for the allocation of time between "pure work" and the production of human capital, although in fact the two activities are intermingled and no meaningful separation is possible. Similarly, it is difficult to distinguish direct outlays on investment in human capital from other household expenditure.

It is clear, however, that if a series on investment in human capital is available some implications of the model can be tested. A series on investment in "on-the-job training" has been constructed by Jacob Mincer.[5] The series is not, of course, a result of direct measurement of investment outlays but is derived from the life cycle of earnings on the basis of the theoretical framework of the human-capital approach.[6] Thus, it is not suitable for a test of the general approach and could be viewed as a test of the specification of the production function, while the general principle is maintained.

The test proposed here is based on the prediction of the model with respect to the time path of investment outlays. Equation 10 predicts a decline of investment with age. Let us now take the derivative of (10) with respect to time and divide it by (10), i.e., obtain the relative rate of change of the relative rate of change of investment. As shown in (16) it turns out to be a very simple expression—it is the rate of interest cor-

---

[5] Mincer, "On-the-Job Training."

[6] For a discussion of the procedure used by Mincer and the relation between our model and this procedure see Appendix.

rected for final life T, and this is the rate at which the decline in investment over the life cycle should accelerate:

$$\widetilde{\widetilde{r}} \equiv \frac{\partial}{\partial_t} \left(\frac{\dot{I}}{I} \right) \bigg/ \frac{\dot{I}}{I} = \frac{r}{1 - e^{-r(T-t)}}. \tag{16}$$

We have here several elements of a test:

a. does $\widetilde{\widetilde{r}}$, as measured, *change* over time only to the very limited extent suggested by the correction for final life in (16)?

b. is the *level* of $\widetilde{\widetilde{r}}$ close enough to what we think is the relevant rate of interest?

c. or, is it close to the level of the (incremental) rate of return used in the calculation of the investment series?

Also note that: $\widetilde{\widetilde{r}}$ together with $\frac{\dot{I}}{I}$ provide, through equation 10 an estimate of μ, the degree of homogeneity in the production function of human capital; $\frac{r}{\mu}$ is then the average rate of return.

Confronting the data one should remember that Jacob Mincer did not prepare the estimates with an eye towards this type of "second derivative" experimentation. The limitations of the estimates, discussed in detail by Mincer, may be responsible for spuriousness in the result and the treatment of the following as an exercise is certainly not overcautious.

In Table 1 (columns 2–4) we have reproduced Mincer's original investment estimates for 1958, which constitute the better-behaved series in his study. The estimates for elementary school are really increments over the 0–4 years of schooling group. The total costs for the group with more schooling are sums of increments up to the respective levels. The rates of change of investment costs (columns 5–7) are piecewise well behaved for the elementary- and high-school levels and much less so for the college level (see Figure 1). The calculated $\widetilde{\widetilde{r}}$'s based on these series are presented in columns 8–10. Because of the irregularities in the original rates of decline, we took the liberty of smoothing the college series with a free hand. The nature of the adjustment is shown in Figure 1.

The estimates of $\widetilde{\widetilde{r}}$ hover in the high twenties for elementary school, in the lower twenties for the high-school level, and in the high teens for the college level. There is a sharp rise in $\widetilde{\widetilde{r}}$, i.e., an acceleration of the rate of decline of investment, as people pass the mid-thirties.

In comparing the different groups of investors, one notes that the level of $\widetilde{\widetilde{r}}$ tends to be lower for the bigger investors—for college compared to high school, high school compared to elementary school (note—this is intergroup and not intertemporal comparison). The levels of inter-

Figure 1. Percentage Annual Rates of Decline in Cost of On-the-Job Training

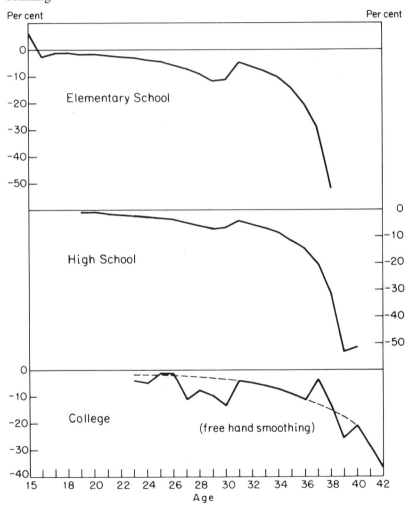

Source: Table 1, columns 5–7.

est rate implied are perhaps not unreasonably high for this type of decision, but are higher than the rates of return calculated by Mincer (19.3 per cent, 15.1 per cent, and 11.5 per cent for the elementary-school, high-school, and college groups respectively) and used in the construction of the investment series.

One also notes that the acceleration in the rate of decline of investment over time beyond the age of thirty-five is higher than could be predicted from equation 15 and at the mid-forties investment stops completely. This may be partly a result of the early flattening of cross-section earning profiles in comparison to longitudinal earning curves.

As indicated, we could use equation 10 and the calculated $\widetilde{\widetilde{r}}$ to calculate the implied μ provided the hypothesis was not rejected. The values of μ that we would get in this way (assuming $T = 65$) are presented in Table 2 and are all in the range .90–.99. Theoretically, they should have been the same for all ages. They fall in a relatively narrow range and are not far from 1, i.e., in terms of the model there would be no great departure from constant returns to scale.

One could start from another end: assume r from the outside, using (10) solve for μ at a given age and then check for how well the pairing r and μ predict the rate of decline of investment at another age. What makes this test weak is that if the resultant μ happens to be close to 1, then very small changes in μ can bring very large changes in $\frac{\dot{i}}{I}$, because in (10) $1 - \mu$ appears in the denominator.[7] The test through the second derivative is thus more conclusive.

IV

ONE might say that the neutrality hypothesis incorporated into the model and discussed in the previous section relegates to the demand side most of the burden of explaining changing behavior over the life cycle, because movements of the demand curve along a stationary marginal-cost curve are responsible for the decline in investment, although the shape of the rising cost function has an effect, as indicated. Mincer, comment-

[7] This paragraph was written in response to comments by Jacob Mincer.

TABLE 2

Estimates of μ at Selected Ages

Age	$100\widetilde{r}$ [a]			$100\frac{i}{T}$			μ [c]		
	Elementary School	High School	College	Elementary School	High School	College	Elementary School	High School	College
25	26.9	20.5	9.5[b]	4.5	3.1	2.0[b]	.95	.94	.99[b]
29	24.9	20.6	11.5[b]	10.5	6.5	3.0[b]	.94	.97	.98[b]
35	30.8	26.0	20.6	14.9	11.5	8.8	.93	.93	.91

[a]Three year averages, centered on the specified age, taken from Table 1, columns 8–10.

[b]Based on the smoothed series.

[c]Caculated on the basis of equation 10: $\dfrac{i}{T} = \dfrac{-r}{1-\mu} \ \dfrac{e^{-r(T-t)}}{1-e^{-r(T-t)}}$ using three-year averages centered on the specific age.

ing on his own estimates, mentions only the demand side by saying that "the decline of training with age is consistent with *a priori* expectations about investment behavior: younger people have a greater incentive to invest in themselves than older ones because they can collect the returns for a longer time."[8] Becker tends to emphasize the role of changing cost conditions.[9]

We should recall that the properties attributed to the neutrality hypothesis hold only at the phase in which there is labor force participation ($s < 1$). In the earlier period, when there is complete specialization in human capital production, cost functions change with K (they actually decline). Most of our analysis thus refers to the period beyond full-time formal education.

We want to end this paper with a few comments on this assumption. Doubts about its validity on *a priori* grounds are linked to the heterogeneity of the ways in which people can invest in themselves. We know that many activities increase earning capacity but leave unaffected the ability to increase earning capacity further. On the other hand, there are activities that do not directly contribute much to earning capacity but increase the ability to produce the kind of human capital which, if produced, would increase earning capacity. Even if any particular type of school, occupation, or job offers a relatively rigid mix of these types of skill, it is possible to choose among activities and to decide on an educational and occupational career that will bring about a desirable mix of the different "capital goods." The market does not make it possible to get something for nothing, so that neutral improvement in human capacity costs more than specialized improvement, and at any period people will choose the optimum early in life. When there is still a large investment program ahead, it is advisable to emphasize devices that reduce future investment costs and make the individual a more efficient producer of human capital. Later in life, when future planned investment is smaller, the fraction of investment outlays devoted to skills that are for purposes of further investment will also be smaller. The formal schooling system, at least in the precollege levels, tends to emphasize skills that are tools for further learning (the more general skills are likely to be produced by

[8] Mincer, "On-the-Job Training," p. 55.
[9] Becker, "Human Capital and the Personal Distribution of Income."

"firms" specializing in the production of skills). On the other hand, certain types of higher education and a large part of on-the-job training impart directly productive skills,[10] building upon the tools previously acquired in school. One presumes, however, that even within the period of labor force participation there is enough variety of opportunity in the labor market to allow a change in the mix. Thus, the structure of the individual's stock of human capital can be expected to change over time and become relatively more market-oriented, reflecting a (planned) shift in comparative advantage. In comparison with the pattern described under the neutrality hypothesis there should be a steeper decline in the production of human capital and an even steeper decline in the time input, because of the substitution of purchased inputs for own time, as the price of the latter increases.

APPENDIX

ON THE ESTIMATION PROCEDURE OF INVESTMENT COSTS

THE purpose of this appendix is to relate the Becker-Mincer procedure of estimating costs of on-the-job training to the model presented in the text (for a more general critique of the procedure see Mary Jean Bowman "The Assessment of Human Investment as Growth Strategy" in the *Compendium on Human Resources* prepared for the Joint Economic Committee of the U. S. Congress, February 1968).

The principle underlying the Becker-Mincer estimating procedure can be described as follows (using our notation): recall the identity $Y \equiv E + I$, i.e., earning capacity equals net earnings plus investment. Think of two (representative) individuals a and b for whom earning

---

[10] If this is indeed true and if these direct skills are of the general type (in Becker's terminology) the initial earning capacity or salary per unit of pure working time of, for example, a high-school graduate should not be higher than that of an elementary-school graduate. But, on the other hand, when on-the-job-training includes specific skills then the employer will, from the start, pay the rent on the superior learning tools that the high-school graduate possesses—he will pay him for his ability to produce efficiently specific skills on the job.

capacities are equal at time 0 and the values of the left-hand side of $(1')$ are known.

$$\Delta E(0) \equiv E^a(0) - E^b(0)$$
$$\Delta I(0) \equiv I^a(0) - I^b(0) \tag{1'}$$
$$\Delta Y(0) \equiv Y^a(0) - Y^b(0) = 0$$

Note that Δ refer always to differences between people and not between periods. Let r be the internal rate of return obtained by equating to zero the discounted differences in net earning between two individuals

$$\int_0^T \frac{\Delta E(z)dz}{1 - e^{-\tilde{r}(T-t)}} = 0 \text{ and assume that it is constant through life. It is then}$$

argued that the following holds true:

$$\Delta I(1) = \tilde{r}\Delta I(0) - \Delta E(1). \tag{2'}$$

The first term on the right-hand side of $(2')$ is the difference in earning capacities in year 1 that was created by the difference in investment in year 0; if, in addition, the bigger investor earns in year 1 less than the small investor does, the difference in their respective investments in year 1 is higher by this term.

This can be repeated and in general incremental costs can be calculated with the aid of $(3')$ which is Mincer's equation 1 (in a continuous form).

$$\Delta I(t) = \tilde{r} \int_0^t \frac{\Delta I(z)dz}{1 - e^{-r(T-z)}} - \Delta E(t) \tag{3'}$$

Rearranging $(3')$ we get:

$$\Delta Y(t) = \tilde{r} \int_0^t \frac{\Delta I(z)dz}{1 - e^{-r(T-z)}}, \tag{4'}$$

by which the difference in earning capacity at time t between two individuals starting with the same earning capacity at time 0 is equal to the internal rate of return times the cumulative difference in investment costs (corrected for final life T). If the increments in costs between the groups compared are small enough, $\tilde{r}$ can be regarded as the marginal rate of return. Sequences of increments in investment for groups facing smaller and smaller rates of interest can be accumulated to obtain total investment of each of the groups.

As far as one can see, the procedure does not depend on a particular form of the production or cost functions and can therefore be described as a general procedure. If, on the other hand, investment differentials, $\Delta I(t)$, are large, then the rates at which investment costs are converted to returns should be *average* rates, which may vary with the size of the investment differentials, and the use of $\tilde{r}$ as a constant through time is not generally justified.

Let us go in what looks like the same direction, using the model of Section I. The addition to earning capacity $Y(z)$ of each period from t to T resulting from the investment of $I(t)$ at time t, is $wQ(t)$, the quantity produced in time t, multiplied by the market rental. If we divide the latter by the former and use (4) and (8) we get:

$$\frac{wQ(t)}{I(t)} = \frac{r}{\mu} \frac{1}{[1 - e^{-r(T-t)}]} \tag{5'}$$

Transposing and accumulating from time 0 we get:

$$Y(t) - Y(0) = \int_0^t wQ(z)dz = \frac{r}{\mu} \int_0^t \frac{I(z)dz}{[1 - e^{-r(T-z)}]}. \tag{6'}$$

The difference between two individuals a and b who have the same earning capacities at time 0 is thus given by:

$$\Delta Y(t) = Y^a(t) - Y^b(t) = \frac{r}{\mu} \int_0^t \frac{\Delta I(z)dz}{1 - e^{-r(T-t)}}. \tag{7'}$$

Compare (7') with (4'), which represents the Becker-Mincer procedure. There is a considerable similarity between the two, but they differ in the assumptions they carry. Equation (7') does not depend for its validity on the size of the investment differentials, $\Delta I(t)$, but rests on the assumption that the two (representative) individuals compared face the same interest rates and have the same μ; in (5') r is the rate of interest and the marginal rate of return is equated to it, and (5') is the *average* rate of return—average over the dollars invested in a given period—the proper translator of total investment into returns.

The reason for the difference in investment that underlies the Becker-Mincer procedure is the difference in the interest rates that different investors face. On the other hand, the investment differentials that (7') claims to measure stem from differences in the cost functions of human capital production, with the severe restriction that the individuals compared have the same elasticities of costs with respect to output Q, i.e., the same μ. The difference in their cost functions are only differences in levels, i.e., in $\widetilde{T}^j$. In addition, the interest rates that they face are assumed to be the same.

One might ask whether the use of a constant average rate of return requires as much as is assumed in the model of Section I. When the quantities of human capital produced vary over time then, with a given marginal rate of return, the constancy of the average rate of return is linked to a constancy of the ratio of marginal to average costs of producing human capital, which in turn implies a constant elasticity of costs with respect to output—the counterpart of a homogeneous production function. It is also difficult to assume a constant average rate of return without accepting the neutrality hypothesis.

COMMENTS

JACOB MINCER
NBER AND COLUMBIA UNIVERSITY

Ben-Porath's contribution to this conference contains a generalization of his recently published model of production of human capital, and an attempt at empirical testing of some of its features. The generalization consists of a weaker specification of the production function: homogeneity and diminishing returns to scale are maintained, but the specific Cobb-Douglass form is dropped. The empirical test refers to age profiles of postschool investment expenditures: According to equations 10 and 16 that profile is predicted to be declining with age at an accelerating rate with a relative acceleration roughly equal to the interest rate r. Given empirical estimates of such age profiles empirical tests are feasible and were carried out.

In my view the Ben-Porath models presented here and in his previous work represent a very useful step forward in the analysis of human capital. The particular specification of the HPF (human capital production function) is less important than the general approach, given the latter's potential flexibility.

As to the particular restrictions in the model, the most important one, as Ben-Porath rightly stresses, is the "neutrality hypothesis," according to which human capital increases productivities in the market at the same rate as it does in the production of additions to the stock of human capital. This is a rather attractive exception to the usual view of "household" (or "nonmarket") production functions. As economists, we tend to ascribe a market bias to most of the effects of human capital, but as educators we are inclined to exempt from the bias the effects of learning on further learning. Perhaps this is correct: Ben-Porath's point is that the issues can be tested, at least in principle.

The hypothesis is a strong one, and for that one must pay a price: It imparts a high degree of rigidity to the Ben-Porath model. Indeed, it

TABLE 1

Predicted and Observed Percentage Declines in Net Investment

	Age					Age of Termination
	25	30	35	40	45	
Elementary						
Predicted	.0 [a]	-.7	- 1.6	-3.8	-8.7	59
Observed	-4.5	-9.2	-14.9	_ [b]	_ [b]	40
High School						
Predicted	-.7	-1.5	-3.3	-7.2	-15.6	56
Observed	-3.1	-6.0	-11.5	-51.7	_ [b]	42
College						
Predicted	-3.2	-4.6	-7.8	-14.7	-25.3	53
Observed	-2.0	-3.6	-8.8	-20.8	_ [b]	45

[a] Almost zero.

[b] Decline to zero (-100 per cent).

neutralizes almost everything, allowing only one source of motion: the finiteness of human life. Unquestionably, this is a major fact. Interestingly, however, finiteness of life is usually of secondary importance in many aspects of the economics of human capital. This is because the discounting of values to be realized decades in the future reduces them to negligibility. The present model is no exception. The age profile of investment predicted by equation 10 declines *only because* of the finite life span T. But with T large the profile is practically horizontal, because the numerator of the second term on the right is almost zero.

The second derivative type of test that was performed indicates that the actual relative acceleration in the decline of "observed" investments is larger than that predicted by equation 16, but perhaps not enough to reject the null hypothesis—particularly in view of the few degrees of freedom. However, the first derivative—the relative speed of decline —is equally amenable to test by equation 10, and is worth considering. Table 1 gives a comparison of actual and predicted speeds of decline in investment at several ages. The predicted magnitudes were calculated by means of equation 10, using $T = 65$, $\mu = .95$, and the values of r for the three schooling groups as given in the original data.

There is a noticeable conformity with prediction in the college series almost up to age forty, and a widening divergence thereafter. In the two lower schooling groups, the divergence is much larger than any similarity: the predicted series is almost completely flat throughout the period when observed investments are positive, with the predicted series reaching zero almost two decades later than the actual.

Note that this test by equation 10 is not independent of the test by equation 16, except that it uses the discount rates from the original data which are produced by equation 16 rather than $\widetilde{\widetilde{r}}$. The same test can also be viewed, independently of 16, as follows: Given the original data for r and for the rate of decline in investments, what values of μ in equation 10 will produce the best fit? The answer is: μ must be extremely close to unity (.99 or so). This is too close for comfort: Unity would mean that all investments take place in the initial period—a clear contradiction; but anything significantly less than unity makes for too slow a decline in investments relative to the observed decline. The specific version of the model is, therefore, substantively fragile and statistically intractable.

If the comparisons of actual with predicted lead to a rejection rather than acceptance of the maintained hypothesis, one may be tempted to blame the results on, or to explain them by, the somewhat conjectural quality of the estimated series. As its producer, I can only say that the series reflects the state of the arts circa 1961, rather than the shoddiness of a surprisingly long-lived monopoly. As Ben-Porath correctly notes, my interest in that work was not in the age profile of postschooling investments, that is in the individual terms of the series, but in their sum, the total investment costs. However, a little reflection suggests that the particular expedients I used to convert the several income intervals into an annual series are not decisive. Shapes of earnings profiles are recognizable and a sizeable stock of them has accumulated in the available statistics. As Ben-Porath's equations 12 and 13 indicate, everything stated about investment profiles can be translated into statements about earnings profiles. Thus, the predicted magnitudes (rows a) imply that earnings profiles, at least below college, are almost exactly linear throughout the first half of working life, long *after* the observed concavity is most noticeable. The other features of the test, which can be rejected simply on the basis of even casual familiarity with earnings profiles, are: (1) the predicted ages of peak earnings (termination of net investment) are systematically later the lower the schooling group, and (2) in this model the slope of the earnings profile is a function of age, not of experience (i.e., length of stay in the labor force).

Incidentally, it is not clear why T is to be put at age sixty-five. If T denotes end of life span, rather than end of working span, it should be a more advanced age, and the predicted profile of investment would be shifted to the right by a corresponding interval, *increasing* the discrepancy between predicted and observed in all schooling groups. The question of the meaning of T and how it is to be brought into the analysis is very important.

One reason this question was left open is the absence of depreciation in the model, or the implicit assumption that it constitutes a fixed fraction of earning capacity throughout life. A depreciation rate rising with age during the second half of the working life seems more realistic and could explain much of the story.

Net investment, not gross, is the factor underlying the earnings profiles. After middle age, gross investment is progressively eroded and eventually outstripped by depreciation. Hence the more rapid decline in net investment and the earlier termination of it—relative to the patterns predicted by the model. The assumption of an exogenously fixed T, whether viewed as end of life or retirement age, may be dropped. A major objective of gross investment at the later stages of the life cycle is to extend the productive years and the life span. With larger gross investments T is postponed to later ages.

As for the earlier ages, other amendments might still be needed, including a "breach of neutrality," possibly along the lines expressed at the conclusion of the paper. This will complicate the model, but it will add life and robustness to the analysis. In the meantime, Ben-Porath is to be applauded for a valiant first step in the right direction.

LESTER C. THUROW
MASSACHUSETTS INSTITUTE OF TECHNOLOGY

Professor Yoram Ben-Porath develops a theoretical model to explain lifetime investment in human capital. The model is then tested against Mincer's estimates of the actual lifetime distribution of human capital investment. Operationally the model must explain why human-capital investment is concentrated in the early years of a person's working life. There are two assumptions in Ben-Porath's model which lead to investment concentration. First, a man is assumed to have a finite working life. The earlier an asset is acquired the longer its working life. Second, the opportunity costs of investing increase as human capital is acquired. Human capital raises a man's marginal product and consequently the opportunity costs of time spent on human investment. Early assets make later assets more expensive.

Although it is interesting to see how these simple assumptions can produce investment concentration, the model is too simple to present a realistic explanation of lifetime human investment. In order to explain human investment, it is necessary to take into account the peculiarities of human capital. I will first outline some of the peculiarities and then indicate how they affect Professor Ben-Porath's results.

1. Human capital is not a negotiable asset. Since it cannot be separated from the person who possesses it, it cannot be sold. Illiquidity lowers its value in an uncertain, risky world, but more importantly it means that a man must accompany his human capital. Capitalists can be

viewed as profit maximizers, but most individual utility maximizers will not be earnings maximizers. Probably no one at this conference can claim that he chose the occupation that maximized his earnings stream.

2. Since a man must accompany his human capital, production and consumption cannot be easily separated. Consumption benefits (positive and negative) come from the process of production and investment. Ideally, these complementary goods should be included in the wage rate used to evaluate an investment. Since they are not, market prices are presumably less reflective of real prices in the human capital area than in the physical capital.

3. The problem goes beyond complementary consumption goods received in the process of production. Much of a man's consumption is self produced. Self-produced goods and services are never priced since they never enter the market place. Yet human capital will be acquired to produce these goods.

4. Human beings possess a collection of human capital assets. Some of these assets are complementary. Many are substitutes or at least cannot be used simultaneously. The worth of a human-capital asset depends on what other assets a man possesses or will possess. One occupational skill may dominate another skill and make it worthless. Physical-capital assets can be separated and used simultaneously. Human-capital assets cannot.

5. Human-capital investment may affect preferences. It may, in fact, be designed to affect preferences. Music appreciation courses are only the most obvious example. Preference functions are needed to make human-capital investment decisions, but they are in turn affected by the investments. Viewed retrospectively, an economically rational individual might say that going to college was a good decision if he had gone to college and that not going to college was a good decision if he had not gone to college. Stable preference functions make much more sense when viewing physical investment.

6. Production and investment costs are not easily separated from consumption costs. How should maintenance costs be treated? Man eats and sleeps to consume as well as to produce or invest. Consumption, production, and investment are joint products of human maintenance activities. There is no way in which to allocate these maintenance costs among different activities since they are joint products of the maintenance costs.

7. Human capital has some of the characteristics of physical capital and some of the characteristics of a natural resource. Some skills, talents, and knowledge are producible; some are not. Most human capital is arrayed between these extremes. It is producible but the costs differ markedly from one person to another. A man may have the ability to acquire one skill and not another. Thus, the human-capital production functions will differ for different individuals. One man cannot acquire another's production function or the most efficient production function. Perfect knowledge allows everyone to acquire the same production functions for physical investment, but not for human investment.

8. The efficiency of the human-capital production function may also change over a person's lifetime. Viewed as a learning machine, a man may become less and less productive as he grows older. Thus, the marginal cost of investment may rise over his lifetime even if it does not rise in any given year. Athletic skills are only the most obvious example. The productivity of physical investment presumably does not depend upon the age of the investor.

9. Human capital investments are lumpy. This is especially true of the major investments in occupational skills. If a man is to work as an electrician, he must acquire most of the skills of an electrician before he can begin to work. To learn to be an electrician efficiently may also require discrete lumps of time.

10. Many investment decisions must be made at an age when the investor is not making his own decisions. Parents make decisions for their children based on their own preferences and not those of their children. In addition, parents may be able to have a major impact on the efficiency of their children's human-capital production functions. Environment may make it impossible for them to acquire many skills.

If Professor Ben-Porath is trying to explain why human-capital investment rapidly decelerates and reaches zero in the middle forties, I suggest that items 8 and 9 cannot be ignored. The available production functions become less efficient with age. It takes longer periods of time to acquire some skills; others cannot be acquired at all. Physical energy for learning or any other activity diminishes as a man grows older. Human-capital investment is also lumpy. We continually learn new skills regardless of our occupation, but initially we must make a major investment to acquire the basic occupational skills. I cannot work as an electrician until I have become an electrician. I may become a better electrician with age, but I must acquire that initial lumpy bundle of skills.

In the model in Ben-Porath's paper, a person invests in each period of time until the rate of return on investment reaches the market interest rate. I would suggest that this definition of equilibrium is too limited for human-capital investment. Each investor is subject to two budget constraints. First, there is a financial or budgetary constraint on his investment behavior. Second, there is a time constraint on his investment behavior. Human-capital investment requires time. Each person possesses a limited amount of time. There is nothing in the human capital market that guarantees that both the financial and time constraints will be effective. The time constraint could easily be the effective one. In this case, markets will not proceed to financial equilibrium. The market rate of interest will not equal the marginal productivity of human capital. The problem is especially acute when we allow different people to have different human-capital production functions. Those with efficient production functions will not drive their rate of return on human-capital investment to market rates of interest. Since the time constraint is their effective constraint the problem is similar to that of imperfect financial markets. Time is rigidly divided among individuals and cannot be transferred to those whose marginal product is higher. Thus, the inability to sell time makes the human-capital market inherently imperfect. Ben-Porath mentions the possibility of boundary solutions while young, but I suggest they are much more extensive than he indicates.

Finally, the "facts" he is trying to explain might be a function of a limited view of human capital. Mincer's investment series is not observed, but calculated from lifetime earnings. Income increases decelerate, so investment must have decelerated. If self-produced goods and complementary consumption goods were measured, real incomes might not decelerate. If real incomes do not decelerate, investment does not decelerate in Mincer's estimation procedure. In any case, we know that wage rates do not flatten out at the same rate as explained by increases in leisure. Using wage-rate-age profiles we obtain different "facts" than earnings-age profiles. Presumably the wage-rate-age profile is the relevant profile. If leisure were not worth more than income, individuals would be working. Consequently, Mincer's data probably overestimates the concentration of human-capital investment.

EDUCATION AND THE
DISTRIBUTION OF INCOME

AN INTERREGIONAL ANALYSIS OF SCHOOLING AND THE SKEWNESS OF INCOME

BARRY R. CHISWICK •
UNIVERSITY OF CALIFORNIA, LOS ANGELES

INTRODUCTION

THE skewness in a distribution indicates its deviation from perfect symmetry around the mean. It reflects the shape of a distribution. The shape of the personal distribution of income is relevant for discussions of the equity of the distribution, as well as for Engel curve and savings-and-investment analyses. The determination of the factors that generate the shape of the distribution is therefore a matter of considerable interest.

The skewness in the distribution of income was considered important in the past, although the scarcity of data restricted empirical studies. A. A. Young wrote in 1917 that skewness, not "concentration," is the relevant parameter for studies of the social desirability of the distribution of income.[1] Three years later, in the first edition of his *Economics of Welfare*, A. C. Pigou tried to reconcile the assumed normal distribution of ability with the positive skewness of income.[2] In spite of the rapid

NOTE: The author is indebted to Gary S. Becker and Linda B. Wedel for many helpful comments on earlier drafts of this paper. The research for this paper was supported, in part, by the Institute of Government and Public Affairs, University of California, Los Angeles.

[1] A. A. Young, "Do the Statistics of Concentration of Wealth in the United States Mean What They Are Commonly Assumed to Mean?" *Journal of the American Statistical Association*, Vol. 15 (March 1917), pp. 471–84.

[2] A. C. Pigou, *Economics of Welfare* (London, 1920), pp. 695–97.

TABLE 1

Annual Earnings During and After Training

Years of Training	1	2	3	...	...	N-1	N	N+1	...
0	Y_o	Y_o	Y_o	...	...	Y_o	Y_o	Y_o	...
1	0	$Y_o(1+r)$	$Y_o(1+r)$	...	...	$Y_o(1+r)$	$Y_o(1+r)$	$Y_o(1+r)$	...
2	0	0	$Y_o(1+r)^2$	...	...	$Y_o(1+r)^2$	$Y_o(1+r)^2$	$Y_o(1+r)^2$	...
⋰ N	0	0	0	...	...	0	0	$Y_o(1+r)^N$	...

increase in data on the distribution of income, the skewness of income has been ignored by most recent studies.[3]

The purpose of this paper is to refocus attention on this important aspect of the distribution of income. In particular, by viewing schooling as a form of capital, this paper attempts to ascertain the extent to which schooling can explain the observed positive skewness in the distribution of personal income. An a priori model is developed in Part I, and then employed in the empirical analysis of the United States and Canada in Part II. The final section consists of a summary and conclusion.

I. THE MODEL

Let us designate Y_N the perpetual annual earnings after N years of training are completed, and Y_o the perpetual earnings if there is no training. It is assumed initially that all persons are of equal ability, that the only private costs of training are earnings foregone, and that during the training period there are no actual earnings. Using these assumptions, Table 1 will help clarify the derivation of the relation between training and earnings.

A person without training would earn Y_o every year, as is shown in the first row of Table 1. A person who invested for one year is assumed to have foregone the amount Y_o, that is, no earnings were received during this year. This is shown by the zero in the second row of the first column. If a rate of return of r were received on his investment, he would earn $Y_1 = Y_o + r Y_o = Y_o (1 + r)$ in year two and all subsequent years, where $r Y_o$ is the perpetual return on the investment Y_o. This is shown in the second row of Table 1. If the rate of return were the same for all

---

[3] There are, however, some exceptions. Income skewness was considered explicitly in Gary S. Becker, *Human Capital and the Personal Distribution of Income* (Ann Arbor, 1967), Barry R. Chiswick, "Minimum Schooling Legislation and the Cross-Sectional Distribution of Income," *Economic Journal* (September 1969), pp. 495–507, Stanley Lebergott, "The Shape of the Income Distribution," *American Economic Review,* Vol. 49 (June 1959), pp. 328–47, Harold Lydall, *The Structure of Earnings* (Oxford, 1968), Thomas Mayer, "The Distribution of Ability and Earnings," *Review of Economics and Statistics,* Vol. 42 (February 1960), pp. 189–95, Herman Miller, "Elements of Symmetry in the Skewed Income Curve," *Journal of the American Statistical Association,* Vol. 50 (March 1955), pp. 55–71, and Jacob Mincer, "Investment in Human Capital and Personal Income Distribution," *Journal of Political Economy,* Vol. 66 (August 1958), pp. 281–302.

years of training, a person with two years of training would have received no earnings during years one and two and after that an amount equal to

$$Y_2 = (Y_o + rY_o) + r(Y_o + rY_o) = Y_o(1 + r)(1 + r) = Y_o(1 + r)^2$$

where $r(Y_o + rY_o) = rY_1$ is the perpetual annual return to the investment in the second year of $Y_o + rY_o = Y_1$. A person with N years of education would receive nothing during the first N years and

$$Y_N = Y_o + r(Y_o) + rY_o(1 + r) + \ldots + rY_o(1 + r)^{N-1}$$

or

$$Y_N = Y_o(1 + r)^N \qquad (1)$$

after the investment period.

If the rate of return were not the same for all years of training, the factors could not be combined, and the post-investment income stream would be represented by

$$Y_N = Y_o \prod_{j=1}^{N} (1 + r_j), \qquad (2)$$

where π is the mathematical symbol for product.

The assumptions that there are no direct costs of training and no actual earnings during the period of investment are not realistic. A year of schooling ordinarily leaves the summer free for working, and for some levels of schooling direct costs (i.e., tuition, school supplies, and other expenses necessitated by schooling) are far from negligible. Those engaged in on-the-job training usually receive positive incomes in excess of direct costs, although in the past, payments for appenticeship programs were quite common. The earnings equation may be modified to make the model more consistent with reality.

Let C_j equal the direct plus foregone-earnings costs of the investment in the jth year of training. Y_{j-1} is the income that would be received after $j-1$ years of training if no further investments were undertaken. Designate by K_j the ratio C_j/Y_{j-1}, that is, K_j equals the proportion of potential income that is invested during year j. We previously assumed that the only cost of education was a full year of foregone earnings, so that $C_j = Y_{j-1}$ and $K_j = 1$. Now K_j may differ from unity. If total costs were greater than potential earnings during the year of training, K_j would be greater than 1. If the potential earnings exceeded total costs, K_j would be less than 1.

The introduction of the investment-income ratio, K, modifies the earnings equation. If there were no investment, Y_o would still be earned. If in year 1, the amount $C_1 = K_1 Y_o$ were invested at a rate of return of r_1, the post-investment income would be

$$Y_1 = Y_o + r_1(K_1 Y_o) = Y_o(1 + r_1 K_1).$$

If N years of investments were undertaken,

$$Y_N = Y_o(1 + r_1 K_1)(1 + r_2 K_2) \ldots (1 + r_N K_N)$$

or

$$Y_N = Y_o \prod_{j=1}^{N} (1 + r_j^*), \tag{3}$$

where $r_j^* = r_j K_j$ is the "adjusted rate of return" to the jth year of education.[4]

Individual differences due to other forms of human capital, physical capital, and luck may be introduced into equation 3 by the inclusion of a residual U_i^*. Differences in "ability" may be introduced by permitting differences in rates of return to a given level of training. The earnings equation becomes

$$Y_{N,i} = Y_o \prod_{j=1}^{N} (1 + r_{ij}^*) U_i^*, \tag{4}$$

where r_{ij}^* is the adjusted rate of return to the ith individual for the jth year of training. Taking logarithms of both sides of equation 4, and using the relation $\text{Ln}(1 + a) \approx a$ when a is small, results in

$$\text{Ln } Y_{N,i} = \text{Ln } Y_o + \sum_{j=1}^{N} r_{ij}^* + U_i, \tag{5}$$

where $U_i = \text{Ln } U_i^*$ and the "approximately equal to" sign has been replaced by the symbol for "equal to." Differences in earnings at the zero investment level may be considered to be in the residual.

The sum of the adjusted rates of return $\sum_j r_{ij}^*$ can be rewritten as

$$\sum_j r_{ij} = \bar{r}_i^* N_i = \bar{r}^* N_i + (\bar{r}_i^* N_i - \bar{r}^* N_i), \tag{6}$$

where $\bar{r}_i^*$ is the ith person's average adjusted rate of return and $\bar{r}^*$ is the

---

[4] That is, the rate of return adjusted for the fraction of potential income that was invested.

average $\bar{r}_i^*$ for the population.[5] If it is assumed that deviations from the population's average adjusted rate of return appear in the residual U', equation 5 can be rewritten as

$$\text{Ln } Y_{N,i} = \text{Ln } Y_o + \bar{r}^* N_i + U_i'. \tag{7}$$

Training can be separated into two components, schooling and on-the-job training. Thus, the earnings equation becomes

$$\text{Ln } Y_{N,i} = \text{Ln } Y_o + \bar{r}_s^* S_i + \bar{r}_j^* J_i + U_i' \tag{8}$$

where S and J designate years of schooling and on-the-job training respectively.

The model can be used for interregional analyses of income inequality or income skewness. The development of the theory and empirical analyses for income inequality have been presented elsewhere.[6] The remainder of the present analysis is specifically concerned with an examination of the skewness of income.

Due to the scarcity of data for on-the-job training, the empirical analysis of Part II is for schooling alone. Consequently, the subsequent theoretical analysis focuses on schooling. On-the-job training is considered a component of the residual.

Let us first assume that income is derived solely from investments in schooling, and then investments in other assets and luck shall be

---

[5] In mathematical terms:

$$\bar{r}_i^* = \sum_{j=1}^{N_i} \frac{r_{ij}^*}{N_i} = \sum_{j=1}^{N_i} \frac{r_{ij}K_{ij}}{N_i},$$

where N_i is the number of years of training and

$$\bar{r}^* = \sum_{i=1}^{p} \frac{\bar{r}_i^*}{p}$$

where p is the size of the population.

[6] Gary S. Becker and Barry R. Chiswick, "Education and the Distribution of Earnings," *American Economic Review,* Vol. 56, No. 2 (May 1966), pp. 358–69; Barry R. Chiswick, "Human Capital and the Distribution of Personal Income" (unpublished Ph.D. dissertation, Columbia University, 1967); and Barry R. Chiswick, "The Average Level of Schooling and the Intra–Regional Inequality of Income: A Clarification," *American Economic Review,* Vol. 58, No. 3, pt. 1 (June 1968), pp. 495–500.

included.[7] If the ith person's income were derived solely from investments in schooling,

$$\text{Ln } Y_i = \bar{r}_i{}^* S_i. \tag{9}$$

In the population, the rate of return and level of schooling have positive means. Then, if it is assumed that $\bar{r}_i{}^*$ and S_i are independent and normally distributed, their product has a small positive skewness.[8] A small positive skewness in the natural logarithm of income implies a considerable positive skewness in income itself.[9]

If the cost of funds for investment in schooling were the same for all, those with higher marginal rates of return (e.g., those with greater ability) would invest more in schooling.[10] This produces a positive correlation between $\bar{r}_i{}^*$ and S_i. The positive correlation is reduced if, as seems plausible, those with higher apparent levels of ability have a lower cost of funds.[11] A positive correlation between the rate of return and the number of years of schooling increases the positive skewness of income.

Thus, income is positively skewed as long as the distributions of the rate of return or of schooling are not sufficiently negatively skewed or as long as the rate of return and the level of schooling are not sufficiently negatively correlated.

One problem with the formulation just presented is the current immeasurability of characteristics, other than average level, of the distribution of the rate of return from schooling. The formulation presented below permits an empirical analysis using the limited data that are available. In addition, it contains a residual, which includes the effects of differences in ability, of capital other than schooling, and of luck.

The earnings or income equation for schooling can be written as

$$\text{Ln } Y_i = \text{Ln } Y_o + \bar{r}^* S_i + [(\bar{r}_i{}^* - \bar{r}^*) S_i + U_{i,s}] \tag{10}$$

where the sum in brackets is the residual. The term $U_{i,s}$ includes the

[7] For an analysis of the effect of chance on the distribution of income, see Milton Friedman, "Choice, Chance and the Personal Distribution of Income," *Journal of Political Economy*, Vol. 61 (August 1953), pp. 277–90.

[8] C. C. Craig, "On the Frequency Function of XY," *Annals of Mathematical Statistics*, Vol. 7, No. 1 (March 1936), pp. 1–15.

[9] See also Mincer, *op. cit.*, and Becker, *Human Capital*, pp. 61–66.

[10] Becker and Chiswick, *op. cit.*, or Becker, . . . *Human Capital*, pp. 2–25.

[11] *Ibid.*

effects on income of on-the-job training, other forms of human capital, physical capital, and luck. The expression $\bar{r}_i^* - \bar{r}^*$ reflects individual differences in adjusted rates of return from schooling.

When the residual is neglected, a normal distribution of S_i produces a normal distribution in the natural logarithm of income. A normally distributed log of income implies that income itself is positively skewed. The greater the skewness of schooling, the greater the skewness of income. Income is positively skewed unless there is a sufficient amount of negative skewness in the distribution of schooling. Given current distributions of schooling, it seems reasonable to predict that if income were due solely to schooling, income would be positively skewed. This is consistent with the most distinctive and apparently universal characteristic of the distribution of income, its positive skewness.

The skewness of income is also a function of the level of the adjusted rate of return. There is reason to believe that, for a given distribution of schooling, the higher the rate of return the greater is the skewness in income. This is easily proved when income (Y) is log-normally distributed. The skewness of Y can be measured by

$$\text{Sk}(Y) = \frac{(Z_3)^{1/3}}{(Z_2)^{1/2}}, \tag{11}$$

where Z_i is the ith moment around the mean.[12] Then,

$$\text{Sk}(Y) = \left(\frac{Z_3}{(Z_2)^{3/2}}\right)^{1/3} = (\eta^3 + 3\eta)^{1/3}, \tag{12}$$

where $\eta^2 = e\sigma^2 - 1$, and σ^2 is the variance of the natural logarithm of Y.[13] If income were due solely to the rate of return from schooling and the level of schooling, and if for individuals these parameters were independent,[14] then

$$\sigma^2 = \text{Var}(\text{Ln } Y) = \bar{r}^2 \text{ Var}(S) + \bar{S}^2 \text{ Var}(r) + \text{Var}(r) \text{ Var}(S). \tag{13}$$

Thus, *ceteris paribus*, the larger the adjusted rate of return, the larger is

---

[12] Kendall suggests this measure raised to the sixth power. M. G. Kendall, *The Advanced Theory of Statistics*, Vol. 1, 4th edition (London, 1948), p. 81.

[13] J. Atchison and J. A. C. Brown, *The Lognormal Distribution* (Cambridge, England, 1957), pp. 7–8.

[14] Leo Goodman, "On the Exact Variance of Products," *Journal of the American Statistical Association*, Vol. 55 (December 1960), pp. 708–13.

the skewness of income. In addition, this procedure predicts that, *ceteris paribus*, the skewness of income is larger at higher levels of schooling.

When a residual term does exist, the conclusions of the last two paragraphs are necessarily valid only for the income predicted by schooling. If the residual is held constant, they are also valid for observed income. I shall demonstrate that several arguments support the hypothesis that the correlation between the skewness of residual income and the skewness of predicted income is positive. If this hypothesis is correct, the skewness of observed income has a positive simple correlation with the predicted skewness, and tends to have a positive simple correlation with the skewness of schooling. In addition, more stringent assumptions result in the hypothesis that observed income skewness is positively correlated with the average level of the rate of return and the average level of schooling.

There is reason to believe that several of the components of the residual also tend to produce skewness in income. The residual of equation 10 is divided into two components. The first, reflecting differential ability, is $(\bar{r}_i^* - \bar{r}^*)\, S_i = d_i\, S_i$. If d_i and S_i were independent, and if both were normally distributed, their product $d_i S_i$ would have a symmetric distribution since the expected value of d_i is zero.[15] The residual is in terms of natural logs, and a lack of skewness in the logarithm of income implies a positive skewness of income itself. As long as the distributions of d_i and S_i are not sufficiently negatively skewed or negatively correlated with each other, the distribution of the antilog of $d_i S_i$ is positively skewed.

We may use the same arguments for other forms of human capital as we used for schooling. As long as the distributions of these other investments, and the rate of return from these investments, are not sufficiently negatively skewed or negatively correlated, their component of residual income will be positively skewed. In addition, the distribution of wealth tends to be highly positively skewed and is likely to produce skewness in its component of the residual income.

There appear to be no simple additive relations for skewness. Although we cannot be certain that positive skewness in its components produces a positively skewed residual, this seems plausible.

Several a priori arguments lead to an expectation of a positive correlation across areas between the predicted skewness and the residual skewness. An increase in the positive skewness of schooling (S_i) results in an increase in the skewness of predicted income and in the skewness of the differential ability ($d_i S_i$) component of the residual. In addition, it seems plausible to assume that the skewness of investments in schooling and the skewness of investments in other assets are positively related. It also seems plausible to assume that the rate of return from schooling and from other forms of capital are positively related across regions. These factors tend to produce a positive relation between the skewness of predicted income and the skewness of residual income.

Since there tends to be greater positive skewness in the ownership of physical capital than in years of schooling, and since investments in these two assets tend to be positively correlated, the residual skewness and the income skewness should be larger than the predicted skewness.[16] The difference would be smaller if earnings rather than total income were under consideration.

The a priori analysis indicates that the higher the level of the rate of return from schooling, the greater is the skewness of income. In addition, the empirical analysis of Part II indicates that the rate of return is important in explaining interregional differences in income skewness. Thus, a brief analysis of the factors that influence interregional differences in the rate of return would be useful.

It is not clear whether poorer regions have a higher or a lower rate of return from schooling than wealthier regions. Although the cost of obtaining a given level of funds for investment in schooling may be higher in a poorer area, the demand for human capital is lower, and the net effect is ambiguous. However, for regions among which there is considerable migration, the poorer ones may have a higher rate of return due to the effects of interregional migration.[17]

Workers with a higher level of education tend to have more knowledge about opportunities elsewhere and perhaps a reduced attachment to place of origin. In addition, they are likely to be wealthier than less educated workers, and thereby find it easier to finance the direct and oppor-

[16] Becker developed a model based on rational investment decisions which predicts a larger positive skewness of investments in physical capital than in human capital. (Becker, . . . *Human Capital*, especially pp. 35–37.)

[17] On this point see Chiswick, *op. cit.* "The Level of Schooling . . . ."

tunity costs associated with migration. Finally, whereas interregional wage differentials may tend to increase in proportion to the wage level for higher levels of skill, costs of migration are not likely to increase in proportion. The less-than-proportionate rise in migration costs is attributable to the direct cost component of migration which is not likely to rise as rapidly as the wage level for increasing levels of skill. These factors provide educated workers with a greater incentive to migrate than less educated workers. This higher migration rate has been found in empirical studies.[18]

The greater mobility implies that educated workers in poor regions face more of a national market for their services than do less educated workers. In the poor regions, those with higher levels of education receive wages relatively closer to the wage for their skill in the wealthier regions, than do workers with less education. Therefore, the rate of return from schooling tends to be higher in poorer regions. This relation between average income and the rate of return appears in interregional analyses for the United States and for Canada.[19]

Thus, holding the distribution of schooling constant, the poorer regions of countries in which there is considerable migration are likely to have a larger skewness of income than the wealthier regions. In an international comparison, however, the rate of return may be uncorrelated with the level of income and the latter may be uncorrelated with income skewness.

The rate of return from schooling may, however, be positively related to the rate of growth of income. If so, *ceteris paribus*, a region experiencing rapid economic development would tend to have a large income skewness. Thus, larger income skewness in rapidly growing countries may be a consequence, and not necessarily a cause, of the rapid growth.

The effect on income skewness of interregional differences in the

---

[18] See Becker, *Human Capital*, p. 89 note and Rashi Fein, "Educational Patterns in Southern Migration," *Southern Economic Journal, Supplement,* Vol. 32, no. 1, pt. 2 (July 1965), pp. 106–24.

[19] Becker and Chiswick, *op. cit.,* and Giora Hanoch, "An Economic Analysis of Earnings and Schooling," *Journal of Human Resources,* Vol. 2 (Summer 1967), pp. 310–29. In addition, it is implied in *Second Annual Review: Toward Sustained and Balanced Economic Growth* (Ottawa: Economic Council of Canada, December 1965), p. 119.

distribution of schooling, due to differences in the level of income, is not clear a priori. The model predicts, *ceteris paribus*, that a higher level of schooling produces a larger income skewness. The level of schooling in a region tends to be negatively related to the skewness of schooling, and the analysis predicts that lower schooling skewness produces lower income skewness. Thus, the simple correlation between income skewness and the level of schooling need not be positive.[20]

A negative correlation between the level and skewness of schooling is found empirically and is easy to understand. The distribution of years of schooling tends to have a central tendency and two finite limits— namely, zero or some minimum required by law as the lower limit, and say twenty years as the upper limit. In almost all regions there would be some at each extreme. As the mean rises from a low to a higher level, the skewness of schooling tends to decline from a positive to a negative value. Therefore, regions with a higher level of income and schooling may tend to have a smaller skewness of schooling, with an ambiguous net effect on the skewness of income. Similarly, economic growth may raise the level but decrease the skewness in years of schooling, with an ambiguous net effect on the skewness of income.

In summary, the rate of return from schooling is likely to be higher in the poorer regions of a country, but uncorrelated with average income across countries. In addition, lower average levels of schooling or income are likely to be associated with higher positive skewness of schooling. There does not appear to be any direct relationship between the rate of return and the skewness of schooling. However, the above suggests that, due to their mutual intercorrelation with the level of schooling, the rate

---

[20] Let X_0 = the skewness of income,
  X_1 = the level of schooling,
  X_2 = the skewness of schooling,
  $X_0 = a_0 + b_{y1.2}X_1 + b_{y2.1}X_2$, and
  $X_0 = a_1 + b_{y1}X_1$,

where the theory predicts that $b_{y1.2} > 0$ and $b_{y2.1} > 0$, and the empirical analysis indicates that $b_{12} < 0$. From statistical theory we know that $b_{y1} = b_{y1.2} + b_{12} b_{y2.1}$. [Arthur S. Goldberger, *Econometric Theory* (New York, 1964), pp. 194–95.]

If the magnitudes of b_{12} and $b_{y2.1}$ are sufficiently large and $b_{y1.2}$ is sufficiently small, b_{y1} will be negative. Thus, a negative correlation between the level and the skewness of schooling could change a positive partial relation between the level of schooling and income skewness into a negative simple correlation.

of return and the schooling skewness are positively correlated across the regions of a country, but are uncorrelated across countries.

The schooling parameters under study can be directly influenced by government educational policies, with accompanying effects on the skewness of income. For example, minimum schooling laws compel those who would otherwise invest in years of schooling below the legal minimum to increase their investments. This increases the skewness of schooling and also the skewness of income.[21]

The analysis also indicates that the skewness of income in a region depends in part on the correlation across individuals between the rate of return from schooling ($\bar{r}_i^*$) and the level of schooling (S_i). Government subsidies designed to increase the level of ability or reduce the cost of schooling to low-ability, poor students (e.g., the Head Start Program or scholarships to students from poor families) reduce the correlation between the rate of return and the level of schooling. *Ceteris paribus*, these policies reduce the skewness of income. Scholarships for high-ability, wealthy students have the opposite effect.

Not all of the hypotheses suggested here lend themselves to empirical testing. The scarcity of compatible international income data prevent an intercountry analysis. In addition, adequate data are not available for a time-series study. Thus, Part II consists of cross-sectional interregional analyses for the United States and for Canada.

The hypotheses tested below are:

1. Schooling parameters can produce a considerable amount of skewness in income.

2. The observed income skewness and the predicted income skewness are positively correlated, and have positive partial correlations with the rate of return, the average level of schooling and the skewness of schooling.

3. The residual skewness is positively correlated with the predicted skewness and the observed skewness.

4. Negative correlations between the level of schooling and the rate of return and schooling skewness may produce biased simple correlations between schooling and income parameters.

---

[21] The effects of minimum schooling laws on the distribution of income are analyzed in Chiswick, "Minimum Schooling Legislation . . .".

II. EMPIRICAL ANALYSIS

Cross-classified data for schooling and income exist for the regions and states of the United States and for the provinces of Canada. This permits the direct calculation of the skewness of earnings or income (i.e., observed skewness), the skewness of schooling, and the average level of schooling. Although average rates of return from schooling have been calculated for a number of regions and countries in recent years, their number is still too small for an effective interregional analysis.

Cross-classified data on schooling and income are used to estimate the average adjusted rate of return from schooling. A least squares linear regression analysis is performed using the equation

$$\text{Ln } Y_{S,i} = (\text{Ln } \hat{Y}_o) + \hat{r} S_i + \hat{U}_i, \tag{14}$$

where $\hat{r}$ and $(\text{Ln } \hat{Y}_o)$ are the regression estimates of the average adjusted rate of return and the average zero schooling level of income respectively. U_i is the residual whose squared deviation from the regression line is minimized. The regression approach appears to generate estimates of rates of return from schooling that are lower than the internal rates of return calculated by others. The bias appears for all regions, and may not alter the relative ranking of rates of return.[22]

If the antilogs of both sides of equation 14 are taken,

$$Y_i = e_{\text{L} \text{n}}{}^{\hat{Y}_o}(1 + r)^{S_i} e^{\hat{U}_i}, \tag{15}$$

where $e_{\text{L} \text{n}}{}^{\hat{Y}_o} (1 + \hat{r})^{S_i}$ is predicted income and $e^{\hat{U}_i}$ is the residual income. The measure of skewness used in this study is equation 11 which is a pure number, and equals zero for a symmetric distribution. Since Ln Y_o is assumed constant within each region, it has no effect on the predicted skewness. The predicted skewness is the skewness of $(1 + \hat{r})^{S_i}$. The residual skewness is the skewness in the residual income $e^{\hat{U}_i}$.

Since we are exploring the relation between schooling and the personal distribution of income, the characteristics of the entire population of a region are not relevant. Students should be removed because the model was developed for those who completed their investments. Wives

---

[22] For an analysis of regression estimates of rates of return, including a comparison with estimates of internal rates of return, see Chiswick, *Human Capital* . . ., chapter 2.

TABLE 2

Skewness Parameters in the United States for Earnings of Males Aged Twenty-Five to Sixty-Four[a]

| | Skewness | | | | Adjusted Rate of Return (5) |
	Observed Income (1)	Predicted Income (2)	Residual Income (3)	Schooling (4)	
1. U. S.	1.69	0.85	1.64	+0.31	.08
2. U. S. White	1.67	0.80	1.64	+0.24	.07
3. North	1.69	0.83	1.63	+0.42	.06
4. North White	1.67	0.80	1.62	+0.39	.06
5. South	1.75	0.92	1.79	+0.57	.09
6. South White	1.71	0.84	1.76	+0.42	.08

[a]Definitions:

1. Skewness:

$$SK = \frac{(Z_3)^{1/3}}{(Z_2)^{1/2}}$$

where Z_i is the ith moment of a variable around its mean.

2. Regression equation:

$$\text{Ln } Y_{S,i} = (Ln \hat{Y}_o) + \hat{r} S_i + \hat{U}_i \; ;$$

3. Observed Income: $Y_{S,i}$;
4. Predicted Income: $_e Ln \hat{Y}_o (1 + \hat{r})^{S_i}$;
5. Residual Income: $_e \hat{U}_i$

The probabilities presented in subsequent tables represent the chance that sample estimates of R will be greater than the values given. The probabilities are based on the number of degrees of freedom equal to, or nearest to, the number of observations minus two. (From R. A. Fisher and F. Yates, *Statistical Tables*, London, 1938, Table VI, p. 36-37.)

SOURCE: *U. S. Census of Population: 1960, Subject Reports. Occupation by Earnings and Education* (Washington: Bureau of the Census), Tables 1, 2 and 3.

should be excluded, since their labor force behavior is strongly influenced by their husbands' income and the number and age distribution of their children. The aged also should be excluded; many of them have low labor force participation due to ill health, discrimination, and pension income which often specifies maximum earnings.

The desired group can be approximated by restricting the data to males aged twenty-five to sixty-four. Although the model was developed for an infinite working life, the reality of a finite work life does not alter the model's basic stucture or its predictions. In addition, where possible

TABLE 3

Means and Standard Deviations of Skewness Parameters for the States (Income of Males Aged Twenty-Five and Over) and the Provinces (Income of Nonfarm Males Ages Twenty-Five to Sixty-Four)[a]

Regions	Skewness				Adjusted Rate of Return (5)
	Observed Income (1)	Predicted Income (2)	Residual Income (3)	School-ing (4)	
1. U. S. total—	1.14	0.93	1.26	−0.20	0.10
51 states	(0.09)	(0.11)	(0.09)	(0.48)	(0.01)
2. Nonsouth —	1.11	0.90	1.22	−0.32	0.10
34 states	(0.07)	(0.10)	(0.07)	(0.46)	(0.01)
3. South —	1.21	0.98	1.35	+0.03	0.12
17 states	(0.07)	(0.09)	(0.07)	(0.46)	(0.01)
4. U. S., white —	1.13	0.92	1.25	+0.00	0.10
51 states	(0.07)	(0.10)	(0.09)	(0.52)	(0.01)
5. Nonsouth, white —	1.10	0.91	1.21	−0.19	0.10
34 states	(0.07)	(0.09)	(0.08)	(0.51)	(0.01)
6. South, white —	1.17	0.95	1.33	+0.40	0.11
17 states	(0.06)	(0.11)	(0.07)	(0.26)	(0.01)
7. Canada —	1.42	1.16	1.55	+0.81	0.09
11 provinces	(0.13)	(0.09)	(0.20)	(0.25)	(0.01)

[a]See notes to Table 2. Standard deviations are in parentheses.

SOURCES: *United States Census of Population: 1960, Vol. 1, Characteristics of the Population,* Parts 2-52 (Washington: Bureau of the Census), Table 138; *Census of Canada: 1961* (Ottawa: Dominion Bureau of Statistics), Table A.11 for the provinces, unpublished.

and practicable, separate calculations are made to remove the effects of differences between races.

The United States data are for adult males and come from the *1960 Census of Population*. For the regions and the United States as a whole, the data are for earnings, and the sample consists of males aged twenty-five to sixty-four with earnings in 1959. At the state level, however, the absence of a cross classification of earnings by schooling in the census necessitated the use of income rather than earnings. Therefore, the sample for the states consists of males aged twenty-five and over with income in 1959. The analyses are performed for males and for "white males," where "white males" are defined as whites in the United States and the regions. In the interstate analysis, however, "white males" are defined as whites only for the sixteen states (including the District of Columbia) with 10 per cent or more nonwhites plus New York State, and as all males in the remaining thirty-four states. Tests indicate that the inclusion of nonwhites in the latter thirty-four states has a negligible effect on the magnitude of the parameters. The Canadian data are for the ten provinces and the Yukon Territory and come from unpublished tables of the *1961 Census of Canada*. The data are for income and the sample consists of nonfarm males aged twenty-five to sixty-four with income in 1960.[23]

An examination of the data for the United States and Canada in Tables 2 and 3 reveals that the predicted skewness is large, but it is smaller than the observed skewness and the residual skewness.[24] Thus,

---

[23] The original data and the calculation of the adjusted rates of return for the United States and Canada are discussed in greater detail in Chiswick, *Human Capital* . . ., chapter 3.

[24] The small size of the observed and residual skewness in the states compared to the regions of the United States seems surprising. The measure of skewness defined in equation 11 is sensitive to the average income of the upper open-end interval. This was estimated from the Pareto equation and its value is sensitive to the grouping of high incomes. Since the point representing the upper open-end interval is considerably above the fitted regression line, the sensitivity of the mean to the value of this interval is greatest for the income and residual skewness and least for the predicted skewness.

Comparisons between the two major regions of the United States, among the states, and among the Canadian provinces can be made because the same grouping is used within each type of area or level of aggregation. It is not valid, however, to compare the states to the regions or provinces unless the same grouping is used. Thus, since the lower bound of the upper open-end interval is $25,000 for the United States, the North and the South, and $10,000 for the states, a comparison between the states and regions would be misleading unless the data were reorganized.

by itself, the distribution of schooling produces a considerable amount of skewness in the distribution of income.

Table 2 indicates that the total South and white South have higher values for the four measures of skewness and for the rate of return than do the total non-South and white non-South. The non-South and the United States results are nearly the same. The removal of nonwhites reduces the magnitude of all of the parameters. The most significant changes are in the skewness of schooling and the skewness of predicted income.

TABLE 4

Correlation Matrix for Skewness in the Fifty-one States for Income of Males Aged Twenty-Five and Over[a]

	Skewness				Adjusted Rate of Return (5)
	Observed Income (1)	Predicted Income (2)	Residual Income (3)	Schooling (4)	
1. Predicted	0.42				
2. Residual	0.86	0.41			
3. Schooling	0.47	0.82	0.41		
4. Adjusted rate of return	0.47	0.77	0.64	0.62	
5. Average schooling	−0.66	−0.58	−0.61	−0.61	−0.66

PROBABILITY	R
.05	.23
.025	.27
.01	.32

[a]Probabilities based on fifty degrees of freedom. See notes to Table 2.

SOURCE: *United States Census of Population: 1960*, Vol. 1, *Characteristics of the Population*, Parts 2-52 (Washington: Bureau of the Census), Table 138.

An examination of Tables 3 through 6 indicates that the states with higher rates of return and larger schooling skewness tend to have larger predicted skewness and observed skewness. The predicted skewness and residual skewness are positively correlated among all the states and within the non-South. Their insignificant negative correlation in the South may be explained by the negative correlation between the schooling skewness and the residual skewness. The observed skewness is positively correlated with the predicted and the residual skewness.

The interstate correlations are weaker when separate analyses are

TABLE 5

Correlation Matrix for Skewness in the Thirty-Four Nonsouthern States for Income of Males Aged Twenty-Five and Over[a]

	Skewness				Adjusted Rate of Return (5)
	Observed Income (1)	Predicted Income (2)	Residual Income (3)	Schooling (4)	
1. Predicted	0.30				
2. Residual	0.76	0.36			
3. Schooling	0.43	0.80	0.45		
4. Adjusted rate of return	0.08	0.70	0.50	0.61	
5. Average schooling	−0.53	−0.27	−0.43	−0.38	−0.06

	PROBABILITY	R
	.05	.30
	.025	.35
	.01	.41

[a]Probabilities based on thirty degrees of freedom. See notes to Table 2.

SOURCE: *United States Census of Population: 1960*, Vol. 1, *Characteristics of the Population*, Parts 2-52 (Washington: Bureau of the Census), Table 138.

performed for the South and the non-South. This is due to the significant differences between the South and non-South.

Similar relationships are found when nonwhites are excluded from seventeen states. Tables 7 through 9 present correlation matrices for all, non-Southern and Southern states after adjustments for nonwhites. The skewness of observed, predicted, and residual income and the adjusted rate of return are positively correlated with each other. The skewness in schooling is positively correlated with these parameters in the country for whites and in the white non-South, but negatively correlated in the white South.

TABLE 6

Correlation Matrix for Skewness in the Seventeen Southern States for Income of Males Aged Twenty-Five and Over[a]

	Skewness				Adjusted Rate of Return (5)
	Observed Income (1)	Predicted Income (2)	Residual Income (3)	Schooling (4)	
1. Predicted	0.20				
2. Residual	0.78	−0.07			
3. Schooling	0.22	0.78	−0.13		
4. Adjusted rate of return	0.30	0.87	0.19	0.45	
5. Average schooling	−0.37	−0.85	−0.09	−0.76	−0.74

PROBABILITY	R
.05	.39
.025	.46
.01	.53

[a]Probabilities are based on fifteen degrees of freedom. See notes to Table 2.

SOURCE: *United States Census of Population: 1960*, Vol. 1, *Characteristics of the Population*, Parts 2-52 (Washington: Bureau of the Census), Table 138.

Table 10 contains a correlation matrix for the Canadian provinces. The adjusted rate of return is positively related to the observed and the predicted skewness. The predicted skewness is positively related to the observed skewness and the skewness of schooling. The residual skewness is highly positively correlated with the observed skewness and weakly negatively correlated with the skewness of schooling. This may explain the insignificant negative correlation between the skewness of schooling and of observed income.

The correlation matrices indicate that across the states and the prov-

TABLE 7

Correlation Matrix of Skewness Parameters for the Fifty-One States of Which Seventeen Are for Whites, for Income of Males Aged Twenty-Five and Over[a]

	Skewness				Adjusted Rate of Return (5)
	Observed Income (1)	Predicted Income (2)	Residual Income (3)	Schooling (4)	
1. Predicted	0.50				
2. Residual	0.83	0.38			
3. Schooling	0.39	0.34	0.49		
4. Adjusted rate of return	0.49	0.72	0.68	0.41	
5. Average schooling	−0.40	−0.59	−0.32	−0.12	−0.37

	PROBABILITY	R
	.05	.23
	.025	.27
	.01	.32

[a]Probabilities are based on 50 degrees of freedom. See notes to Table 2.

SOURCE: *United States Census of Population: 1960*, Vol. 1, *Characteristics of the Population*, Parts 2-52 (Washington: Bureau of the Census), Table 138.

inces, the skewness of observed, predicted, and residual income tend to be positively correlated. In addition, they tend to be positively correlated with the regression estimate of the adjusted rate of return and the skewness of schooling, when the latter are positively correlated with each other. When the rate of return and schooling skewness are not positively correlated, it is the effect of the rate of return which dominates.

The correlation matrix tables indicate that the average level of schooling tends to be negatively related to the predicted and the observed

TABLE 8

Correlation Matrix of Skewness Parameters for the Thirty-Four Non-Southern States of Which Three Are for Whites, for Income of Males Aged Twenty-Five and Over[a]

| | Skewness | | | | Adjusted Rate of Return (5) |
	Observed Income (1)	Predicted Income (2)	Residual Income (3)	Schooling (4)	
1. Predicted	0.50				
2. Residual	0.83	0.44			
3. Schooling	0.30	0.45	0.34		
4. Adjusted rate of return	0.30	0.76	0.51	0.32	
5. Average schooling	-0.42	-0.76	-0.39	-0.02	-0.54

PROBABILITY	R
.05	.30
.025	.35
.01	.41

[a]Probabilities are based on thirty degrees of freedom. See notes to Table 2.

SOURCE: *United States Census of Population: 1960,* Vol. 1, *Characteristics of the Population,* Parts 2-52 (Washington: Bureau of the Census), Table 138.

skewness. This is contrary to the model's prediction, *ceteris paribus*, that the level of schooling is positively related to the skewness of income. The analysis of Part I and Tables 4–10 indicate that the level of schooling tends to be negatively correlated with the estimate of the average adjusted rate of return and the skewness of schooling. The data in Table 11 are intended to test the hypothesis that for the regions of the United States and Canada, the observed simple negative correlation between the level of schooling and the skewness of income is due to the effects of

TABLE 9

Correlation Matrix of Skewness Parameters for the Seventeen Southern States of Which Fourteen Are for Whites, for Income of Males Aged Twenty-Five and Over[a]

| | Skewness | | | | Adjusted Rate of Return (5) |
	Observed Income (1)	Predicted Income (2)	Residual Income (3)	Schooling (4)	
1. Predicted	0.38				
2. Residual	0.72	0.07			
3. Schooling	-0.19	-0.30	-0.19		
4. Adjusted rate of return	0.41	0.71	0.55	-0.34	
5. Average schooling	-0.37	-0.43	-0.19	-0.11	-0.20

PROBABILITY	R
.05	.39
.025	.46
.01	.53

[a]Probabilities are based on fifteen degrees of freedom. See notes to Table 2.

SOURCE: *United States Census of Population: 1960*, Vol. 1, *Characteristics of the Population*, Parts 2-52 (Washington: Bureau of the Census), Table 138.

TABLE 10

Correlation Matrix for Skewness in the Provinces for Income of
Nonfarm Canadian Males Aged Twenty-Five to 64[a]

| | Skewness | | | | Adjusted Rate of Return (5) |
	Observed Income (1)	Predicted Income (2)	Residual Income (3)	Schooling (4)	
1. Predicted	0.49				
2. Residual	0.96	0.44 '			
3. Schooling	−0.07	0.60	−0.12		
4. Adjusted rate of return	0.66	0.75	0.64	0.28	
5. Average schooling	−0.45	−0.67	−0.35	−0.23	−0.58

PROBABILITY	R
.05	.52
.025	.60
.01	.69

[a]Probabilities based on nine degrees of freedom. See notes to Table 2.

SOURCE: *Census of Canada: 1961* (Ottawa: Dominion Bureau of Statistics), Table A.11 for the provinces, unpublished.

Notes to Table 11

[a]Row 1, partial slope or correlation coefficient; row 2, Student's *t* ratio (in parenthesis). The levels of significance of the coefficients are in row 3. *NS* = not significant at 5.0 per cent level. Degrees of freedom equal the number of observations minus two (for the simple correlation coefficient) or minus four (for the partial regression coefficients). Significance levels from H. M. Walker and J. Lev, *Statistical Inference* (New York, 1953), p. 465 and p. 470.

SOURCES: *United States Census of Population: 1960, Vol. 1, Characteristics of the Population,* Parts 2-52 (Washington: Bureau of the Census), Table 138; *Census of Canada: 1961* (Ottawa: Dominion Bureau of Statistics), Table A.11 for the provinces, unpublished.

TABLE 11

Average Schooling and the Skewness of Observed and Predicted Income in the United States and Canada[a]

Region—No. of Observations	Row No.	I Skew—Obs. Inc. Partial Slope Coeff. (t values) Significant at: (per cent) $\bar{S}$	$\hat{r}$	Skew($\hat{S}$)	II Skew—Pred. Inc. Partial Slope Coeff. (t values) Significant at: (per cent) $\bar{S}$	$\hat{r}$	Skew($\hat{S}$)	III Skew Obs. Inc./Skew Pred. Inc. Simple Cor. Coeff. Significant at: (per cent) Skew Obs. Inc. $\bar{S}$	Skew Pred. Inc. $\bar{S}$	IV Change in Coefficient of S: Less Neg +, More Neg −, No Change 0 Skew Obs. Inc.	Skew Pred. Inc.
U.S., Total— 51	1	-0.065	0.093	0.020	0.009	3.388	0.126	-0.661	-0.583	0	+
	2	(-3.822)	(0.097)	(0.763)	(0.700)	(4.763)	(6.320)				
	3	0.05	NS	NS	NS	0.05	0.05	0.05	0.05		
U.S., white 51	1	-0.029	1.643	0.034	-0.055	4.145	0.013	-0.403	-0.588	+	0
	2	(-2.092)	(2.153)	(1.851)	(-4.014)	(5.491)	(0.691)				
	3	2.50	5.00	5.00	0.05	0.05	NS	0.50	0.05		
Nonsouth total— 34	1	-0.063	-1.205	0.061	-0.005	3.272	0.134	-0.527	-0.269	+	0
	2	(-2.368)	(-0.952)	(1.897)	(-0.206)	(2.620)	(4.244)				
	3	2.50	NS	5.00	NS	1.00	0.05	0.50	NS		
Nonsouth, white— 34	1	-0.063	-0.269	0.040	-0.102	3.062	0.057	-0.445	-0.764	+	0
	2	(-2.423)	(-0.203)	(1.768)	(-6.257)	(3.690)	(3.980)				
	3	2.50	NS	5.00	0.05	0.05	0.05	1.0	0.05		
South, total— 17	1	-0.046	0.070	-0.026	+0.000	4.602	0.096	-0.373	-0.852	0	+
	2	(-0.898)	(0.030)	(-0.390)	(0.016)	(6.499)	(4.771)				
	3	NS	NS	NS	NS	0.05	0.05	NS	0.05		
South, white — 17	1	-0.021	1.459	-0.030	-0.039	5.087	-0.059	-0.372	-0.434	0	0
	2	(-1.316)	(1.162)	(-0.482)	(-1.821)	(3.091)	(-0.727)				
	3	NS	NS	NS	5.00	0.50	NS	NS	5.00		
Canada— 11	1	-0.022	7.035	-0.155	-0.036	3.060	0.138	-0.449	-0.672	0	+
	2	(-0.398)	((2.032)	(-1.039)	(-1.486)	(2.053)	(2.161)				
	3	NS	5.00	NS	NS	5.00	5.00	NS	2.50		

other variables, namely, the skewness of schooling and the rate of return from schooling.

Table 11 contains the results of a multiple regression of the skewness of observed income (column I) and predicted income (column II) on the level of schooling, the rate of return, and the skewness of schooling. Column III contains the simple correlations of the level of schooling with observed skewness and predicted skewness. Column IV is a summary which indicates whether holding the skewness of schooling and the rate of return constant decreases the negative (sign +), increases the negative (sign −) or does not change the significance (sign 0) of the correlation of level of schooling with observed and predicted skewness.

The correlation never becomes more significant in a negative direction, but frequently becomes less negative. In only two instances (among the states of the United States and the South for predicted income), the negative simple correlation becomes a positive partial correlation, but both positive correlations are insignificant. Thus, it appears that when the rate of return and skewness of schooling are held constant, the magnitude of the negative correlation between the level of schooling and income skewness is reduced, but there is no significant change in sign. Note, however, that for the total and white non-South the positive simple correlations between the rate of return and the skewness of observed income become insignificant negative partial slope coefficients. It is not clear why the level of schooling does not behave as expected while the rate of return generally follows the predicted pattern.

Testing the hypotheses developed from the theoretical analysis reveals that:

1. Schooling alone can produce a considerable amount of skewness in the distribution of income.

2. The observed income skewness and that predicted by schooling are positively correlated. When the rate of return and the skewness of schooling are positively correlated, each tends to be positively correlated with the predicted and the observed skewness. When they are not positively correlated, it is the rate of return which dominates. Indeed, the rate of return appears to be more important than the skewness of schooling in explaining income skewness.

3. The residual skewness tends to be positively correlated with the observed and the predicted skewness.

4. The average level of schooling tends to be negatively related to the rate of return from schooling and to the schooling skewness. Thus, a priori, it is not clear how changes in the distribution of schooling due to a higher level of income affect the skewness of income. Empirically, the significance of the simple negative correlation between the level of schooling and the skewness of observed and predicted income is reduced when the rate of return and the schooling skewness are held constant.

III. SUMMARY AND CONCLUSIONS

The a priori analysis of Part I and the empirical analysis of Part II indicate that income skewness can be related to rate of return and schooling parameters, and that these parameters are important for explaining interregional differences in income skewness. In particular, it has been demonstrated that the distribution of schooling by itself tends to produce a considerable positive skewness in the distribution of income. This suggests that income would have a considerable positive skewness even if human capital were the only source of income.

The model predicts that the skewness of income in a region has a positive partial correlation with the level of the rate of return from schooling, the skewness of schooling, the level of schooling, the skewness of predicted income, and the skewness of the residual income. In general, the predicted signs were found for simple correlations for all of the explanatory variables, except the level of schooling. It was argued, and demonstrated empirically, that the level of schooling tends to be negatively correlated with the rate of return and the skewness of schooling across the regions of a country. The partial correlation between income skewness and the level of schooling, when the rate of return and the skewness of schooling were held constant, was less negative than the simple correlation.

Since the rate of return from schooling tends to be higher in the poorer regions of a country, the analysis predicts, *ceteris paribus*, that poorer regions have a larger income skewness. The theory also suggests that the lower level of schooling in a poorer region should produce, *ceteris paribus*, a lower income skewness. Lower levels of schooling, however, tend to be related to larger schooling skewness, and therefore, larger income skewness. A priori, the net effect of these factors is ambiguous.

Empirically, income skewness is larger in poorer regions of the United States and Canada.

No international empirical analyses were performed. Economic theory does not suggest any clear relationship across countries between the level of income and the rate of return. In addition, the effects of a lower level of schooling and a larger schooling skewness in poorer countries tend to offset each other. Therefore, no prediction is offered as to whether, across countries, income skewness is related to the average level of income. If, however, rapid rates of economic growth are associated with high rates of return from investments, rapid economic development may generate a larger income skewness.

COMMENTS

MARY JEAN BOWMAN
UNIVERSITY OF CHICAGO

The remarks that follow will center around three topics: (1) meanings and measurements of skewness and of "inequality" in the analysis of the "shape" of an income distribution; (2) Chiswick's empirical analysis and statistical interpretations; (3) his attempt to integrate his empirical analysis with a Becker-style human-investment decision theory, as the theoretical starting point of his work.

CONCERNING THE "SHAPES" OF INCOME DISTRIBUTIONS
AND THEIR MEASUREMENT

In his opening paragraph, Chiswick argues the importance of studying determinants of the skewness of a distribution, on two main grounds: the relevance of "shape" (asymmetry) for discussions of the equity of the distribution, and its relevance for "Engel curve and savings-and-investment analyses." I fully agree with his emphasis on the importance of asymmetry in the distribution of incomes. Furthermore, I have no objection to his particular choice of a measure of skewness. But this is only one among many possibilities, and I am disturbed by the lack of any mention of the fact that such measures can be various, and that they do not necessarily give identical rankings because skewness (however measured) may be raised, or lowered, by quite diverse kinds of changes in the shapes of the various segments of the distribution. The omission of any comment at all on this point is the more disturbing in view of the fact that Chiswick asserts that while skewness was considered important in the past, "it has been ignored by most recent studies." He mentions a few exceptions, but he sweeps aside, as though they did not exist, recent preoccupations with poverty and the tailing out of incomes to the bottom, the increasing use of the Gibrat coefficient or of variance in the logarithms as an inequality measure, the increasing tendency to compare results of alternative measures of "inequality" that incorporate nonsymmetrical weighting systems, and the renewed concern with "welfare" concepts in the selection of measures to describe the forms of income distributions generally.[1] It is true enough that interest in the Pareto measure of "inequality" has declined, and that Pareto's index was in fact a measure of an important component of skewness—the stretching out of the upper tail. And it is equally true that the use of third-moment measures of skew, though they pile out of the computers along with other univariate statistics, have received comparatively little attention as interesting end products in themselves. But this does not signal a lack of concern in recent literature with the asymmetries of income distributions.

Basically, Chiswick's lack of attention to just what his measure of skewness means seems to go back to neglect of three interconnected facts. First, "shape" is clearly a matter of an entire distribution, and no single parameter can give us an adequate picture of "shape." This does not mean that single parameters are not useful—and, indeed, indispensable. But it does mean that we must (and for simple measures, as of central tendency, we do) interpret them in the light of underlying characteristics of the distribution they are summarizing. Second, the only inequality measures that are free of skewness components are those that weight

[1] For the most recent such contribution (to my knowledge) see D. J. Aigner and A. J. Heins "A Social Welfare View of the Measurement of Income Equality," *Review of Income and Wealth,* Series 13, No. 1, March 1967, pp. 12–25.

deviation of an income from the mean (or of any pair of incomes from each other) by their arithmetic differences. Even the standard deviation is in fact a skew-biased measure of dispersion when the underlying distribution is not symmetrical—which is of course one of the reasons we so often switch to the use of logarithms of incomes (tacitly assuming a log-normal income distribution, or a good approximation thereto). And third, to repeat, skewness, by any measure that attempts to describe the asymmetry of an entire distribution, may rise or fall as a result of quite different sorts of changes in component parts of the distribution. Thus, for example, the skewness of the income distribution in the United States may decline either because there is a lesser tailing out at the top or because there is more tailing out at the bottom (as modal incomes rise leaving the bottom still very low); conversely, skewness could become greater either because the top incomes are pulling further away from the mode or because the lowest incomes are rising toward it. A recognition of these facts might have helped Chiswick interpret some of his results, even if he did not choose to go on to look at "shape" using other indicators of asymmetry in his statistical analysis.

THE EMPIRICAL ANALYSIS AND FINDINGS

Although the heart of Chiswick's paper is in his effort to build a rate-of-return human-investment decision model into the analysis and interpretation of income skewness, it will be easier to see just what he has done if we begin by stripping away all the theoretical paraphernalia to ask what his statistical operations are and what they tell us. So stripped, Chiswick's mean "adjusted rate of return," $\bar{r}^*$, becomes simply the slope coefficient $\hat{r}$ in regressions of the natural log of earnings (or incomes) on schooling. Starting from that point, Chiswick derives his predicted skewness of income from the skewness of the schooling term (taking antilogs) of $(1 + \hat{r})^{s_i}$. As he shows, his equation states that *ceteris paribus* income will be more skewed (1) the higher the slope coefficient $\hat{r}$, (2) the higher the mean level of schooling $\bar{S}$, and (3) the more skewed the distribution of schooling. Using various sets of states and the Canadian provinces in a series of regressions, he then presents correlation matrices including these three attributes along with the skewness of observed, predicted, and residual incomes. He gets his expected positive zero-order correlation with observed income for $\hat{r}$ in all cases and for skewness in schooling in all except the subsets of the seventeen Southern states (fourteen white) and the Canadian provinces. However, correlations of observed income skew with average schooling level, $\bar{S}$, emerge very substantially negative, exceeding those with $\hat{r}$ in four of the seven zero-order matrices, and never coming closer to zero than −.30, though in one case the correlation between $\hat{r}$ and observed income skew was only .08. In multiple regressions, taking observed skewness as the dependent variable, the negative coefficients of $\bar{S}$ are reduced, but remain significant at 2.5 per cent or better in all sets except those for the Southern states only and for the Canadian provinces. On the other hand, in these regressions, the partial coefficients for $\hat{r}$ were nonsignificant except for the set that used all fifty-one states but whites only (significant at 2.5 per cent) and that for the Canadian provinces (significant at 5 per cent). When the "predicted skewness" is the dependent variable in multiple regressions, the relative effectiveness of $\bar{S}$ and $\hat{r}$ as explanatory variables is reversed, with $\hat{r}$ coming through much more strongly, but this is clearly not a test of his model.

In revising his paper Chiswick has become much more cautious in his statements concerning the "dominant importance" of $\hat{r}$, and is less inclined to dispose of the question of the "wrong" (negative) signs on $\bar{S}$, with the observation that they are less negative in a multiple than in a zero-order correlation. Furthermore, he is quite explicit about the importance of the negative zero-order correlations between levels of schooling on the one hand, skewness of the schooling distribution and the value of $\hat{r}$ on the other—and the multicollinearity problems involved. Nevertheless, he still stresses the good performance of $\hat{r}$ and seems to regard that of $\bar{S}$ as puzzling. I wonder if he would still be puzzled if he stepped outside of the model developed in this paper to use his insights (and he has such insights) to try another, complementary approach. A simple preliminary example might be the use of path coefficient analysis or a two-stage regression in which $\hat{r}$ would be treated in the first instance as a function of $\bar{S}$. I am not suggesting that Chiswick should have done yet another analysis before presenting the results of this one. What I do suggest is that his findings thus far indicate that if study of determinants of skewness is worth while, then it would also be worth while to try some other, complementary approaches. This is the more true in view of the fact that there may be very little resemblance empirically between $\hat{r}$ ($= \bar{r}^*$) and an internal rate of return—the base on which his theoretical construct is built.

THE RELATIONSHIP BETWEEN $\hat{r}$ AND AN INTERNAL RATE OF RETURN TO SCHOOLING

There are several reasons why $\hat{r}$ and the internal rate of return are different things: (a) Working life is not infinite, as Chiswick in effect assumes. We may dismiss this as unimportant, however, in view of the fact that he is concerned with schooling only. (b) Cross-section income data are by no means the same thing as the income prospects of an individual through time. But let us set that also aside, accepting the cross-section data as an approximation to expected income streams of the future. (c) Much more important is the simplifying assumption that this is a world in which all that men learn they learn in school, that they forget none of it, that none of it becomes obsolete, and so on. I shall come back to this, but for the moment let us accept it too. Even under such circumstances, the "adjusted rate of return" is an odd animal. Let us take a look at it. Under these circumstances, any given incremental investment by an individual in the jth year of schooling yields a permanent incremental income stream. Omitting subscripts specifying an individual, let us designate the incremental investment as I_j and the associated incremental lifetime income (rental value) stream as W_j. Under the specified conditions, the internal rate of return will equal the mean rental value ratio to costs, which is of course W_j/I_j. If we take Y_j as the potential earnings if the individual were to go directly into the labor market, and assume that k_j is an adjustment factor (as in Chiswick) such that $I_j = k_j Y_j$, we can write $r_j = W_j/k_j Y_j$. Now Chiswick's "adjusted rate of return" is $r_J^* = r_j k_j = W_j/Y_j$. But note that by this time we have eliminated any assessment of costs from the denominator. What we have, of course, is simply the ratio of the income increment associated with the jth year of schooling to mean lifetime income were schooling to stop at the lower schooling level. To call this a "rate of return," adjusted or not, is to contribute, in my judgment, to the deterioration of the language of economics—though I must admit that Chiswick has respectable company in this usage. Semantics aside, the important question is, of course, the magnitude of k, and its stability or variability among the various sub-populations to which the analysis is applied.

(d) Returning to the real world, from which Chiswick's observations were in fact obtained, it is clearly not so that all learning is in school (or at least before leaving school), and that there is no subsequent obsolescence of skills or learning of them—with or without cost. The magnitude of this effect is substantial. I have shown elsewhere[2] that for U. S. data the internal rates of return as conventionally computed from cross-section data equal about half or less of the ratio of an average individual's mean incremental annual income to investments in the associated increment of schooling. Chiswick's finding (in his dissertation) that his $\hat{r}$ values are not much changed when computed within age categories, excepting for a reduction of the estimate in the youngest age category, does not answer this challenge.

(e) Since Chiswick (correctly) uses observed incomes, without discounting, we might expect a priori that his estimates of rates of return would exceed the internal rates of return computed in conventional human-investment decision models. Yet, in fact, he obtained lower values for $\hat{r}$ than those found in internal rate-of-return comparisons. This reflects the fact that this foregone income or cost proxy is the mean income of men *of all ages* who are in the next lower level of schooling or, when he does the analysis by age groups, the mean incomes of men in the designated age categories. Those incomes incorporate returns to postschool learning. Although, in revising his paper, Chiswick has agreed that this is likely to cause a cost overestimation, and hence downward bias in his "rate-of-return" estimates, it seems to me that he still fails to appreciate the broader implications. Those implications are critical in any interpretation of his $\hat{r}$ as though it were a legitimate measure of $\bar{r}^*$, and especially in an analysis that attempts to explain and interpret variations in the skewness of income distributions.

[2] *The Assessment of Human Investments as Growth Strategy,* Joint Economic Committee, 90th Congress, 2nd Session, 1968, pp. 84–99.

DUNCAN FOLEY

MASSACHUSETTS INSTITUTE OF TECHNOLOGY

This paper sets out to study the relation between the positive skewness of distributions of income and the distribution of schooling which is presumably one of several variables that affect income. In studying this problem, the author leans very heavily on the assumption that the relation between schooling and income takes a particular form: that the logarithm of income depends linearly for an individual on years of schooling. Given this functional form, much of the paper follows analytically. As the author points out, this log-linear specification transforms a zero or small negative skewness in the distribution of schooling into a positive skewness in the distribution of income.

Since this assumption is of such fundamental importance, it is somewhat disturbing that it is not tested in any very direct way. The author takes the "rate of return" formulation for this function without question. Rates of return are very convenient ways to summarize the performance of any investment *ex post*, but it is not self-evident, at least to me, that the only possible functional relation between income and years of schooling is log-linear. One curious consequence, for example, of these specifications is that the marginal product of schooling increases with years of schooling.

Other functional forms might also be fitted to the data to see if there is any good empirical basis for preferring the log-linear hypothesis. The consequences of other functional forms on skewness would also be an interesting problem in this connection.

The author indicates at one point that educational policy might be employed to alter the skewness of the distribution of income. He bases this comment on his finding that the distribution of schooling affects the distribution of income in a particular way. But we see from his original formulation that the distribution of schooling affects the distribution of income through the distribution of the rate of return to schooling. This fact is obscured in the empirical part of the paper when variations in rates of return are lumped into the residual because of lack of data.

Given the author's earlier model, policy recommendations concerning the relation between schooling and income distributions depend crucially on the distribution of rates of return, that is, on the distribution of part of his residual. These recommendations would be clearer and more strongly founded if they were based explicitly on some statistically testable property of the residual. The paper as it stands contains no detailed study of the residual in the regression to back up the policy argument.

What is a good strategy for achieving a coherent economic explanation of the distribution of income? It seems to me that this paper offers substantial food for methodological thought. Certainly the forces working on the distribution of income are numerous and their interaction complex. The author mentions on-the-job training and the distribution of wealth in addition to schooling, and there are many other phenomena of importance, such as discrimination, the distribution of natural talent and temperament, and so on, affecting the distribution of income. Is it possible to deduce a great deal about the sources of skewness in the income distribution without a fairly detailed and well articulated model which takes several of these factors into account?

The author chooses to test his model only very indirectly, by looking at the relation between the skewness parameters he predicts on the basis of the distribution of schooling and observed skewness. If the model he has set up and begun to estimate correctly reflects an important relation, it should predict many features about the distribution of income besides skewness. To approach the problem in this way would involve specifying the residual distribution more carefully and testing hypotheses about the residual itself, in addition to looking at somewhat indirect consequences of the model, such as predicted skewness.

EDUCATION AND HUMAN CAPITAL
IN INTERNATIONAL ECONOMICS

SKILLS, HUMAN CAPITAL, AND COMPARATIVE ADVANTAGE •

PETER B. KENEN • COLUMBIA UNIVERSITY

This paper will deal with two important questions: (1) What have we already learned about the role of skills, human capital or, more broadly, knowledge, in determining national comparative advantage and, therefore, the structure of external trade? (2) What are the chief implications of the facts we have at hand, and what do we need to learn, whether by the speculative methods of the theorist or the patient efforts of the empiricist? My answers to these questions will be incomplete. I shall, indeed, spend more time posing a series of subsidiary questions under each main rubric than answering the two I have already asked. This exercise, however, may inspire new research on what may be the most exciting single issue facing specialists in foreign trade and those who are concerned with problems of development.

RESEARCH ON HUMAN CAPITAL AND FOREIGN TRADE

RESEARCH on this subject stems from two quite different papers by Kravis and Leontief.[1] The former, on wage rates in major trading industries, found that, in the U. S. case, the chief export industries pay somewhat

NOTE: I am grateful to Carol Gerstl and Constantin Voivodas for research assistance, and to the International Economics Workshop, Columbia University, for constructive criticism. Remaining blunders are my own.

[1] Irving Kravis, "Wages and Foreign Trade," *Review of Economics and Statistics,* February 1956; and Wassily W. Leontief, "Domestic Production and Foreign Trade: The American Capital Position Re-examined," reprinted in *Readings in International Economics,* R. E. Caves and H. G. Johnson (eds.), Homewood, Ill., 1968.

higher wage rates than import competitors. The latter found that U. S. trade is, on balance, labor using and, paradoxically, capital conserving. Kravis gave no explanation for his results, which seem superficially to contradict common views. Leontief, disturbed that the United States, a capital-rich country, could disobey the famous Heckscher-Ohlin theorem, offered a tentative rationalization. American labor, he suggested, is three times as efficient as foreign labor, the difference being due to "entrepreneurship and superior organization," rather than cooperation with abundant capital.[2]

Subsequent research inspired by these papers suggests that both phenomena—high wages and relative labor intensity in U. S. export industries—have a single cause: the substantial use of skill in U. S. export industries or, in current parlance, the intensive use of human capital.

A recent paper by Helen Waehrer reproduces Kravis' work for 1960 and tests it for significance.[3] She finds that twenty-two major export industries pay a yearly wage of $5,649, while an equal number of import competitors pay only $4,932. Further, there is a statistically significant relationship between an industry's trade balance, B, and its yearly wage, W.[4] Taking all major trading industries together:

$$B = -18.48 + 0.003 \, W \qquad r = 0.43$$

Waehrer goes on to ask why this is so, and generates two more significant regressions that shed new light on Kravis' problem. Constructing an occupational index, I, to measure the fraction of each industry's labor force employed in jobs that call for skill,[5] she shows that:

$$B = 16.15 + 0.31 \, I \qquad r = 0.50$$
while
$$W = 1923.4 + 67.89 \, I \qquad r = 0.86$$

---

[2] Wassily W. Leontief, "Domestic Production and Foreign Trade," p. 525.

[3] Helen Waehrer, "Wage Rates, Labor Skills, and United States Foreign Trade," in *The Open Economy: Essays on International Trade and Finance*, P. B. Kenen and R. Lawrence (eds.), New York, 1968, especially pp. 23, 30 and 37. Waehrer's paper derived from her dissertation (Columbia, 1966).

[4] Waehrer's trade balance, B, is the difference between exports and imports, divided by industry shipments. It differs from the index B_i used later in this paper; B_i is divided by the sum of exports and imports.

[5] Waehrer's skill index, I, is the sum of professional, managerial, clerical, sales and service workers, and craftsmen and foremen, divided by total industry employment.

An industry's skill mix, *I*, gives a somewhat better statistical account of its trade balance than does its yearly wage, and its skill mix goes a long way to explain its wage rate. In Waehrer's view, Kravis' findings represent the role of skills in structuring our foreign trade, with wage rates (strongly linked to skills) serving as a proxy for skill intensity.

Leontief himself took the first important step toward a systematic explanation of his paradox. In a second article refining his results, he classified total employment in export and import-competing production according to occupation:[6]

	Per cent of Total Labor Force	
Occupation	Export Production	Import-Competing Production
Professional, technical, etc.	13.75	12.24
Clerical, sales and service	22.07	17.00
Craftsmen and foremen	15.15	11.79
Operatives	30.05	28.38
Laborers	18.98	30.59

Translating these numbers into a crude estimate of the human capital employed by the two sectors, one can say that American export production is the more intensive in this species of investment. I have, in fact, performed this particular translation, on the limiting assumption that unskilled laborers have no human capital and that all wage differences (the excess over laborer) are due to education and on-the-job training. For all trading sectors (and all supplying sectors), I obtained these estimates of the human capital used to manufacture 1947 trade:[7]

[6] Wassily W. Leontief, "Factor Proportions and the Structure of American Trade: Further Theoretical and Empirical Analysis," *Review of Economics and Statistics,* November 1956, p. 399.

[7] The results reported here are summarized in my "Nature, Capital and Trade," *Journal of Political Economy,* October 1965, pp. 456–58; for additional detail, see P. B. Kenen and E. B. Yudin, *Skills, Human Capital and U.S. Foreign Trade,* International Economics Workshop, Columbia University, New York, 1965. The particular figures cited in this table and the next derive from mean wage data (not medians), were deflated by consumer prices (not hourly earnings), and related to all sectors of the economy (Leontief's estimate A). Other computations, some less successful, can be found in Kenen and Yudin, pp. 21–23 (and a separate analysis of direct requirements is given on pp. 26–34).

	Human Capital per Man Year (thousands of 1959 dollars)	
1959 Wage Differences Capitalized at	Export Production	Import-Competing Production
9.0 per cent	24.78	21.10
11.0 per cent	20.27	17.26
12.7 per cent	17.56	14.95

Next, I have converted these statistics into 1947 dollars in order to merge them with Leontief's statistics and generate a comprehensive capital-to-labor ratio for each trading sector:[8]

	Total Capital per Man Year (thousands of 1947 dollars)	
1959 Wage Differences Capitalized at	Export Production	Import-Competing Production
9.0 per cent	30.61	29.83
11.0 per cent	27.16	26.89
12.7 per cent	25.08	25.12

In two of these three cases (and a handful of others), converting skills data into human capital suffices to reverse the well-known paradox.[9]

Four other studies, using a variety of models and techniques, forcefully emphasize the strategic role of skills. In an input-output study of West German trade in 1954, Roskamp was surprised to find that German exports were capital intensive, relative to those of the United States, even though labor seemed then the abundant factor in West Germany.[10] Re-

---

[8] This amalgamation invokes another limiting assumption concerning the long-run fungibility of all forms of capital. It counts upon society's ability to choose deliberately between investing in men and investing in things. The same supposition, involving strong assertions about the efficiency of capital markets, underlies much other work on human capital, especially comparisons of rates of return, and is the explicit basis for my own elaborate model in "Nature, Capital and Trade."

[9] One might still argue, however, that the paradox survives, for Leontief's computations continue to imply that U.S. trade conserves tangible capital, and all evidence suggests that the United States is well endowed with this form of capital. If, further, one rejects the limiting assumption set forth in the preceding note, this counterargument acquires great strength.

[10] Karl W. Roskamp, "Factor Proportions and Foreign Trade: The Case of West Germany," *Weltwirtschaftsliches Archiv*, No. 2, 1963.

cently, however, Roskamp and McMeekin have taken a new look at that same year's trade, using somewhat different methods and taking explicit account of human capital.[11] This reexamination had two results. First, it revealed that, neglecting human capital, German exports were, after all, more labor intensive than U. S. exports. Second, it found that West German exports were quite intensive in human capital. In the authors' own words, ". . . one has to conclude that human capital was the most abundant factor of production relative both to physical capital and to labor. Labor was the abundant factor relative to physical capital but not to human capital. Physical capital was the scarce factor of production. When factors actually moved [internationally] it was human capital which left the country and physical capital which flowed in. This corroborates our findings."[12]

A second major contribution to this new subject is the series of papers contributed by Keesing.[13] He has used U. S. "skill coefficients" to measure the skills content of many countries' trade and has come forth with several striking results. Devising a list of occupations different from those used in other studies, Keesing ranks fourteen countries' exports and imports according to the skills their trade flows would embody if all countries' industries used skilled labor as do their U. S. counterparts.[14] He then shows a powerful inverse correlation (a Spearman coefficient of -0.87) between the skill content of exports and the skill content of

[11] Karl W. Roskamp and Gorden C. McMeekin, "Factor Proportions, Human Capital and Foreign Trade: The Case of West Germany Reconsidered," *Quarterly Journal of Economics,* February 1968. The chief difference in method consists in using factor incomes, rather than physical factor data, to measure factor use in each industry; this was done because "revenue streams emanating from assets, capital or labor, determine how large those assets are" (p. 155).

[12] Roskamp and McMeekin, "Factor Proportions, Human Capital and Foreign Trade," p. 160.

[13] Donald B. Keesing, "Labor Skills and International Trade: Measuring Many Trade Flows with a Single Measuring Device," *Review of Economics and Statistics,* August 1965; "Labor Skills and Comparative Advantage," *American Economic Review,* May 1966; and "Labor Skills and the Structure of Trade in Manufactures," in *The Open Economy,* pp. 3–18. The summary furnished here draws mainly on the last-named work.

[14] Keesing ranks countries by means of an index which sums up scientists and engineers, technicians and draftsmen, and other professionals, gives them double weight, then adds machinists, electricians, and tool- and diemakers, and divides this weighted total of "skilled workers" by the corresponding industry total of semi-skilled and unskilled workers.

imports; countries that "supply" large amounts of skill by way of their exports "absorb" very little skill by way of their imports. Keesing goes on to show that skill content of exports correlates impressively with income per capita (a Spearman coefficient of 0.93), this despite the fact that his study is confined to major industrial countries that do not display huge income differences. Finally, Keesing demonstrates remarkable consistency in the bilateral trade of the industrial countries; if a country exports skill-intensive goods to a trading partner, it is likely to import less skill-intensive goods from that same trading partner. Working separately with scientists and engineers, Keesing finds just two exceptions to a strong ordering of pairwise trade patterns; working with machinists, electricians, and tool- and diemakers, he finds only one exception.

Keesing's work is open to several objections,[15] and yields only roundabout results on the role of skills. It does not link the factor content of a nation's trade directly to that nation's factor endowment, but couples consistency in national rankings with the Heckscher-Ohlin theorem to *infer* differences in nations' skill supplies. Another cross-national analysis, however, gives us direct evidence that the stock of skills (or skill-generating power) shapes the production pattern within manufacturing and, therefore, affects a nation's foreign trade. Working with data for twenty-six countries, including less-developed countries, Yahr finds that certain industries pay high wages in all countries and, with Waehrer, treats these as the industries using large amounts of skill.[16] She then asks how large a part of each nation's output comes from these same industries. Finally, she employs a schooling index (Harbison-Myers) as a crude proxy for total skill supply (or the capacity to generate skill), and asks if countries with high scores on the schooling index do, in fact, specialize in skill-intensive products. Computing a separate cross-national regression for each industry, she seeks to "explain" that industry's share in each nation's total output by that nation's schooling score. Her results

[15] See, e.g., Johnson's comments on "Labor Skills and Comparative Advantage," and A. O. Krueger's comments following my paper.
[16] Merle I. Yahr, "Human Capital and Factor Substitution in the CES Production Function," in *The Open Economy*, pp. 91–97, especially Table 6. Yahr's paper derives from her dissertation (Columbia, 1967). Her industries are composites of two-digit ISIC groups. Two out of thirteen could not be classified consistently according to relative wage (rubber products and nonmetallic mineral products); five others were classified as high wage and the remaining six as low wage.

are-impressive. In four out of five high-wage industries, the regression coefficients are, as anticipated, positive and statistically significant (the coefficients of determination range as high as 0.47). In five out of six low-wage industries, the regression coefficients are, instead, negative and statistically significant (the coefficients of determination range as high as 0.43).[17] Clearly, countries with large amounts of skill specialize in industries needing much skill, while countries with limited amounts of skill specialize in industries needing little skill.

Finally, let me mention one more result, tangentially related to this general survey. In an early theoretical investigation of human capital and foreign trade, I argued that standard Heckscher-Ohlin models do allow for differences in incomes per capita, but seem to offer too few reasons for those same differences. If all factor prices were equalized by trade, there could be only two causes of differences in incomes: differences in labor-force-participation rates and differences in over-all capital-to-labor ratios. But models including investment in man introduce two more causes of differences in incomes: differences in stocks of human capital per worker and differences in the innate quality of labor (its "susceptibility to improvement by investment").[18] Recent work by Krueger, using an ingenious model, emphasizes the importance of these extra elements. A very large portion of most income differences can be attributed to measured differences in nations' stocks of human capital.[19] In sixteen of twenty-one countries studied, more than half the difference between U. S. income and that of the other country is due to a shortfall in human capital. In no fewer than eight cases, moreover, the shortfall accounts for more than three-fifths of the income difference.

---

[17] The sole exception among high-wage industries was chemicals production (including petroleum); the regression coefficient was negative but nonsignificant. The sole exception among low-wage industries was wood manufacture (including furniture); the regression coefficient was positive but nonsignificant. Yahr notes that the coefficients of determination are in general lowest for industries with close ties to natural-resource exploitation.

[18] See "Nature, Capital and Trade," p. 451, and "Toward a More General Theory of Capital and Trade," in *The Open Economy*, p. 118 and note 27.

[19] Anne O. Krueger, "Factor Endowments and *Per Capita* Income Differences Among Countries," *Economic Journal*, September 1968, especially pp. 651–53. Note Krueger's observation that her model understates accountable differences in income insofar as measured income is understated for poor countries and insofar as barriers to free trade prevent full factor-price equalization (pp. 651, 657).

Yet, some work on this subject leads to deep puzzlement. Bharadwaj and Bhagwati have made human-capital estimates for India very similar to those I have made for the United States.[20] Measuring the skills employed by Indian exports and import substitutes, converting these to human-capital equivalents, and adding their figures to tangible capital, they find, as expected, that India's external trade is labor using and human-*cum*-tangible capital saving, but, quite surprisingly, that the adjustment for human capital works to decrease, not increase, the relative labor intensity of India's exports. The two authors offer several explanations for this paradox and argue that more recent data might well resolve it.[21] But doubts and suppositions, however plausible, do not alter numbers, and these numbers do suggest that skills may not be all-important for comparative advantage.

Consider, moreover, the quite different recent work of Keesing and others, advancing a "dynamic" view of U. S. foreign trade. A pioneer in research on the role of skills, Keesing has now supplied a second, competing explanation for the behavior of U. S. exports. Spending on research and development, he argues, explains U. S. success in foreign markets better than any other variable tested, from which it is reasonable to conclude that "the world economic role of the United States involves the systematic export of new products."[22]

[20] Ranganath Bharadwaj and Jagdish Bhagwati, "Human Capital and the Pattern of Foreign Trade: The Indian Case," *Indian Economic Review,* October 1967.

[21] One, in particular, deserves complete quotation: "On the one hand, the weight of plantations, mining and textiles in Indian exports, for our period, is very considerable; and these sectors have a high percentage of 'skilled' workers. On the other hand, the over-all skill content, in labour, in import competing activities such as iron and steel and light engineering industries (many of which have a large base in the small-scale sector in India) turn out to be lower; the growth of more complex technology in these industries, involving perhaps greater over-all skill levels, must have come in the period *beyond* that covered by our wage rates and occupational data, which generally span the period 1955–1959" (pp. 139–40).

[22] Donald B. Keesing, "The Impact of Research and Development on United States Trade," in *The Open Economy,* pp. 175–89, and the several authors cited in Keesing's first footnote (especially Hoffmeyer, Lary, Hufbauer, and Vernon). See, too, William Gruber, D. Mehta and Raymond Vernon, "The R & D Factor in International Trade and International Investment of United States Industries," *Journal of Political Economy,* February 1967, and S. F. Kaliski's comment in the same journal, October 1967.

Keesing's chief evidence for this new view comprises a series of simple correlations (using sixteen or more sectors) between the U. S. share in major countries' exports during 1962 and the several constructs listed here:

Independent Variable[a]	Linear Correlation[b]
Company R & D as a percentage of sales	0.59
Federal R & D as a percentage of sales	0.84
Total R & D as a percentage of sales	0.90
Scientists and engineers in R & D as a percentage of the total labor force	0.91
Scientists and engineers outside R & D as a percentage of the total labor force	0.67
Semi- and unskilled workers as a percentage of the total labor force[c]	−0.59
Value added per establishment (standing for plant economies of scale)	0.44

[a] All data for 1960, save for value added per establishment (1958).

[b] All but last significant at the 0.05 level.

[c] Keesing gives simple correlations for two other skill groups ("other professionals" and "skilled manual workers") but does not aggregate his groups to test the role of all skilled labor outside R & D. Hence, I reproduce his correlation for all unskilled labor [as a proxy (with sign reversed) for skilled labor as a whole].

Clearly, expenditure on research and development and the corresponding professional employment in R & D have the highest correlations with export performance—higher than the correlations that relate to skills per se.

One observer has suggested that we need not choose between the skills hypothesis and the R & D approach, as the former is static and the latter is dynamic.[23] The R & D approach, however, is not dynamic in any conventional sense; it does not explain *changes* in the trade pattern. Instead it has to be viewed as treadmill dynamic, explaining the trade

---

[23] Edward J. Mitchell, "Explaining the International Pattern of Labor Productivity and Wages: A Production Model with Two Labor Inputs," *Review of Economics and Statistics,* November 1968, p. 467.

pattern at each point in time by ongoing innovation.[24] One is obliged to make a choice between the two approaches.

But Keesing's tests may not be the best basis for that choice. Note, first, that research input—employment or expenditure—is an imperfect proxy for research output, and it is the latter that must govern export shares.[25] Moreover, it is not clear that one year's R & D is, alone, decisive for export performance in another year, or that R & D undertaken in a single sector has its chief effects on the exports of that sector.[26] Note, finally, that Keesing reports high intercorrelations between several pairs of his "independent" variables, so that the sequential use of R & D and skills, in simple correlations with export performance, does not permit the perfect ranking of competing suppositions.[27]

This last point has led me to augment his analysis by running and reporting (in Appendix A) a series of multiple-regression relationships. These do not resolve the most important difficulties inherent in testing the R & D approach, but do help to clarify certain of the issues. Starting with Keesing's own dependent variable, X_i, the U. S. share in world exports of ith sector output is:

$$X_i = 19.16 - 14.988K_{1i} + 4.037R_i + 1.725S_{1i} \qquad \bar{R}^2 = 0.88$$
$$(2.850) \qquad (5.515) \qquad (1.728)$$

where K_{1i} represents the (direct) capital-to-output ratio for 1947, derived from Leontief's original data; where R_i is Keesing's scientists and engineers working in R & D; where S_{1i} is Keesing's scientists and engineers outside R & D (but recomputed as a fraction of the total labor force

[24] If it were dynamic in conventional terms, the R & D approach might best be tested by correlation R & D input (or output) with the *change* in export share (or some "stock" of R & D with the share itself). One such test was performed in connection with this paper and was unsuccessful; there is no correlation between scientists and engineers in R & D (1960) and the change in export share (1962 to 1965). See Appendix A, Table 1. Note, however, one objection to this test (suggested orally by Richard Nelson): The R & D approach postulates prompt imitation of most innovations, so that old R & D grows obsolete very fast, and current or quite recent R & D represents the whole stock relevant to export shares.

[25] To make matters worse, available statistics on R & D are imperfect input measures; the classification of scientists and engineers (between R & D and other activities) is somewhat arbitrary, and one must also classify supporting personnel, not (as here) treat all of them as production workers.

[26] For more on this last point, see Keesing, "The Impact of Research and Development," pp. 176–77.

[27] For several of these correlations, see Appendix A, Table 3.

outside R & D); and where the several numbers in parentheses are "t" coefficients (not standard errors). In this and several other computations, the argument representing research and development is, indeed, more powerful than all others tried. The proxy for skills input, S_{1i}, and several broader aggregates serving the same purpose did not attain statistical significance (and did little to increase $\bar{R}^2$).

But when one employs a different measure of success in foreign trade, the ith industry's trade balance, B_i, one generates a very different series of results:

$$B_i = 23.94 - 87.782K_{1i} + 2.656R_i + 16.020S_{1i} \qquad \bar{R}^2 = 0.46$$
$$(2.168) \qquad (0.471) \qquad (2.084)$$

Keesing's proxy for research and development, R_i, falls far short of significance (and actually reduces $\bar{R}^2$), while S_{1i} attains statistical significance. Further, a broader index of skill use (less closely correlated with R_i) gives a better explanation of the trade balance:

$$B_i = -14.51 - 97.097K_{1i} + 5.828R_i + 2.671S_{5i} \qquad \bar{R}^2 = 0.60$$
$$(2.772) \qquad (1.579) \qquad (3.252)$$

where S_{5i} includes scientists and engineers outside R & D, other professionals, and all skilled manual workers. Here, R_i comes closer to significance (and helps slightly to increase $\bar{R}^2$), but the index of skill use, S_{5i}, does the most to explain trade-balance performance.

One is led, in the end, to choose Keesing on skills over the more recent Keesing on R & D, for when one looks at imports along with exports (at B_i instead of X_i), skill use seems to be the more important variable.[28] Research and development may still play a vital role in sustaining U. S. exports (which is all that Keesing claims) and may be quite important in some other instances.[29] A cautious eclecticism is surely in order. Yet Keesing's work on skills, with that of many others, appears to open a more intriguing avenue for study, promising more general, comprehensive explanations of the structure of production and comparative advantage.

---

[28] Notice, however, that this B_i equation has a lower coefficient of determination than that obtained with X_i.

[29] See, e.g., Ozawa's work relating transferred knowledge—research output—to the rates of growth of Japanese exports. (Terutomo Ozawa, "Imitation, Innovation, and Japanese Exports," in *The Open Economy,* pp. 190–212.)

AN AGENDA FOR RESEARCH: POSITIVE ANALYSIS

THE several studies surveyed in the preceding section argue impressively that skills or human capital are an important determinant of trade flows. But this finding only serves to pose a series of questions that trade theorists and others have yet to examine. Statements that countries well endowed with skills will export skill-intensive products are no different from and no more illuminating than statements that countries well endowed with machines will tend to export machine-intensive goods. The fixed-endowment factor box used in every trade course helps us to describe national endowments and the two-way trade flows that endowments generate, but it is inadequate for a long-run analysis. It does not tell us how endowments come into being and why they should differ between countries.

To carry the analysis one vital step further, one must ask why some countries have acquired large supplies of skill and why others have acquired large stocks of machinery. "In the dynamic case," Valivanis argues, "the producible factors of production, given time, adjust precisely to the pattern of final demand. It makes no sense to speak of 'original endowments' unless one is speaking of the immediate short run."[30] This reminder gains new force when, as now, the labor force has to be regarded as a producible factor of production. One might, perhaps, adopt an intermediate view, supposing that financial capital and capital goods move across frontiers more readily than labor and that, in consequence, "the human resources of a country are subject to slower change than its man-made material resources."[31] This view, however, makes too much of a difference in degree to serve as the basis for general theorizing. Furthermore, it faces factual challenge. Many skills can be imported via foreign schooling and on-the-job training, and others can be borrowed by hiring foreigners.[32]

When, instead, stocks of skill and capital equipment are viewed as the end products of decisions to save and decisions to invest, an elemen-

[30] Stephan Valivanis, "Leontief's Scarce Factor Paradox," *Journal of Political Economy*, December 1954, p. 524.

[31] Keesing, "Labor Skills and the Structure of Trade in Manufactures," pp. 5–6.

[32] On imported skills, see A. D. Scott's important paper in this conference volume; on borrowed skills, see Elinor B. Yudin, "Americans Abroad: A Transfer of Capital," in *The Open Economy*, pp. 40–69.

tary answer starts to take shape. High-income countries, capable of saving, are likely to accumulate all forms of capital—labor skills, machinery, and disembodied knowledge. So, too, are those poorer countries, like Japan, which appear to generate unusually large savings. Note, again, Keesing's point that high-income countries are the ones that export skill-intensive products.[33]

But how are savings allocated—how much to training, to physical plant, and to the development of new techniques? I lay claim to the first, tentative reply. In two papers on this subject,[34] I have tried to convert conventional "point" theory, using the factor box, into "situation" theory, using a species of factor-transformation curve. That curve shows how savings should and will be allocated between the improvement of the nation's labor force and the production of tangible capital. Its shape and size depend upon the savings rate and the innate quality of labor and land. The point chosen on the curve depends upon the interest rate and prevailing factor prices (Valivanis' "pattern of final demand").

My approach is not without intriguing implications. It helps, for instance, to explain the ACMS finding that "the American advantage in efficiency tends to be least in capital-intensive industries,"[35] and shows

[33] But note that skill abundance, as reflected in trades flows, does not strongly correlate with tangible-capital abundance; countries that export skill-intensive products seem also to conserve tangible capital. This point is implicit in Leontief's analysis, is made again by Keesing ("The Impact of Research and Development," p. 181), and is reaffirmed by my own multiple regressions (in which K_{1i} and K_{2i} have negative weights, while S_{1i} and S_{5i} have positive weights). It is, of course, possible that skill-intensive *processes* are not also tangible-capital intensive, and this would make for similar regression results, but there is little evidence to this effect. There is no correlation, positive or negative, between the two measures of capital intensity and the three measures of skill intensity in Appendix A, Table 3.

[34] "Nature, Capital and Trade," pp. 442–49, and "Toward a More General Theory of Capital and Trade," pp. 101–07.

[35] The finding in question is in K. J. Arrow, H. B. Chenery, B. S. Minhas and R. M. Solow, "Capital-Labor Substitution and Economic Efficiency," *Review of Economics and Statistics,* August 1961, p. 247. My note on the problem, attributing the bias to neglect of skills (labor augmentation), is "Efficiency Differences and Factor Intensities in the CES Production Function," *Journal of Political Economy,* December 1966, pp. 635–36. Recently, incidentally, Arrow, *et al.,* concede that "there is little to choose between neutrality [their first choice] and pure labor-augmentation." See their reply, furnished by a protégé, to Gupta's comprehensive treatment of the problem (Suraj B. Gupta, "Some Tests of the International Comparisons of Factor Efficiency with the CES Production Function," and Archen Minsol, "Reply," *Review of Economics and Statistics,* November 1968, pp. 470–80). Minsol's university, Lower Slobbovia, would seem to have acquired a brilliant economist!

why international capital movements can occur even when free trade has equalized all input prices.[36] Yet I do not recommend much more work along these lines. First, my own approach relies on the existence of diminishing returns to capital formation in man and land (the latter representing all tangible assets). This is far from realistic, if not with respect to man, surely with respect to land. Second, my approach leaves no room for direct use of simple, unskilled labor and, therefore, loses touch with much of the research summarized above, dealing with differences in the skill requirements of various activities and related trade flows. Third, my approach gives no place to the production of pure disembodied knowledge—research and development—although this species of investment seems to play a role in the explanation of U. S. exports.

Future work on human capital and foreign trade must surely answer the same questions studied in my model, but should now be focused less abstractly on two basic issues: (1) How does human capital enter the production function? (2) Why do certain countries seem to have an edge in the acquisition of human capital? Taken together, answers to these questions would lead us to modify factor-endowments theory and furnish an incisive analysis of foreign trade, especially of trade in manufactured products.

Trade theorists would be quite pleased if other economists were to reply to the first question; we do not care to poach on colleagues' preserves. But we cannot refine our own methods without knowing more about the links between skilled and unskilled labor and their relationship to physical capital. Are we now to use three-factor production functions, allowing for the joint employment of both types of labor? If so, should we treat the two as far from perfect substitutes? This view is endorsed by Mitchell and is the rationale for most of Keesing's computations on skill requirements.[37] Alternatively, should we use simple labor augmentation?

[36] "Nature, Capital and Trade," pp. 451–55, and "Toward a More General Theory of Capital and Trade," pp. 118–23.

[37] See Mitchell, "Explaining the International Pattern of Labor Productivity and Wages," especially pp. 466–68, and Keesing, "Labor Skills and the Structure of Trade in Manufactures," pp. 8–9. Others would appear to take a similar position, including Roskamp and McMeekin, Krueger, Waehrer, and Yahr, all cited previously. (Yahr's work on factor substitution, however, may fit more neatly into a labor-augmentation model; see pp. 70–85).

This view seems to have Griliches' support (see his paper in this volume) and was the explicit basis for my own theorizing.[38] If, finally, we are told that labor augmentation makes the most sense, how should we then interpret Keesing's computations, based as they are on fixed skill requirements?[39] Trade theorists are frequent lenders of technique. This time, we must be net borrowers of knowledge, and are likely to display strong preference for present over future goods or, at least, for quick service from the rest of the profession.

Meanwhile, we must deal with the second question—the reasons for differences in stocks of human capital. Here, then, are three conjectures, each of which may help explain the apparent concentration of human capital in a small handful of high-income countries:

I. SCHOOLING AND TRAINING MAY BE SUBJECT TO INCREASING RETURNS.

This conjecture is derived from two other suppositions. First, there are obvious economies of scale in formal education (measured in quantity and quality of output): large institutions can employ expensive, indivisible physical equipment and can gather staff in numbers that permit advanced, specialized instruction. Second, as countries accumulate skills, they may well encounter diminishing returns to the *use* of skills in manufacturing, so that the diversion of skilled workers to the supervision of on-the-job training makes for a smaller absolute sacrifice of current output than would be the case in countries with small stocks of skill.

II. THE OPPORTUNITY COST OF OBTAINING SKILL MAY DECREASE AS INCOME RISES.

This conjecture is derived from the further supposition that the marginal utility of current consumption does, in fact, decline and is, in

---

[38] It is likewise consistent with my computations amending Leontief (and may also be consistent with Krueger's work on income, even though her model is cast in multifactor form).

[39] One could, of course, treat Keesing's skill-mix computations as proxies for differences in degrees of augmentation or, more precisely, as measures of (augmented) labor intensities (which must differ systematically across sectors for the strong factor ordering required by factor-endowments analysis).

any case, quite high when income nears subsistence.[40] Put less controversially, personal savings and discretionary spending are, together, very small at prevailing income levels in many countries, so that too many youngsters and adults cannot pay the costs of training (whether tuition fees or foregone earnings).[41]

III. IMPERFECT CAPITAL MARKETS TEND TO DIVERT SAVINGS TOWARD TANGIBLE CAPITAL, AND IMPERFECTIONS ARE SEVERE IN ALL BUT A FEW MARKETS.

This conjecture does not call for much elaboration. Few observers would deny that capital markets are underdeveloped in a surprising number of countries (and even those that are developed have only recently begun explicitly to finance personal investments in formal education). Furthermore, imperfect capital markets tend to favor short-term lending against very visible, salable collateral. (In most countries, of course, formal education is financed by the state, not from private savings, but even here, differences in levels of development may correlate with biases against human capital. Less-developed countries are notorious for spending public funds on tangible symbols of economic sovereignty.)

Putting these conjectures into different form, the first suggests that the supply curve of training shifts out with rising income; the second suggests that the demand curve moves in the same direction; and the

[40] Note, however, Krueger's point (in her comment on this paper) that training to high skill levels may involve large opportunity costs to the individual and society, since those who receive this training are already skilled and forego high incomes to obtain more skill.

[41] This point applies to formal schooling and general training, since specific training is financed by employers. In fact, however, most of the skills employed in the poorer countries are probably low-level manual skills (and the markets for them are sufficiently competitive to treat them as general). Precisely because professional skills are in such short supply, production is patterned toward low-skill processes. On specific and general skills, see Gary S. Becker, *Human Capital,* New York, NBER, 1964, pp. 11–29. On manual and professional skills, see Keesing, "Labor Skills and the Structure of Trade in Manufactures," pp. 9–10, where he asserts that certain manual skills are "ubiquitously required in every manufacturing industry," and are, therefore, general in Becker's sense.

third conjecture reinforces the second. If one or more of them is true, human-capital formation is quite likely to proceed faster, absolutely and compared to other forms of investment, in high-income countries. If, further, this prediction is combined with the chief inference from Krueger's work—that human capital adds mightily to real income—one is brought to forecast the continuing concentration of human capital in the wealthy countries, with a corresponding concentration on those activities making intensive use of high-level skills.

Consider, finally, one more topic for investigation. Distinctions among types of skill may help to explain the sequence and migration of industrial development over long periods and the corresponding evolution of foreign trade. If a particular level or type of skill is used by a particular technology or subset of activities, a country pioneering in that technology may well acquire a comparative advantage in all the activities using that technology. In effect, a "leading" industry using that technology can furnish the "followers" with a low-cost input (or with the trained workers they will need as teachers). Put differently, the skills employed by a technology will be more or less specific to the leading industry— the first to be developed—and training costs will be borne by the first firms, but the same skills will be general for subsequent users of the same technology, and further training costs will be borne by workers. Yet a country that accumulates one level or type of skill may have no particular comparative advantage in other industries or upon the advent of a new technology. It is as likely to lag as lead in the development of those other industries or in the exploitation of the new technology.

More concretely, could one show that the international migration of the industrial revolution from Britain to the Continent and the United States was related to differences between the skill requirements of the "leading" product groups in its successive phases, first textiles, then metals, then motorcars, chemicals and electrical equipment? As human-capital endowments may well change more slowly than physical endowments, inherited differences in skill supplies may have been more important in governing the pace and locus of development than inherited differences in stocks of machinery. Could one also show that the migration of disembodied knowledge and of small numbers of highly skilled workers, serving as temporary teachers, is strategic to the further spread of industrialization? The Japanese example may be a leading case in point.[42] Lastly, could one show that the well-documented tendency toward a more sophisticated specialization among industrial countries—the tendency toward larger two-way trade flows inside product groups—reflects the very specialized technologies and, therefore, specific skill requirements of the newer manufactures?[43] By doing so, one would attach a new operational significance to the Heckscher-Ohlin theorem, especially if one could show why one country has a comparative advantage in producing the techniques and the labor skills connected with its own differentiated exports.

AN AGENDA FOR RESEARCH: NORMATIVE ANALYSIS

MUCH of our research on human capital has been inspired by normative concerns, not mere curiosity. Are we investing enough in education? Are the several outputs of our schools well matched to the needs of our economy? Are we using the right input mix—teachers and professors, buildings and equipment—in the production of knowledge and skills? The bulk of the research called forth by these questions is, quite rightly, positive; one must have facts before one can give advice. Yet I should like to make a new plea for theoretical and normative investigations, and to ask that those investigations span a wider range of questions than the one to which research has already been addressed. There are, in particular, some problems in trade theory that acquire new dimensions when one takes account of skills.

[42] See, again, Ozawa, "Imitation, Innovation, and Japanese Exports," and Yudin, "Americans Abroad." My comments here constitute a modified version of the familiar "late-comer" hypothesis, stressing the late-comer's exploitation of the leader's assets, not his mistakes. Incidentally, the importance of skilled labor to development was well known to the mercantilists centuries ago. Colbert's decrees, for example, offered large bounties to lure master craftsmen from Flanders to France.

[43] For evidence on intraindustry trade and further thoughts on its causes, see Bela Balassa, "Tariff Reductions and Trade in Manufactures among the Industrial Countries," *American Economic Review*, June 1966, and his *Trade Liberalization among Industrial Countries*, New York, 1967, pp. 86–94.

The costs and benefits of training would seem to provide the most compelling case for infant-industry protection. The accumulation of human capital has two important aspects. First, it absorbs resources. Manpower and materials are consumed by education and by other forms of training, and there is an output loss (the counterpart of income lost by the students and trainees). Second, education is a time-consuming process. Most manual skills can, perhaps, be learned quite quickly, but professional and managerial skills are imparted very slowly; these involve continuous learning-by-doing over a large fraction of one's working life. Taken in tandem, these two aspects of the process justify temporary tariffs or subsidies for skill-using industries during the early stages of development. Protection may be most potent in fostering the acquisition of specific skills (as the training costs involved are borne by the firm, and the quite specific managerial skills which seem often to be scarcest take much time to acquire). But tariffs or subsidies may also be needed to promote investments in general training, as personal incomes are quite low and capital markets are imperfect in the less-developed countries, so that firms may be unable to shift any training costs onto their apprentices.[44]

In some cases, however, the gains from investment in human capital may justify permanent tariff protection for import-competing skill-using industries. Protection could increase the demand for skills, encouraging additional investment in training and raising real income. This possibility is explored in a two-sector model outlined in Appendix B. The model displays most of the properties of standard Heckscher-Ohlin constructs, but seeks to make explicit—if primitive—allowance for the costs and benefits of using skilled labor.

One sector of the two-sector economy produces and exports a primary commodity, using unskilled labor and embodied capital (permanent improvements in natural land). The second sector manufactures an import-competing consumer good, using skilled labor and imported machines. Skilled workers earn a higher wage and are trained by sacrificing current manufactured output (in a fixed amount per newly trained worker); skilled workers never die and machines do not depreciate.

[44] An analogous argument is made by Steffan Linder, (*An Essay on Trade and Transformation*, Stockholm, 1961, pp. 27–28).

Investments in skill are governed by rational calculations; future earnings due to skill are discounted at the market rate of interest and their present value equated to the cost of training. But because training costs are measured in consumer goods and these are subject to a tariff, investments in skill may be valued in two ways. The consumer goods absorbed by training have a social cost (their world price) and a private cost (their tariff-distorted domestic price). One's impulse is always to opt for social cost, all the more so in this instance, because the social cost is lower, making for additional investments in skill. But this impulse may be harmful. One has also to remember that the marginal product of skilled labor is distorted by the tariff on the skill-intensive good. We enter the unhappy world of the second best!

To round out the model, savings and tax revenues (from tariffs and income taxes) are used jointly to finance all forms of investment—further permanent improvements in the land, imports of additional machines, and the education of more skilled workers. Imports of consumer goods and machines are exactly equal to primary exports (a result which may depend on the exchange rate, though this rate does not appear directly in the model, because all prices are defined in foreign currency).

When set out most compactly (equations 2.1–2.14), the model still contains twenty-two variables, eight of them exogenous and fourteen endogenous. It is much too large for complete analysis. I have, therefore, extracted a subset of equations (the matrix 2.16) to analyze partially the role of the tariff, t, unit training costs, g, and growth in the labor force. This partial analysis has as its chief defect that it fixes net investment (by fixing the sum of savings and tax revenues) and the allocation of investment between the two sectors (by fixing the difference between total exports and consumer-destined imports). Note, however, that it does not fix the distribution of investment between machines and skills used in manufacturing. The partial analysis summarized below examines the effects of changes in t and g on the equilibrium position of the system and on the equilibrium growth rates of the skilled labor force and net national product.

Taking first the impact on the stock of skills (equation 2.18), an increase in the tariff on manufactures reduces, once and for all, the stock of skills, rather than increasing it, but has no direct effect on the rates of growth derived from population change and capital formation.[45] Furthermore, the mode of valuation of human capital (at social or private cost) makes no difference whatsoever at this juncture. Finally, an increase in unit training costs has no direct effect on the stock of skills, but does slow down the rates of growth attached to population change and capital formation.

Turning next to the effects on real income (valued at world prices), one encounters strange results (equation 2.19). If one asks what will happen when a tariff is imposed (not when an existing tariff is raised) and when human capital is valued at social cost, the answer is clear: real income will fall. If, instead, one asks about an increase in a tariff, the answer is not clear: real income will not fall so much and, indeed, may increase if the tariff rate and return to skill are quite high to start. Further, when human capital is valued at private cost, the argument grows more complex, since two new terms appear in the relevant coefficient, each with a different sign. One can say that valuation at private cost reduces the income loss consequent upon the introduction of a tariff (for one of the two terms drops out again), but one cannot evaluate the cost of change in a preexisting tariff.

To make matters worse, a tariff change has complex direct effects on the real growth rates attached to population change and to capital formation.[46] When human capital is valued at social cost, an increase in the tariff on manufactures will decrease the growth rate of real income caused by population change, will increase the growth rate caused by net investment in export production, and will decrease the growth rate caused by net investment in manufacturing (including net investment in human capital). Its over-all effect, of course, depends on the relationships among population growth and the two investment flows. When human capital is valued at private cost, the outcome is less certain. By way of illustration, consider the effects of an increase in the tariff, t, on the growth of real income due to population change: If $t > 1$, an increase

---

[45] This result is diametrically opposed to my initial supposition. But note the several *caveats* in footnotes 52 and 54.

[46] The word "direct" is meant to warn that the results reported here exclude effects of tariff change on several of the variables entering the argument of equation 2.19. This is a second sense in which Appendix B constitutes an incomplete, partial analysis.

in t will cause an even larger decrease in the growth rate. If $t = 1$, the two modes of valuation have identical (retarding) effects. But if $t < 1$, the outcome depends on the relationship between t and the wage differential due to skill, denoted by w:

    a. When $(w - 1) < t(1 + w)$, an increase in t will be adverse to growth in real income.

    b. When $(w - 1) = t(1 + w)$, an increase in t will have no effect on growth in real income.

    c. When $(w - 1) > t(1 + w)$, an increase in t will actually promote growth in real income.[47]

One could perhaps refine all of these results, thereby explaining the source of their complexity. One could also generate additional results, pertaining to the consequence of higher training costs and to the effects of changes in t and g on other variables.[48] Most importantly, one should continue the search for a firm answer to the basic question: What is the precise interaction between tariff rates, wage differentials, and the real costs of training? This was the question with which I began, but I have not answered it in this account or in the appendixes.

APPENDIX A

THE data on skills and U. S. foreign trade used in the body of this paper are taken from Keesing,[49] Leontief,[50] and United Nations publications.

---

[47] Note the clearer implication of these findings for the imposition of a tariff (when $t = 0$ to start). If $w < 1$, the introduction of a tariff will reduce the growth rate due to population change; if $w = 1$, it will have no effect; and if $w > 1$, it will raise the growth rate.

[48] I have found that an increase in training costs (expenditure per worker) will raise real output, but have not tried to analyze its direct effect on the rates of growth of output linked to population change and the two investment flows. The task is not easy, and I doubt that much more effort should, in fact, be lavished on the partial model used in Appendix B.

[49] Donald B. Keesing, "The Impact of Research and Development on United States Trade," in *The Open Economy*, P. B. Kenen and R. Lawrence (eds.), New York, 1968.

[50] W. W. Leontief, "Factor Proportions and the Structure of American Trade: Further Theoretical and Empirical Analysis," *Review of Economics and Statistics*, November, 1956.

Precise definitions follow:

X_i U. S. exports of ith industry output, expressed as a percentage of Group-of-Ten ith industry exports, 1962.

G_i The over-all percentage change in X_i from 1962 through 1965.

B_i U. S. exports of ith industry output *less* U. S. imports of ith industry output expressed as a percentage of their sum, 1961.

R_i Scientists and engineers engaged in research and development, expressed as a percentage of total ith industry employment, 1960.

S_{1i} Scientists and engineers *not* engaged in research and development, expressed as a percentage of adjusted ith industry employment, 1960 (adjusted employment being total employment *less* scientists and engineers engaged in research and development).

S_{2i} Other professionals, expressed as a percentage of adjusted ith industry employment, 1960.

S_{3i} Skilled manual workers, expressed as a percentage of adjusted ith industry employment, 1960.

S_{4i} The sum of S_{1i} and S_{2i}.

S_{5i} The sum of S_{1i}, S_{2i}, and S_{3i}.

K_{1i} Direct capital requirements per dollar of ith industry output, 1947.

K_{2i} Direct *plus* indirect capital requirements per dollar of ith industry output, 1947.

The trade data used for X_i, G_i and B_i derive directly from Keesing's paper and from *Commodity Trade Statistics*. The skills data used for R_i and for S_{1i} through S_{5i} also come from Keesing's paper, but S_{1i}, S_{2i} and S_{3i} have been redefined to exclude from the labor-force denominator scientists and engineers engaged in research and development. The capital coefficients K_{1i} and K_{2i} are export-weighted averages of the coefficients given by Leontief. (As these weights and coefficients pertain to 1947, they are not well matched with the trade and skills data for 1960–62, but should not be wholly irrelevant.)

The eighteen industries studied here are those used by Keesing and account for the bulk of manufactured exports. The chief exclusions are atomic energy devices, communications equipment and electronic components, ordnance and guided missiles, petroleum, and food and kindred products.

TABLE 1

Simple Correlations Between Trade Indexes and Input Indexes

Input Indexes	Trade Indexes		
	X_i	B_i	G_i
R_i	0.9126^a	0.5861^a	0.0152
S_{1i}	0.6962^a	0.5957^a	0.1270
S_{2i}	0.7151^a	0.5844^a	0.1693
S_{3i}	0.0343	0.3145	0.2303
S_{4i}	0.7315^a	0.6061^a	0.1614
S_{5i}	0.4071	0.5843^a	0.2821
K_{1i}	-0.3432	-0.3629	-0.3034
K_{2i}	-0.4813^a	-0.4320	-0.0849

[a]Significantly different from zero at the 0.05 level.

TABLE 2

Simple Correlations Between Trade Indexes

	X_i	B_i	G_i
X_i	1.0000	$-$	$-$
B_i	0.6793^a	1.0000	$-$
G_i	0.0918	0.3616	1.0000

[a]Significantly different from zero at the 0.05 level.

TABLE 3

Simple Correlations Between Trade Indexes

	R_i	S_{1i}	S_{4i}	S_{5i}	K_{1i}	K_{2i}
R_i	1.0000	$-$	$-$	$-$	$-$	$-$
S_{1i}	0.7092^a	1.0000	$-$	$-$	$-$	$-$
S_{4i}	0.7536^a	0.9295^a	1.0000	$-$	$-$	$-$
S_{5i}	0.4108	0.6018^a	0.5049^a	1.0000	$-$	$-$
K_{1i}	-0.1528	0.1271	0.0084	0.2384	1.0000	$-$
K_{2i}	-0.3972	0.0044	-0.1968	0.1224	0.7552^a	1.0000

[a]Significantly different from zero at the 0.05 level.

TABLE 4

Multiple Regression Equations Using K_{1i}

Trade Index		Regression Coefficients on Input Indexes[a]			$\overline{R}^2$
X_i	=	$20.33 - 11.918\,K_{1i}$ (2.261)	$+\ 4.977\,R_i$ (9.551)		0.86
X_i	=	$21.36 - 25.063\,K_{1i}$ (2.954)		$+\ 5.818\,S_{1i}$ (5.062)	0.63
X_i	=	$18.97 - 19.957\,K_{1i}$ (2.311)		$+\ 1.769\,S_{4i}$ (4.858)	0.61
X_i	=	$18.40 - 26.661\,K_{1i}$ (2.214)		$+\ 0.644\,S_{5i}$ (2.459)	0.29
X_i	=	$19.16 - 14.988\,K_{1i}$ (2.850)	$+\ 4.037\,R_i +$ (5.515)	$1.725\,S_{1i}$ (1.728)	0.88
X_i	=	$18.92 - 13.125\,K_{1i}$ (1.482)	$+\ 4.248R_i\ +$ (5.337)	$0.402\,S_{4i}$ (1.200)	0.86
X_i	=	$17.38 - 14.184\,K_{1i}$ (2.582)	$+\ 4.644R_i\ +$ (8.022)	$0.160\,S_{5i}$ (1.234)	0.86
B_i	=	$34.73 - 59.267\,K_{1i}$ (1.406)	$+\ 11.387R_i$ (2.731)		0.34
B_i	=	$25.38 - 94.411\,K_{1i}$ (2.554)		$+\ 18.713\,S_{1i}$ (3.737)	0.49
B_i	=	$19.80 - 77.938\,K_{1i}$ (2.021)		$+\ 5.442\,S_{4i}$ (3.346)	0.44
B_i	=	$-\,13.22 - 112.754\,K_{1i}$ (3.201)		$+\ 3.278\,S_{5i}$ (4.276)	0.56
B_i	=	$23.94 - 87.782\,K_{1i}$ (2.168)	$+\ 2.656R_i\ +$ (0.471)	$16.020\,S_{1i}$ (2.084)·	0.46
B_i	=	$19.76 - 72.072\,K_{1i}$ (1.774)	$+\ 3.647R_i\ +$ (0.596)	$4.268\,S_{4i}$ (1.657)	0.41
B_i	=	$-\,14.51 - 97.097\,K_{1i}$ (2.772)	$+\ 5.828R_i\ +$ (1.579)	$2.671\,S_{5i}$ (3.232)	0.60

[a]Numbers in parentheses are "t" coefficients, not standard errors.

TABLE 5

Multiple Regression Equations Using K_{2i}

Trade Index		Regression Coefficients on Input Indexes[a]			$\bar{R}^2$
X_i	=	$19.44 - 3.152\,K_{2i} + 4.841\,R_i$ $(1.293)\quad(7.852)$			0.83
X_i	=	$26.99 - 10.821\,K_{2i}$ (3.541)		$+\ 5.402\,S_{1i}$ (5.106)	0.69
X_i	=	$22.77 - 7.840\,K_{2i}$ (2.264)		$+\ 1.596\,S_{4i}$ (4.273)	0.61
X_i	=	$25.79 - 12.047\,K_{2i}$ (2.800)		$+\ 0.588\,S_{5i}$ (2.457)	0.38
X_i	=	$19.67 - 4.848\,K_{2i} + 3.774\,R_i$ $(1.851)\quad(4.017)$		$+\ 1.729\,S_{1i}$ (1.465)	0.84
X_i	=	$18.40 - 3.529\,K_{2i} + 4.212\,R_i$ $(1.417)\quad(4.483)$		$+\ 0.334\,S_{4i}$ (0.892)	0.83
X_i	=	$17.58 - 3.899\,K_{2i} + 4.537\,R_i$ $(1.489)\quad(6.290)$		$+\ 0.123\,S_{5i}$ (0.836)	0.83
B_i	=	$37.54 - 19.586\,K_{2i} + 10.315\,R_i$ $(1.076)\quad(2.241)$			0.31
B_i	=	$38.74 - 35.999\,K_{2i}$ (2.491)		$+17.142\,S_{1i}$ (3.426)	0.48
B_i	=	$27.91 - 26.943\,K_{2i}$ (1.695)		$+\ 4.843\,S_{4i}$ (2.825)	0.40
B_i	=	$5.53 - 42.344\,K_{2i}$ (3.102)		$+\ 2.982\,S_{5i}$ (3.925)	0.55
B_i	=	$39.97 - 37.009\,K_{2i} - 0.639\,R_i$ $(2.038)\quad(0.098)$		$+17.763\,S_{1i}$ (2.170)	0.45
B_i	=	$25.04 - 24.119\,K_{2i} + 2.759\,R_i$ $(1.260)\quad(0.412)$		$+\ 4.016\,S_{4i}$ (1.504)	0.36
B_i	=	$-1.56 - 35.309\,K_{2i} + 3.917\,R_i$ $(2.234)\quad(0.900)$		$+\ 2.580\,S_{5i}$ (2.914)	0.54

[a]Numbers in parentheses are "t" coefficients, not standard errors.

Table 1 sets out simple correlations between X_i, G_i and B_i and the several measures of research input, skill use, and capital intensity. Table 2 sets out simple correlations between the three trade indexes themselves. Table 3 sets out simple correlations between R_i, S_{1i}, S_{4i}, S_{5i}, K_{1i} and K_{2i}. Table 4 supplies a comprehensive set of multiple regressions "explaining" X_i and B_i. Table 5 supplies a similar series using K_{2i} instead of K_{1i}.

APPENDIX B

THE model set out here describes a two-sector economy operating under pure competition, with constant returns to scale, and trading with the outside world. The first of its two sectors produces a primary commodity, A, using unskilled labor, L_a, and a stock of capital, K_a, which does not depreciate and can be augmented by sacrificing current production of A. By implication, K_a is measured in A, its rate of change is nonnegative, and K_a is exogenous (representing irretrievable investments in the past). In the first sector, then:

$$A = f_a(K_a/L_a, 1)L_a \tag{1.1}$$
$$p_a[(A/L_a) - (K_a/L_a)f_a'] = w_a \tag{1.2}$$
$$f_a' = r \tag{1.3}$$

where p_a is the world price of A and w_a the wage of unskilled labor (each of them expressed in foreign currency), and r is the rate of interest.

The second sector manufactures a consumer good, C, using skilled labor, L_c, and a stock of capital, K_c, consisting of imported machines that do not depreciate. By implication, used machines can be exported without discount, the rate of change of the stock can be negative, and K_c is not exogenous (being susceptible of instant adjustment). In the second sector, then:

$$C = f_c(K_c/L_c, 1)L_c \tag{1.4}$$
$$p(1 + t)[(C/L_c) - (K_c/L_c)f_c'] = w_s = (1 + w)w_a \tag{1.5}$$
$$p_c(1 + t)f_c' = p_k \cdot r \tag{1.6}$$

where p_c is the exogenous world price of C, p_k the exogenous world price of a machine, and w_s the wage of skilled labor (each of them expressed in foreign currency), where w is $(w_s - w_a)/w_a$, the wage differential due to skill, and t is the ad valorem tariff on C.

The skills used in this second sector are created by sacrificing current production of C at a fixed rate, g, per skilled worker. Skill, like other stocks, does not depreciate (workers do not die). By implication, L_c^*, the total stock of skills, has attributes similar to those of K_a; its rate of change is nonnegative, and L_c^* itself is exogenous.[51] Investments in skill are governed by rational cost-benefit calculations of the ordinary sort. In consequence:

$$g \cdot p_c(1 + nt) = \sum_{i=1}^{\infty} \frac{w \cdot w_a}{(1+r)^i} = \frac{w \cdot w_a}{r} \tag{1.7}$$

where $n = 0$ if investments in skill are valued at social cost, and $n = 1$ if they are valued at private (tariff-distorted) cost. All skilled labor is employed in manufacturing—none of it is left to do the work of unskilled workers—and the whole labor force is fully employed. Formally:

$$L_c = L_c^* \tag{1.8}$$
$$L_a + L_c = L \tag{1.9}$$

where L is the whole labor force. Next, define gross (and net) national product, using the price of the exportable as numeraire and counting output sacrificed to capital formation.[52] At domestic prices:

$$Y_d = A + (p_c/p_a)(1 + t)C \tag{1.10}$$

and at world prices:

$$Y_w = A + (p_c/p_a)C \tag{1.11}$$

---

[51] One could, of course, reduce L_c^*/L (where L is the whole labor force) if L itself were growing, and this is how I shall interpret certain subsequent results. To put the same point in a general context; formulae that describe changes in the stock of skills or real income consequent on changes in tariffs or training costs must be viewed as pertaining to once-over movements between equilibria, accomplished by departing from the rates of growth associated with those equilibria. Formulae that describe changes in rates of growth must be viewed as pertaining to once-over changes in the equilibrium rates themselves.

[52] This sort of accounting will be valid provided the outputs in question (measured by $K_a \cdot \dot{K}_a$ and $gL_c^* \cdot \dot{L}_c^*$) are included in the definition of investment.

Further, define gross (and net) investment, including additions to K_a and to $L_c{}^*$:

$$I = K_a \cdot \dot{K}_a + (p_k/p_a)K_c \cdot \dot{K}_c + (p_c/p_a)(1 + t)gL_c{}^* \cdot \dot{L}_c{}^* \qquad (1.12)$$

where dotted terms denote percentage rates of change. Tax revenues consist of tariff proceeds and of an income tax levied at a fixed rate, y. Savings are a fraction, s, of after-tax income. Continuing to use p_a as numeraire:

$$T = (p_c/p_a)t \cdot C_m + y \cdot Y_d \qquad (1.13)$$
$$S = s(1 - y)Y_d \qquad (1.14)$$

where C_m are imports of the manufactured good. Total imports are C_m *plus* the machinery used to manufacture C. Using the same numeraire:

$$M = (p_c/p_a)C_m + (p_k/p_a)K_c \cdot \dot{K}_c \qquad (1.15)$$

Furthermore:

$$C_m = C_c + gL_c{}^* \cdot \dot{L}_c{}^* - C \qquad (1.16)$$

where C_c is final domestic demand, a function of relative prices and total private spending:

$$C_c = C[(p_c/p_a)(1 + t), (1 - y)(1 - s)Y_d] \qquad (1.17)$$

Export demand, in turn, depends on the relative price of the primary product:

$$X = A_f = A[(p_a/p_c), \phi] \qquad (1.18, 1.19)$$

where ϕ impounds all exogenous elements affecting export demand. Finally, assume that foreign trade is always balanced and that all government spending is for capital formation. These assumptions give:

$$X = M \qquad (1.20)$$

$$I = S + T \qquad (1.21)$$

The system set out here can be rendered more compact and, in the end, determinate. Combine equations (1.1), (1.4), (1.9), (1.10), (1.11), (1.17) and (1.19) into five equations using the ten variables L_a, $L_c{}^*$, L, Y_d, Y_w, C_c, A_f, R_a [for K_a/L_a], R_c [for $K_c/L_c{}^*$], and q_c [for p_c/p_a], and the four parameters t, ϕ, y and s' [for $s(1 - y)$]:

$$L_a + L_c{}^* = L \tag{2.1}$$

$$Y_d = Y_w + q_c \cdot t \cdot f_c(R_c, 1)L_c{}^* \tag{2.2}$$

$$Y_w = f_a(R_a, 1)L_a + q_c \cdot f_c(R_c, 1)L_c{}^* \tag{2.3}$$

$$C_c = C[q_c(1 + t), (1 - y - s')Y_d] \tag{2.4}$$

$$A_f = A(1/q_c, \phi) \tag{2.5}$$

Then combine the rest of the original equations into five more, using the six additional variables w, $\dot{R}_a$, $\dot{R}_c$, $\dot{L}_a$, $\dot{L}_c{}^*$ and q_k [for p_k/p_c], and the remaining parameters, g and n:

$$\left(\frac{1 + w}{1 + t}\right)\left[\frac{f_a(R_a, 1) - R_a \cdot f_a'}{f_c(R_c, 1) - R_c \cdot f_c'}\right] = q_c \tag{2.6}$$

$$(1 + t)(f_c'/f_a') = q_k \tag{2.7}$$

$$g\left(\frac{1 + nt}{1 + t}\right)f_a' = \left(\frac{w}{1 + w}\right)[f_c(R_c, 1) - R_c \cdot f_c'] \tag{2.8}$$

$$K_a \cdot \dot{L}_a + q_c(g + q_k \cdot R_c)\dot{L}_c{}^* \cdot L_c{}^* + K_a \cdot \dot{R}_a + q_c(q_k \cdot K_c)\dot{R}_c = J_1 \tag{2.9}$$

$$q_c(g + q_k \cdot R_c)L_c{}^* \cdot \dot{L}_c{}^* + q_c(q_k \cdot K_c)\dot{R}_c = J_2 \tag{2.10}$$

where $J_1 = q_c(C_c - C)t + (y + s')Y_d$, net revenues plus savings; where $J_2 = A_f - q_c(C_c - C)$, the difference between total exports and imports of consumer goods; and where, by additional assumption, $A_f > q_c(C_c - C) > 0$.[53] Finally, differentiate (2.1), (2.6), (2.7) and (2.8) to form four more equations using the six additional variables L, w, q_k, q_c, g and t, and determining the sector allocation of investment and of any increase in the total labor force:

---

[53] The variable C appears in J_1 and J_2, but does not count among the endogenous variables entering this compact version. Here and hereafter, C and A are used in place of the more cumbersome functions $f_c(R_c, 1)L_c{}^*$ and $f_a(R_a, 1)L_a$, whenever convenience will not be misleading. Notice, in passing, that $J_1 - J_2 = K_a \cdot L_a + K_a \cdot R_a = K_a \cdot K_a$, investment in primary production, and this is nonnegative. Notice, further, that subsequent procedures in which J_1 and J_2 are held constant imply an arbitrary allocation of fixed tax revenues and savings between primary production, on the one hand, and skills *plus* machines, on the other. It is of course possible to fix these two terms, despite changing incomes, exports, imports, prices, and tariffs; one could change the tax rate, y, to stabilize J_1, and one could impose export taxes or export subsidies to manipulate A_f and stabilize J_2 (while altering y again to offset the fiscal consequences for J_1). But a constant allocation of tax revenues and savings may not be optimal (and may, indeed, be inconsistent with some equilibria). This is the major defect of the method I adopt below.

$$L_a \cdot \dot{L}_a + L_c^* \cdot \dot{L}_c^* = L \cdot \dot{L} \tag{2.11}$$

$$[A_{kk}(p_a/w_a)r \cdot R_a]\dot{R}_a - \left[C_{kk}(p_a/w_a)\left(\frac{1}{1+w}\right)(q_c \cdot q_k)r \cdot R_c \right]\dot{R}_c$$

$$+ \left(\frac{w}{1+w}\right)\dot{w} - \left(\frac{t}{1+t}\right)\dot{t} - \dot{q}_c = 0 \tag{2.12}$$

$$A_{kk} \cdot \dot{R}_a - C_{kk} \cdot \dot{R}_c + \left(\frac{t}{1+t}\right)\dot{t} - \dot{q}_k = 0 \tag{2.13}$$

$$\dot{g} - A_{kk} \cdot \dot{R}_a - \left[C_{kk}(p_a/w_a)\left(\frac{1}{1+w}\right)(q_c \cdot q_k)r \cdot R_c \right]\dot{R}_c - \left(\frac{1}{1+w}\right)\dot{w}$$

$$- \left(\frac{t}{1+t}\right)(1-n)\dot{t} = 0 \tag{2.14}$$

where $A_{kk} = -f_a''(R_a/f_a')$ and $C_{kk} = -f_c''(R_c/f_c')$, and each may be deemed positive.

This second version of the model has twenty-two variables, but eight of these should be regarded as exogenous: the size and rate of change of the total labor force (L and $\dot{L}$); the size and rate of change of the import price ratio ($\dot{q}_k$ and q_k); the stocks L_c^* and K_a, representing investments brought forward from the past; and changes in the tariff and in unit training costs ($\dot{t}$ and $\dot{g}$). There are, then, fourteen endogenous variables and the same number of equations.

I seek now to ascertain the principal effects of changes in the tariff and in unit training costs. To do so totally, however, would be quite difficult, requiring the simultaneous solution of fourteen equations. Hence, I shall develop partial answers, neglecting all changes in J_1 and J_2,[54] and concentrating on two questions:

1. What are the effects of changes in g or t on the equilibrium *position* of the system, especially upon the stock of skills and upon national income at world prices?

2. What are the effects of changes in g or t on the equilibrium *rates of growth* of L_c^* and Y_w when and if the system has attained the equilibrium position implied by a new g or t? To answer these two questions,

---

[54] For *caveats* concerning this procedure, see notes 51 and 53.

one has first to use equation (2.3) to define the rate of change of national income:

$$Y_w \cdot \dot{Y}_w = A \cdot \dot{L}_a + (q_c \cdot C)\dot{L}_c^* + f_a'(R_a \cdot L_a)\dot{R}_a + f_c'(q_c \cdot R_c \cdot L_c^*)\dot{R}_c$$
$$+ (q_c \cdot C)\dot{q}_c \tag{2.15}$$

Notice, however, that equations (2.9) through (2.14) contain the same five variables that affect $\dot{Y}_w$ and that there is only one other endogenous variable, $\dot{w}$, in that subset of equations. In consequence, one can attach (2.15) to that six-equation subset, then use this central portion of the whole system to answer the questions just posed. First, set $(p_a/w_a) = q_c = q_k = 1$, by an appropriate choice of the relevant physical units. Then remove $\dot{q}_c$ from (2.15), using the arguments of (2.12). Finally, add (2.13) to (2.14) to simplify the latter, and subtract (2.10) from (2.8) for similar purposes. After these manipulations:

$$\begin{bmatrix} L_a & L_c & 0 & 0 & 0 & 0 \\ 0 & 0 & A_{kk} & -C_{kk} & 0 & 0 \\ 0 & 0 & 0 & U_1 & 1 & 0 \\ 1 & 0 & 1 & 0 & 0 & 0 \\ 0 & g+R_c & 0 & R_c & 0 & 0 \\ A & C & U_2 & U_3 & -w \cdot C & -1 \end{bmatrix} \begin{bmatrix} \dot{L}_a \\ \dot{L}_c^* \\ \dot{R}_a \\ \dot{R}_c \\ \dfrac{-\dot{w}}{1+w} \\ Y_w \cdot \dot{Y}_w \end{bmatrix} = \begin{bmatrix} L \cdot \dot{L} \\ \dot{q}_k - \left(\dfrac{t}{1+t}\right)\dot{i} \\ \dot{q}_k - \dot{g} - n\left(\dfrac{t}{1+t}\right)\dot{i} \\ (J_1 - J_2)/K_a \\ J_2/L_c^* \\ C\left(\dfrac{t}{1+t}\right)\dot{i} \end{bmatrix}$$

$$\tag{2.16}$$

where $U_1 = -\left(\dfrac{r \cdot R_c}{1+w} + 1\right)C_{kk}$, $U_2 = r(L_a + C \cdot A_{kk})R_a$, and $U_3 =$

$r\left(\dfrac{1}{1+w}\right)\left[\left(\dfrac{1+w}{1+t}\right)L_c^* - C \cdot C_{kk}\right]R_c.$

This system has a simple, nonsingular determinant:

$$/D/ = -[L_a(g + R_c)C_{kk} + L_c^* \cdot R_c \cdot A_{kk}] < 0 \tag{2.17}$$

It also supplies straightforward solutions for changes in the stock of skills and national income. Solving first for $\dot{L}_c{}^*$:

$$\dot{L}_c{}^* = (R_c/Q)\left\{L_a\left[\dot{q}_k - \left(\frac{t}{1+t}\right)\dot{i}\right] + (L \cdot A_{kk})\dot{L} + \dot{H}\right\} \qquad (2.18)$$

where $Q = -/D/ > 0$, while $\dot{H} = (1/K_c)[(K_a \cdot C_{kk})J_2 - (K_c \cdot A_{kk})(J_1 - J_2)]/R_a \gtrless 0$.[55]

An increase in the tariff, t, reduces the equilibrium level of $L_c{}^*$ (slowing or halting investment in human capital until the economy has achieved the requisite reduction in $L_c{}^*/L$). Further, the mode of valuation of human capital, whether at social or private cost, has no effect on the influence of changes in the tariff; the term $n\left(\frac{t}{1+t}\right)\dot{i}$ in (2.16) does not appear in (2.18). Finally, an increase in $\dot{q}_k$—in the price of the machinery used to manufacture C relative to that of C itself—augments the equilibrium value of $L_c{}^*$.

Consider, next, two continuing effects—population growth, denoted by $\dot{L}$, and gross investment, denoted by $(J_1 - J_2)$ and J_2. Clearly, population growth raises $L_c{}^*$. Notice, moreover, that the tariff rate does not appear in Q or in any other part of the coefficient attaching to $\dot{L}$. Once, then, the economy has attained the equilibrium implied by a new tariff rate, that rate has no direct effect on the allocation of subsequent additions to the total labor force.[56] But changes in training costs do have a direct effect; as g appears in Q, an increase in unit training costs will shunt a larger share of additional labor into primary production. The joint effects of investment, denoted by $\dot{H}$, cannot reduce the stock of skill, but the separate effects of $(J_1 - J_2)$, investment in primary production, and of J_2, investment in manufacturing, have unambiguously opposite signs. The former tends to reduce $L_c{}^*$; the latter tends to raise it. In each case, moreover, the tariff rate does not affect the impact of investment, but higher training costs, increasing Q, diminish the influence of both forms of investment.

[55] The sign attached to $\dot{H}$ derives from the fact that $(J_1 - J_2)$ and J_2 are continuing processes, not single acts like $\dot{i}$ or $\dot{g}$, and have continuing effects on $L_c{}^*$, regardless of the size of $\dot{L}$. But $\dot{L}_c{}^*$ is nonnegative, so $\dot{H}$ must be nonnegative.

[56] The tariff, however, will influence the equilibrium values of R_c, L_a and $L_c{}^*$ (appearing in R_c/Q) and will then have an indirect effect on the allocation of additional labor.

Now solve (2.16) for $\dot{Y}_w$, the rate of change of real income valued at world prices:

$$\dot{Y}_w = \left(\frac{1}{Y_w}\right)\{[C(r \cdot R_c) - (K_c/C_{kk})V - (1/Q)(K_c \cdot L_a)W]\dot{q}_k$$

$$+ [w \cdot C]\dot{g}$$

$$- [(L_a/A_{kk})(Z - 1) + C(1 + r \cdot R_c - n \cdot w)]\left(\frac{t}{1+t}\right)\dot{t}$$

$$+ [L \cdot Z]\dot{L}$$

$$+ [r - (Z - 1)/R_a](J_1 - J_2)$$

$$+ \left[r\left(\frac{1}{1+t}\right) - V - (1/Q)(L_a \cdot C_{kk})W\right]J_2\} \qquad (2.19)$$

where $V = (C/Q)[w + r(R_c - R_a)]C_{kk} \cdot A_{kk}$, and $V > 0$ if $R_c > R_a$ (the familiar strong factor-intensity assumption); where $W = \left(\frac{t}{1+t}\right)\left[1 - \left(\frac{n \cdot w}{1+t}\right)\right]$, and $W > 0$ if $n\left(\frac{w}{1+t}\right) < 1$; and where $Z = [1 + (g + R_c)V - (1/Q)(K_c \cdot A_{kk})W] = \left[(L_a/Q)(g + R_c)C_{kk} + (K_c/Q)\left(1 + \frac{n \cdot w \cdot t}{1+t}\right)\left(\frac{1}{1+t}\right)A_{kk} + (g + R_c)V\right]$, so that $[1 + (g + R_c)V] \gtrless Z > 0$.

The first three arguments of (2.19) pertain to the effects of once-over changes ($\dot{q}_k$, $\dot{g}$ and $\dot{t}$) on the equilibrium level of income. Unfortunately, two of them are ambiguous, even after one invokes strong factor ordering (to set $V > 0$). One can say that an increase in expenditure on training ($\dot{g} > 0$) causes a permanent increase in income (and that the influence of changes in training costs is not directly dependent on the tariff rate or the mode of valuation of human capital). But one cannot know the impact of changes in q_k or t.

If human capital is valued at social cost ($n = 0$), the second portion of the tariff coefficient has to be positive. If, further, $t = 0$ to start, Z will exceed unity (as W is zero). The *introduction* of a tariff will reduce Y_w. If $t > 0$ to start, however, Z could be less than unity, diminishing the adverse impact of a higher tariff. If human capital is valued at private cost ($n = 1$), the argument grows more complex. With or without a tariff to start, this mode of valuation activates the final term in the tariff coefficient, working to reduce, if not to reverse, the impact of the tariff change. When $t = 0$ to start, then, the introduction of a tariff could increase real income (and is the more likely to do so, the larger the wage difference earned by skill). When $t > 0$, however, W reappears, reducing Z, and the net effect of a higher tariff is again in doubt.[57]

The last three terms of (2.19) relate to the effects of population growth and the two forms of investment. Once more, however, two of them have uncertain signs. An increase of the labor force ($\dot{L} > 0$) raises real income, but the fixed pattern of investment denoted by ($J_1 - J_2$) and J_2 could work to reduce it.[58]

Consider, next, the impact of the tariff rate on the rates of change of income associated with $\dot{L}$ and with investment.[59] Neglecting indirect effects (those on L_a, $L_c{}^*$, K_a, K_c, w, and r):

$$(\delta Z/\delta t) = -(1/Q)(K_c \cdot A_{kk})(\delta W/\delta t) \tag{2.20}$$

where:

$$(\delta W/\delta t) = \left(\frac{1}{1+t}\right)^2\left[1 - n\left(\frac{1-t}{1+t}\right)w\right] \tag{2.21}$$

If, then, human capital is valued at social cost ($n = 0$), an increase in the tariff rate will lower the $\dot{Y}_w$ induced by $\dot{L}$ (but cannot turn it negative). If human capital is valued at private cost ($n = 1$), an increase in the tariff may have different consequences:

a. If $t > 1$, an increase in t will be even more adverse to growth in income due to growth in population;

b. If $t = 1$, an increase in t will have the same effect as when $n = 0$;

c. If $t < 1$, there are three possibilities:

(i) With $(w - 1) < t(1 + w)$, an increase in t will be adverse to growth in income;

---

[57] Notice, however, that W declines as w rises, so that, with high returns to skill, the whole coefficient could be positive.

[58] The uncertain signs of the coefficients multiplying ($J_1 - J_2$) and J_2 themselves may well derive from the fact that fixed rates of investment will not always maximize growth in real income.

[59] Changes in training costs are equally significant for the population and investment coefficients, but their effects are more difficult to analyze (and the partial analysis used thus far is even less appropriate).

(ii) With $(w - 1) = t(1 + w)$, an increase in t will not affect growth in income; and

(iii) With $(w - 1) > t(1 + w)$, an increase in t will actually promote growth in income due to growth in population.

Turning, finally, to investment, when $n = 0$, the argument multiplying $(J_1 - J_2)$ rises with a higher tariff. Investment in primary production will make a larger contribution to $\dot{Y}_w$. This is because the higher tariff raises W, reducing Z (see equation 2.21). When $n = 1$, however, one must go through all the cases listed above, turning them around. In case c(i), for instance, an increase in t will reduce the contribution of $(J_1 - J_2)$; the positive derivative of $-Z$ will be reduced, so that the whole coefficient multiplying net investment will not rise as much. Again, when $n = 0$, the argument attached to J_2 alone is decreased by a higher tariff, for $r\left(\dfrac{1}{1 + t}\right)$ will fall and W will rise. Investment in manufacturing, including human capital, will make a smaller contribution to $\dot{Y}_w$. When $n = 1$, of course, one must again apply the serial analysis developed from (2.21), but without reversing the substance of the argument. In case c(i), for instance, an increase in the tariff will reduce the adverse impact (or enhance the contribution) of capital formation in manufacturing.

COMMENTS

ANNE O. KRUEGER
UNIVERSITY OF MINNESOTA

As Kenen's paper amply demonstrates, the role that human capital plays in determining comparative advantage is not yet well understood, even in a static sense. The solution of the question of the determinants of individual countries' paths of accumulation of various productive factors will be even more difficult. Kenen has done a masterful job of surveying the results to date and outlining the approaches with which future work is likely to have the highest payoff.

No matter how well-founded the reasons given, the ultimate test of such speculations about future research is the outcome. By and large, my own hunches are in accord with Kenen's. I shall, nonetheless, confine my remarks to those areas where there are differences in emphasis between us.

I. THE PRESENT STATE OF KNOWLEDGE

Kenen is, in my judgment, somewhat too charitable in accepting the work on research and development to date. While the question of the relative importance of R & D and human capital in explaining comparative advantage is still open, Kenen seems to accept two aspects of the work that are surely questionable. First, there are serious questions about the meaning of the variables used by Keesing and others to represent the role of R & D. Second, there is good reason to question the appropriateness of a skill index to measure a human capital stock.

The R & D variable used in most regression analysis is either the number of scientists and engineers engaged in R & D as a percentage of total employment in the industry, or current expenditures on R & D as a percentage of sales (which undoubtedly contains a high percentage of scientists' and engineers' salaries). Both are flow variables. If one were to consider the stock of "disembodied knowledge," one would surely wish something like cumulated expenditures on R & D or the present value of past investments. Even then, there is a question whether R & D is a factor of production or a produced good. Scientists and engineers, after all, represent a certain very highly skilled group of employees. To the extent that a production process requires specific design and engineering skills carried on in an R & D department, the production process requires a large human capital input. It may be that R & D activities, essential to production, are human-capital-intensive activities, and as such, are carried on most successfully in countries with a large stock of human capital relative to other factors. The collinearity which Kenen notes suggests that human capital inputs to an industry and its R & D performance are not independent.

As Kenen shows, a broader skill index reverses the results in terms of relative importance of scientists and engineers in R & D and in other skill categories. This raises the second question. That is, to what extent can the importance of human capital in determining comparative advantage be tested using a skill index of the type constructed by Keesing and others? The skill indexes are all derived by taking certain skill groups as a percentage of total employment in the industry. In one sense, this implies that there is perfect substitution among all groups included in the numerator and no substitution between those groups and other groups excluded from the numerator. Surely, by standards of some developing countries, some American industries must have more than one skilled worker per worker.

Measurement of physical capital stock, despite all the conceptual problems, is usually in some sort of homogeneous unit. Investing in humans constitutes the same sort of capital accumulation, yet the fraction of workers with skills (above some minimal level) is regarded as an adequate proxy for the human capital content of the labor force. A similar procedure with machines would be to take machines of more than twenty-five horsepower, for example, as a fraction of all machines. It can also be argued that investing in human capital results in an addition to capital stock, not the substitution of one kind of labor for another.

A skill index, such as that used by Keesing and others, is therefore highly suspect as a test of the role of human capital in determining comparative advantage. In view of the suspicions which must attach to both indexes, it is doubtful how much weight can be given to regression results of the type reported by Keesing and others.

II. AGENDA FOR RESEARCH: POSITIVE ANALYSIS

I fully agree with Kenen's conclusion that use of a multifactor model, incorporating not only the static aspects of the Heckscher-Ohlin theory, but also an explanation of how factors are accumulated, will stimulate productive research.

I would, however, add several queries to his list. First, what is the role of population growth (and rates of change in it) in determining the relative allocation of investable resources between skills and machines? This question has two parts because: (a) insofar as population growth comes from increasing life expectancy, it surely must raise the rate of return (or the present value) of investment in man relative to investment in machines; and (b) one can envisage families with limited resources to invest in future generations: they can either invest intensively in a few children (for education, health, nutrition, and the like) or extensively in many children, allocating fewer resources to each one. Given the systematic patterns observed in the birth rate-death rate pattern as a function of income levels, it is difficult to believe that economic incentives are unimportant in determining the choice. One can imagine growth models incorporating mechanisms of this kind which might go far to explain the systematic factor-endowment differences observed among countries at different income levels.

My second question is, in a sense, an expression of doubt about two of Kenen's empirical assumptions. He believes that the real costs of training vary inversely with the skills on hand. This is questionable because increasing the skills of an already skilled person requires a higher foregone income. In rich countries, increasing skill levels involves the additional training of already skilled persons, whereas in poor countries, increasing skill levels may well involve training unskilled persons. The a priori reasons for believing that the real costs of the latter are higher are not clear. Kenen's second assumption is that learning-by-doing is less costly for high-income countries. This is questionable for much the same reasons expressed in the first assumption. High-income countries have more human capital invested in the learners, which would tend to make foregone income during on-the-job training higher.

Kenen makes these assumptions in attempting to explain why different countries have different human- to physical-capital ratios. His research, reported in his paper, provides the most fruitful starting point for analysis of the question, and raises additional questions. Focus upon the role of the interest rate and population growth (which capital theory suggests may be interrelated) in determining the allocational pattern between skills and machines, rather than on training costs, appears promising. Investment in man generally takes longer, and depreciates over a longer period of time than does investment in physical capital. One would, therefore, expect that at a higher interest rate, it would pay to invest relatively more in machines than at a lower interest rate. Similarly, a higher rate of population growth due to increasing life expectancy would increase the present value of investment in man, whereas a higher birth rate would reduce it.

Kenen's discussion of migration suggests one other line for research, both positive and normative. Trade will, in general, tend to lower the wage of relatively scarce factors of production and raise the wage of abundant factors. If the amount invested in skills (and machines) is an increasing function of the return to investment, trade may reduce investment in human and physical capital in capital-scarce countries by lowering the return on it. Offsetting this is the higher real income a country can attain through trade, which tends to increase the country's saving and therefore its investable resources. If skills are acquired partly in response to the incentive to do so, and trade reduces those incentives, there may be a justification for infant-industry intervention somewhat different from that suggested by Kenen. A subsidy or tariff for capital- (physical and human) using industries will tend to raise the rate of human and physical capital accumulation by increasing incentives and returns on it, and lower the rate of accumulation by lowering real income and therefore saving. An infant industry subsidy or tariff would then be set at a level where the increase in investment in human and physical capital generated by the higher incentives exactly offsets the reduction in investment occasioned by lower present real income as a consequence of reduced trade.

III. NORMATIVE ANALYSIS

Kenen's plea for more theoretical normative analysis is well taken. His own heroic attempt illustrates the difficulties of model formulation, either positive or normative. His model is a worth-while starting point, although one might question the focus upon training costs, for the reasons I have outlined.

Even if one believes that training costs are the appropriate focal point for analysis, there remain significant problems, which Kenen pointed out in his earlier discussions. Perhaps the most important is the question of how skills are incorporated in the production function. Kenen's production function (equation 1.4) has constant returns to scale. In form, the production function for manufacturers (1.4) is no different from that in agriculture (equation 1.1), even though it is assumed that manufacturing requires skilled workers and agriculture only unskilled workers. (Is this a good assumption?)

If investing in skills adds to resources, a satisfactory treatment would require a production function of the form:

$$C = f_c[K_c/L_c, S_c/L_c, 1] \cdot L_c \qquad (1.4')$$

where S_c/L_c represents skills per worker, just as K_c/L_c represents capital per worker. In Kenen's treatment, the difference between skilled and unskilled workers on the demand side is only that skilled workers must receive a higher wage, and therefore must have a higher value of marginal product.

At a more technical level, Kenen has amply demonstrated the difficulties inherent in attempting to develop a dynamic model of human and physical capital accumulation. He set out to analyze the effects of changes in training costs and tariffs on the growth paths of real income and human capital accumulation. Yet he succeeds only at the cost of holding constant: (1) imports of machinery to produce consumer goods (J_2); and (2) total investment (J_1).[1] In a model where all growth occurs through factor accumulation, it is reasonable to question whether a model in which there is one degree of freedom in the factor accumulation path —the allocation of fixed investable resources between the primary sector's physical capital and the manufacturing sector's human capital—will answer the questions he poses. One can only conclude, with Kenen, that additional research is badly needed.

ROBERT E. BALDWIN
UNIVERSITY OF WISCONSIN

International trade theory is presently in the interesting but somewhat confusing state in which there are almost too many promising hypotheses with which to supplement the traditional, simple factor-proportion approach to explaining the structure of trade. For example, as Peter Kenen

---

[1] Kenen asserts (footnote 54) that ($J_1 - J_2$) equals investment in primary production. Since, however, J_1 is total government revenue plus government saving (equals investment, by equation 1.21) and J_2 is the difference between export earnings and consumer good imports (1.15), J_2 must equal the net addition to manufacturing physical capital stock.

points out, both relative differences in labor skills and in research expenditures have tested out as highly significant variables in recent investigations of trade patterns. Moreover, there are a number of other variables that seem to be important determinants of a country's trade pattern. It has been suggested, for example, that the existence of natural resource scarcities in conjunction with a complementary relationship between these natural resources and physical capital explains Leontief's paradoxical results. There are also those who claim their analyses show that factor-intensity reversals within relevant factor-price ratios are so pervasive that they make the entire factor-supply approach irrelevant. Tariffs and other market perfections are another set of factors that apparently play an important role in accounting for actual trade patterns.

What is very much needed in the trade field are careful empirical efforts to determine the relative importance of these various factors. As Kenen notes, there are several players in the drama, and we should stop the common practice of trying to show that some one player is really the star, if only one is willing to ignore certain other players or concentrate on some particular scene. It is in this spirit of eclecticism that he considers the relative importance of labor skills and research activities. From this analysis he concludes that skills may be a more significant determinant of the U. S. trade pattern than production function differences related to relative research expenditures.

Although there seems to be no doubt that relative supplies of skilled labor play a major determining role in the composition of U. S. trade, I should like to underline a few of the well-known difficulties of measuring skill data in human capital terms and also to caution against underestimating the importance of research. One method of approaching the skill problem is to assume that wage differences are a consequence of differences in skill levels, which, in turn, are the result of differences in investment in education and on-the-job training. Kenen has performed the exercise of capitalizing such wage differences among skill groups employed in U. S. export and import industries and has shown that exports are considerably more intensive in human capital terms than imports. Moreover, he is able to reverse the Leontief paradox by capitalizing these wage differences at rates less than 12.7 per cent and then combining them with Leontief's measure of tangible capital.

A drawback of computing human capital by capitalizing income differentials is, of course, that this procedure assumes all income differences to be the result of differences in education, on-the-job training, and other forms of human investment.[1] However, there is growing evidence that market imperfections associated with various economic and social factors as well as differences in ability are also important explanatory factors accounting for wage differences. Nevertheless, other measures of skills and human capital do indicate that in 1962 U. S. export industries employed a higher proportion of skilled workers than U. S. import-competing industries.[2] For example, the average years of education of workers employed in export industries was greater than in import-competing industries. Similarly, as is consistent with Leontief's findings, export industries employed relatively more professional and managerial employees as well as craftsmen and foremen than did import-competing industries. The opposite relationship held with respect to operatives and nonfarm laborers.[3]

As an indicator of the relative importance of research efforts, a class of research workers was constructed from the detailed occupational statistics of the 1960 sample census and the number of such individuals employed directly and indirectly in export- versus import-competing industries was then calculated. A representative bundle of exports turned out to require about 50 per cent more workers of this type than a representative bundle of import substitutes. Similarly, using the R & D sector in the 1958 input-output table, it was found that the R & D expenditures associated with export industries were also about 50 per cent higher than with import-competing industries. In running multiple regressions between an industry's net trade balance and such variables as years of education, earnings, capital/labor ratios, and various skill groups, the research-worker measure invariably turned out to be highly significant. The proportion of skilled workers and of farmers and farm laborers employed in each industry are two other variables that were significantly correlated in a positive manner with the trade-balance variable.

---

[1] By not including the human capital represented by unskilled laborers, Kenen's procedure tends to overstate the ratio of human capital in export compared to import-competing production, since in 1959 there were more unskilled laborers involved in a million dollar's worth of import-competing production than export activities.

[2] In making these calculations, I used the 1958 input-output table, capital and labor coefficients estimated for that year, and the 1960 1/1000 sample census of population.

[3] However, there are slightly more farm plus nonfarm laborers engaged in producing a representative export- than import-competing bundle of commodities.

It would seem, therefore, that as far as the U. S. trade structure of the early sixties is concerned both research and skills are important explanatory variables. Furthermore, using a single gross measure of human capital such as years of education, cost of education, or earnings does not appear to capture all the labor force qualities that influence the pattern of trade. This suggests that other factors are also important in accounting for the qualitative composition of a country's labor supply. We need a better empirical and analytical understanding of what these other variables may be and how they are interrelated with the notion of human capital. Moreover, we need to explore further the relations between the nature of technological progress and such factors as natural resource conditions and the nature of the labor skills available in a country.

Kenen and those who have been working with him in the trade workshop at Columbia have in recent years made substantial analytical and empirical contributions to questions of this sort. As he points out, the models that have been developed are still quite simple and restrictive but they are important first steps in moving trade theory away from the simple factor-proportion approach that has dominated it for too long. Consequently, I strongly second his point that—partly as a result of research in the human investment field—international trade theory is at a stage where a whole series of promising lines of inquiry have opened up and are much in need of research. Hopefully, those with special competence in the human investment field will not only help to influence the nature of this research but also will actually participate in it themselves.

D. J. DALY
YORK UNIVERSITY

This paper continues the valuable work on the contribution of skills and human capital to the composition of commodity trade of the United States. It emphasizes the role of the high levels of human skills and education in the U. S. labor force, and the differences in education and skill requirements in broad commodity groups.

It is worth emphasizing that a new range of empirical data relevant to this question is available in a recent Brookings study.[1] In this study the contribution of a wide range of factor inputs and other topics are estimated and assessed for the United States and eight European countries. A Canadian study, using the same framework, has also been prepared.[2] These countries provide data in a comprehensive framework for a group of countries that dominate world trade, especially in manufactured products.

Although this framework and these data were developed initially to deal with differences in the levels of real output and growth experience between countries, they can be easily applied to international trade. For example, the data on factor supplies per employed person and output in relation to total factor inputs can be used to test the relevance and relative importance of the theories of Ricardo and Heckscher-Ohlin to international trade and comparative advantage in the main industrial countries.

Kenen's data on human capital use the percentages having various skills or the percentage engaged in R & D, and Anne Krueger's comments raise questions about these measures. Denison measures the whole education distribution and provides a measure with the desired characteristics.

This point can be illustrated for Canadian data, which have been assembled and published along the same lines as developed in the Brookings study. Although the levels of education in Canada are lower than in the United States, the supplies of other factors of production per employed persons are higher (e.g., construction, inventories, and natural resources). In total, the supplies of the total levels of all measured factor inputs are almost identical in the two countries, when weighted by their importance in national income. On the other hand, the levels of output per employed person and output in relation to total factor inputs is about 20 per cent lower than in the United States for the economy as a whole, and the differences are much larger for total manufacturing. The Canadian data are much more consistent with the Ricardian assumption

[1] Denison, E. F. and Poullier, J. P., *Why Growth Rates Differ: Postwar Experience in Nine Western Countries,* Washington, 1967.
[2] Walters, Dorothy, *Canadian Income Levels and Growth: An International Perspective,* Staff Study No. 23, Economic Council of Canada, Ottawa, 1969.

of different production functions in different countries (or quite different observable positions on a similar production function), than the Heckscher-Ohlin theory which emphasizes the role of different factor prices and factor supplies and similarities in production conditions.

I hope that future work on trade and comparative advantage can incorporate more analysis and use of the new material on international comparisons of real incomes, factor supplies, and output in relation to input.

THE BRAIN DRAIN—IS A
HUMAN-CAPITAL APPROACH
JUSTIFIED? • ANTHONY SCOTT •
UNIVERSITY OF BRITISH COLUMBIA

INTRODUCTION

TEN years ago, Brinley Thomas' excellent conference volume on international migration[1] contained papers mentioning the skills and education of immigrants, but almost no reference to the special problem of the emigration of scientists, professionals, and other highly qualified persons. The recognition of this special problem has been delayed, in my opinion, by the fact that in most decades the international flow of intellectuals has been in the form of voluntary exile (caused by political and religious developments) and involuntary flight (brought about by persecution). However, paralleling the waves of Jewish, White-Russian, Hungarian, Polish, Irish, and Baltic refugee and emigré intellectuals, was a steady stream of trained people from the United Kingdom, Scandinavia, the Low Countries, Spain, Portugal, France, and Italy who were going to the newly opened lands in the United States, Latin America, and the various nineteenth century empires. These migrations, moreover, were

NOTE: This paper has benefited from the research assistance of Mr. L. Brown, Mrs. M. Darrough, and from written comments from Mary Jean Bowman and Robert Myers. It reflects an earlier study undertaken jointly by H. Grubel and me at the University of Chicago, aided by a Rockefeller Foundation research grant directed by Harry Johnson. The present research was aided by the Canada Council and the UBC Research Committee.

[1] Brinley Thomas, ed., *Economics of International Migration*, London, 1958.

often only the beginning—the same people or their children moved on to better prospects, sometimes again as refugees, but more often as a new "upper class" of migrants soon to be assimilated among the professionals of their new homeland.

It was, of course, not at all unusual in earlier centuries also to regard the movements of trained workers and professionals as the best—perhaps the only—practical means of transmitting information and technology. My inexpert reading of economic history, for example, conveys the impression that the geographic transfer of textile technology, like that of printing and publishing, was usually accomplished by the flight or migration of specialists. That these two industries are believed to have expanded and shifted in this way is important for general economic history, for they are usually said to be among the leaders, or even harbingers, of general economic growth.[2]

Such transmissions of information and technology are today the subject of research by international trade specialists rather than manpower scholars. The latter, apparently overwhelmed by the difficulties of conceptualizing manpower planning in developing societies, usually ignore the outflow of trained personnel, the gain of such personnel from other countries, and the in- and outflows of students moving from their homes to schools, or back to final occupations. It is not surprising, therefore, that the "brain drain" has emerged as a topic publicized and studied by economists not usually associated with population, migration, or scientific policy.[3]

The purpose of this paper is to draw attention to three types of economic research which have been applied to the policy question of the

[2] This observation is not essential for what follows. It appears to be substantiated, however, in the first four sources which I consulted: Stevan Dedijer, " 'Modern' Migration," in W. Adams (ed.), *The Brain Drain*, New York, 1968, pp. 9–28; W. W. Rostow, *The Stages of Economic Growth*, Cambridge, 1960; Herbert Butterfield, *The Origins of Modern Science*, New York, 1960; and W. C. Dampier, *A Shorter History of Science*, New York, 1957.

[3] Frederick Harbison, for example, after some important work on education and manpower planning, has turned to the brain drain. But his earlier volume, C. A. Myers and F. Harbison, *Education, Manpower and Economic Growth*, New York, 1963, neglected the existence of a world open economy in the market for trained personnel.

brain drain.[4] The first of these in time is concerned with welfare theory— helping to resolve whether and in what sense there *could* be a brain drain problem. This body of literature, of course, stems from official investigations and reports from the United Kingdom, the Organization for Economic Cooperation and Development, the United States, and Canada, and first attracted attention in Harry Johnson's "The Economics of the 'Brain Drain': the Canadian Case," published in 1965 (see footnote 35), followed by "The International Flow of Human Capital," by Grubel and Scott, published in 1966 (see footnote 36). Although there were elements of other approaches in both papers, they depended primarily upon a search for externalities to indicate whether the departure of scientists and professionals hurt or helped the country of origin.

A second approach seeks to obtain and explain the demographic data about migration. Authors have, therefore, specialized in making the best of censuses, migration returns, and special questionnaires, and in testing the explanatory power of income, distance, race, religion, and so forth, as determinants of the migration of skilled and highly qualified persons. Little of this work has proceeded beyond the working-up of tables and charts, but some of it has followed the lead of L. Sjaastad in his path-breaking "The Costs and Returns of Human Migration" (see footnote 6).

A third set of writings has attempted an application of the human capital approach, pioneered by T. W. Schultz and Gary Becker, for the analysis not only of education and manpower policies but also of individual behavior. In the hands of Grubel and Scott, Wilkinson, Parai,

---

[4] Among general Anglo-Saxon economists, almost the only important exception to the claim in this statement is Brinley Thomas, whose earlier studies of transatlantic migration are well-known. On the other hand, the work of mobility specialists working *within* a society has turned out to be very useful. One thinks here of Sjaastad, Weisbrod, Fein, and many others.

To attempt footnotes to establish the integrity of these three approaches would require a bibliographic article. In any case, the need is greatly reduced by the existence of two excellent bibliographies: S. Dedijer and L. Svenningson, *Brain Drain and Brain Gain,* Research Policy Program, Lund, Sweden, 1967; W. G. Scheurer, John C. Shearer and others, "Selected Bibliography International Movement of High-Level Human Resources (The 'Brain Drain') by Sender Area," Pennsylvania State University and University of Chicago Comparative Education Center, May 1967 (mimeographed); and by the bibliographies appended to recent articles by Bowman and Myers, Grubel and Scott, and Brinley Thomas.

Bowman and Myers, Rashi Fein, and a few others, human capital studies of migration have not proceeded very far beyond the onerous stage of obtaining the demographic data according to age, status, education, and occupation; all that has been attempted is to value the various categories created, either backward-looking, in terms of the costs and foregone production embodied in the migrating human capital, or forward-looking, in terms of the expected future earnings (wealth) of the migrants.

Of course, it is impossible to separate cleanly an exploratory literature into such distinct methodological "traditions," especially when the writers are themselves involved in the complex policy questions which inspired the whole blossoming of the subject. Thus, Johnson's most recent analyses used international trade theory more than Pigovian welfare economics; Weisbrod's work on migration has transcended public finance and manpower studies; and a number of authors have branched off their original trails to consider either the general problems of migration for growth and development in low-income countries or the particular problem of the return or nonreturn of students obtaining higher education abroad. The uninitiated may, therefore, be particularly grateful for the appearance of two compilations of papers: *The Brain Drain*, edited by Walter Adams, and the forthcoming *Proceedings* of the 1967 conference of the International Association for Research in Income and Wealth which was held in Ireland and which concentrated on the subject of the brain drain.

Similarly, it is impossible to classify the literature by the various *policy* questions to which the authors were, speculatively or econometrically, addressing themselves. Instead, what follows is concerned with three approaches to migration. The first part deals with the decision to migrate, referring to a set of studies not apparently consulted by many economists; the second part deals with migratory human capital, especially its measurement; and the third, with other policy questions about migration.

THE DECISION TO MIGRATE

A LIST OF THE DETERMINANTS

1. *Income differentials.* The pioneering study by Sjaastad concentrated on this explanation of migration, which is the one economists would think of first. Most studies and many policy documents have made much of it. The British Jones Report estimated that young graduates or Ph.D.'s in the United States might expect from two to three times the initial salary obtainable in the United Kingdom; larger ratios of course apply to differentials between less developed countries (LDC's) and western economies. Economists would naturally think that the present value of income, or permanent income, would actually be the relevant concept. A study by Grubel and Scott summarizes the possible decision rule thus:[5]

$$\sum_{i=1}^{N_o} \frac{Y_{o,i}}{(1+r_o)^i} + \sum_{i=1}^{N_o} \frac{P_{o,i}}{(1+r_o)^i} \underset{<}{>} \sum_{i=1}^{N_d} \frac{Y_{d,i}}{(1+r_d)^i} + \sum_{i=1}^{N_d} \frac{P_{d,i}}{(1+P_d)^i} - C$$

where

Y is expected real income,

r is rate of discount,

N is expected life,

P is psychic income,

C is cost of living,

o is the subscript for the country of origin, and

d is the subscript for the country of destination.

If the left-hand side is exceeded by the right-hand side, migration is "rational."

As the dating and discounting of the real-income items suggest, it is not merely the initial level but the time-shape of the alternative income streams which will exercise the most leverage. Indeed, some studies have explicitly mentioned the different rates of increase of salaries in countries

[5] Herbert G. Grubel and Anthony D. Scott, "Determinants of Migration: The Highly Skilled," *International Migration,* 5, No. 2, 1967, p. 128. For fuller information, see M. J. Bowman and R. G. Myers, "Schooling, Experience and Gains and Losses in Human Capital Through Migration," *Journal of the American Statistical Association,* 62, September 1967, pp. 875–98.

TABLE 1

Motivation Studies

I. The Wilson Study of British Scientists, 1964: Reasons for Emigrating to North America

Reason	Percentage[a]
Low status for scientists in United Kingdom; Science in United Kingdom is "demoralized"	14.1
Britain "frustrating and depressing"	12.5
Lack of facilities in United Kingdom	10.4
Dissatisfied with conditions (of scientific work) in United Kingdom	17.5
Greater professional opportunities in North America	38.6
Low salaries in United Kingdom	6.2
Higher salaries in North America	18.0
Higher standard of living in North America	10.6
Higher social standing of scientists in North America	6.5

II. The Hatch-Rudd Study of Graduate Students, 1957-58: Reasons for Overseas Study

Reason	Percentage[b]
Desire to travel	39
To gain scientific, academic experience	26
To gain other or unspecified forms of experience	18
To work in a particular department or study a particular subject	15
Availability of better research facilities	6
Financial reasons, higher salary	22
Better opportunities; offered better job but finance not specified	23
Dissatisfaction with conditions and opportunities in Britain	19
Sent by employer	4
Other reasons	14
Reasons not stated	3

Notes to Table 1

SOURCE: *The Brain Drain: Report of the Working Group on Migration,* Committee on Manpower Resources for Science and Technology (London: HMSO, Cmnd. 3417, 1967), pp. 69–70. The origin of the studies embodied in the report is as follows: James A. Wilson, "The Depletion of Natural Resources of Human Talent in the United Kingdom; a Special Aspect of Migration to North America, 1952–64," doctoral dissertation, University of Pittsburgh. (The majority of Wilson's respondents were young natural scientists with a high academic background.) Stephen Hatch and Ernest Rudd, University of Essex, U. K.; survey of the employment former postgraduate students. The survey included some 3,400 graduates in 1957.

[a]Total of 517 respondents.

[b]Total of 678 students were or had at some time been graduate students overseas.

of Europe and in the United States as important determinants of migration. The higher American starting salaries are contrasted by potential migrants with slower subsequent pay increases.

The psychic income items will be dealt with as part of the discussion on living and working conditions. The rates of interest are presumably equal only if all factors are perfectly mobile and all markets are perfect. Otherwise one would expect that highly qualified potential migrants would discount future incomes at rates which reflected both their superior access to capital markets and their greater certainty about the future. Whether the formulation is realistic in ascribing to the potential migrant the imaginative capacity to discount foreign incomes at foreign rates is a matter for debate, as is the question of whether the factor of risk is small enough to justify leaving it out of the calculation.

2. *Openings and opportunities.* It is not obvious that scientists and professionals are more specialized in any technical sense than are some less educated members of the labor force. However, many of the latter are willing to start new lives in new countries by abandoning their old occupations, while the brain-drain literature suggests that highly educated manpower frequently moves in search of the precise opening to justify past training or experience.

Two other aspects of opportunity may be important for scientific manpower. First, to the extent that scientists are confined by their work to universities or institutional laboratories, they may be very concerned about obtaining opportunities for future advancement and promotion which are missing in their country of origin. Second, for similar reasons they may wish to escape from countries in which one or a few institutions comprehend all their opportunities and to emigrate to countries offering more ample scientific facilities and in which sideways mobility makes possible escape to other hierarchies.

3. *Living conditions.* This is really an omnibus category like "psychic income." Leaving aside quests for political, religious, or racial non-discrimination and freedom, many professionals obviously move simply to obtain better living conditions for themselves, their wives, or their families. Climate, holiday facilities, schools, welfare, social attitudes, and styles of living may be magnets. Once again, manpower which customarily communicates with, or travels among, colleagues all over the world is well qualified to know of such differences.

4. *Working conditions.* The more creative is highly qualified manpower, the greater its desire for suitably equipped, secluded, or serviced facilities and premises. Obviously, rich countries can provide potential immigrants with the greatest promise of research funds, appropriate colleagues, time, space, and apparatus.

THE RELATIVE IMPORTANCE OF THE DETERMINANTS

It is easier to list these determinants than to discover their relative importance. A few studies, however, have been made, chiefly in the United Kingdom. (See Table 1, which is based on two of these studies.) Before presenting a summary of this evidence, the limitations of these studies should be stressed. First, they deal explicitly with emigrants from the United Kingdom. While that country is an important source of emigrant scientists, it should be noted that there is an immense number of migrants from the less developed countries. Second, as in many questionnaire-based studies, they report only the percentage of respondents mentioning one or more particular suggested motivations, and the researchers' classifications of these mentions. In particular, these frequencies are not weights or regression coefficients. The two surveys were published separately, but the tables are taken from summaries prepared for the 1967 report of the British working group on migration, *The Brain Drain*. (See Table 1, Source.)

The Wilson study concentrates on approximately 500 scientists, while the broader Hatch-Rudd study considers the about 20 per cent of a group of 3,400 former British graduate students who had ever gone overseas. It is not surprising, therefore, that the former study appears to indicate the greatest importance for scientific and professional opportunity—"working conditions"—in our own listing. Other surveys and the opinions of experts who have dealt with scientists and Ph.D.'s also frequently assert that money is not the important factor in a migration. The point is difficult to test because most migrations do appear to bring both higher lifetime incomes and better facilities to the migrant.

There are, of course, many studies of migration, but few of them attempt to analyze data on incomes, distance, and cost of moving. One of the best known is L. Sjaastad's "Costs and Returns of Human Migration," based in part on his earlier doctoral thesis.[6] Attempting to study disaggregated gross internal U. S. migration, he finds an extraordinary sensitivity to distance, so that, in miles and 1947-49 dollars, it would take $106 per year in extra income to induce a migrant already on the move to migrate an extra 150 miles. Sjaastad's explanation of this immobility is that his data neglect the uncertainty and loss of psychic income involved in the extra distance; income is not the only explanatory variable.[7]

Sjaastad's discovery that income differences may be overshadowed by other explanations is, of course, consistent with motivation and questionnaire studies of highly educated manpower, which tend to stress the importance of work opportunities and facilities for research and the absence of impediments of culture and language. A rather special version of this finding is set out in R. G. Myers' doctoral thesis[8] in which he investigates the foreign students' nonreturns from study in the United

[6] L. Sjaastad, "Costs and Returns of Human Migration," *Journal of Political Economy*, 70, October 1962, pp. 80–93.

[7] There are, of course, many recent studies of labor mobility. See the *Journal of Human Resources*, spring and summer, 1967.

[8] R. G. Myers, "Study Abroad and the Migration of Human Resources," (Ph.D. dissertation, University of Chicago, 1967), p. 97.

States, by country of origin. It is found that nonreturn rates are positively correlated with the level of per capita income in the sending country, though the correlation is not impressive until national levels of education, fields, and types of immigration status are also considered. However, this is a surprising finding on incomes alone: it suggests that the *smaller* the differential between parent-country and United States per capita income, the greater the tendency of nationals to remain after studies in the United States.

Myers also questioned a large sample of Peruvians studying in the United States, obtaining guesses from each respondent as to his alternative income streams in the United States and Peru. To paraphrase his summary of his very complex results, he obtained no firm answer to the question of whether expected earnings distinguished those who had decided to return home from those who planned to stay in the United States. It was found that students of low social status on grants and scholarships in the United States were planning to return to expected low incomes in Peru. Clearly, considerations other than incomes or expected earnings were influencing migration decisions.[9]

FACTORS STRENGTHENING THE DETERMINANTS

It is obvious that conditions in certain countries will create incentives to come or to leave. The literature has given much attention to these conditions because their removal would do much to reduce the brain drain. Consequently, it is enough simply to list a few of the more important suggestions.

1. *Foreign training.* In the present context, the main significance of foreign training is that it familiarizes students with incomes, opportunities, and working and living conditions elsewhere. While it is possible that study abroad simply gives would-be emigrants easy access to their new country, many writers believe that scientists and professionals leave their native countries *because of* their experiences as students abroad. Countries which lack higher education facilities, though able to supply a

[9] *Ibid.,* p. 242.

flow of persons at the university or professional school entrance level, are bound to see many of these students go abroad for their education and stay abroad. It is probable that, in some fields at least, starting professional schools at home will not only produce a domestic flow of qualified persons, but also reduce the loss of those who would otherwise stay abroad after training. (Obviously this assertion holds only if the local graduates do not go on to foreign postgraduate training. And even then, as a comparison of migrating physicians from Pakistan and the Philippines shows, foreign training cannot be the chief explanation of migration.)

2. *Domestic income distribution.* Each economy may, either as an interpretation of egalitarianism or in furtherance of other aims, pursue policies which point up or water down the economic structure of incomes and occupational status, thus affecting migration behavior. The incomes of scientists and engineers may be the result of government policy designed to benefit universities and the government itself by providing personnel for its own departmental organizations. As one example, the European custom of overpaying "the professor" of each subject in a university often not only places the incumbent advantageously with respect to his professional colleagues at home and even overseas, but also places him ahead of them in relation to other occupations and social groups. Senior men in such positions are therefore loath to migrate, except for political reasons; their juniors, however (perhaps as a direct financial consequence), are ill paid, of low social status, and interested in migration.

A second example is well known in the literature. Physicians in the United Kingdom, following an almost free medical education, receive low stipends as part of social policy on incomes and on welfare. It is possible that the rate of return on their own input is as high for doctors in Britain as in countries where doctors pay more for their training and get higher money incomes later. However, where the two systems coexist, it pays students to get free training in the United Kingdom and then migrate elsewhere, which is what they do.

A third example comes from India. The high status and relative salaries of a few intellectuals, civil servants, and scientists attract thousands of emulators from the same social classes, so many, in fact, that colleges are flooded by indifferent scholars and the market is flooded with unplaceable graduates. It is said that emigration comes naturally to both good and bad products of this system, frustrated by the oversupply. Note the similarity to the European professorship system already mentioned.

Income redistribution may also be accomplished through taxation and expenditure policy. Scientists who would be highly paid in the United States may be victims of steeply progressive income tax rates elsewhere; more generally, their net fiscal position may be negative, thus driving them out of the country.

Indeed, all too little has been said about the positive (as opposed to the normative) effects of taxation on the brain drain, or on migration generally. It is frequently asserted that high tax rates drive people away, but the information comes from former migrants whose views are not completely reliable. What about a priori judgments from public finance? The literature of federal finance, for instance, is full of suggestions about migration from one province to another, because of net fiscal pressure (fiscal residuum, in Buchanan's terminology). One would want to know whether taxes and public services do have this alleged effect on the retention or repulsion of persons contemplating migration, and whether it is closely related to other alleged effects, such as the demand for leisure and other untaxed factor allocations.

In particular, debates about the brain drain make it important to know whether scientists and engineers, relative to other would-be migrants, are more heavily taxed; are more sensitive to marginal tax increments; and, are more responsive to the availability of public goods, transfers, and social services. One aspect of the welfare debate has centered on the "debt" of the emigrant to his home country—is he a debtor for the services absorbed in his youth, and is he morally bound to repay this debt? The positive aspect of this question is whether small changes in services and repayments (i.e. taxes) would alter his choice about leaving.

3. *Language and culture.* We have already noted that scientists and engineers are well informed about the advantages and opportunities elsewhere. Their education and background also help them to feel at home in a new country. On the other hand, it is conceivable that they are more sensitive than are less educated persons to the loss of their own culture, religion, or language. Such considerations may help to explain

TABLE 2

Hatch-Rudd Survey: Reasons for Returning to Britain

Reason	Percentage[a]
Family, domestic	36
Prefer "British way of life"	13
Patriotism, "obligation to this country"	6
Dislike of life overseas	7
End of temporary visit	41
Offer of a good job in Britain	19
Dissatisfaction with job or prospects overseas	11
Other reasons	7
Reasons not stated	3

SOURCE: *The Brain Drain: Report of the Working Group on Migration,* HMSO p. 71.

[a]The total number returning to Britain was 335.

why migration within the English-speaking world is so high, and why the much smaller migration within the French-speaking world rarely crosses over into English-speaking countries.[10]

THE TIME DIMENSION OF MIGRATION

It should not be assumed that every highly qualified person who leaves his country, even to work elsewhere, is necessarily adding to the brain drain. Far from it—the brain drain is both larger and smaller than this.

It may be larger because, in spite of its name, the brain drain is measured by the movement of people with certain occupations or educations, not by their brains or potential. For many attributes, the rankings of people vary. Thus, it is obvious that young children, geniuses or not, will not be counted as part of the brain drain when they move but only

---

[10] See Michel Olivier, "Algerians, Africans and Frenchmen," *Interplay,* 1, May 1968, pp. 20–25; and Robert Mosse, "France," *The Brain Drain,* Walter Adams (ed.), New York, 1968, pp. 157–65.

when they have acquired higher degrees or acquired academic or scientific positions. The same is true of adults classified as "managerial and administrative" personnel—the group is usually excluded because it contains many managers and owners of small businesses, some of them failures and bankrupts. Yet among them are also trained or experienced entrepreneurs, innovators, consultants, and industrialists. It is doubtful whether statisticians would have counted Andrew Carnegie in the brain drain when he moved to the United States at the age of twelve, or Albert Einstein when he entered Switzerland at seventeen.

Nevertheless, in spite of these serious exclusions, the brain drain is probably *smaller* than current statistics suggest because of the difficulty of netting out the reflux of returning nationals. They return because of (a) disappointment in their fortunes or conditions in the new country, or (b) fulfillment of a plan to return after obtaining schooling, training, experience, or simply the pleasures of living and traveling abroad. A British study (see Table 2) has attempted to discover by questionnaire why British scientific emigrants return home, although the statistical difficulties, both of locating former emigrants and of obtaining "correct" answers from them, are, of course, formidable.

It must also be pointed out that, until death makes return impossible, it must never be concluded that emigration is "permanent." All academics know colleagues who have made one or more return journeys to their homeland. They know that this process can take place at various ages and for a variety of personal reasons as well as for motives easily classified as "economic." The difficulties here are similar to those confronting the demographer estimating "average size of family" for a still fertile population. Just as parents add to their families after their first batch of children are nearly grown up, so older emigrants may begin to seek or accept positions in their homelands. Such a reflux has understandably long been visible among former European political refugees, but is also evident among those whose move was purely economic or professional. Hence, flow estimates of the brain drain must always be overestimates of permanent emigration.

However, the most important category of returning emigrants is undoubtedly the group of students and short-term appointees (often postdoctoral fellows). The accompanying panels (see Table 3) give some estimates of the Swedish, British, and Canadian reflux from this source—

TABLE 3

Brain Drain: Sweden, United Kingdom, and Canada

	Drain	Reflux	Net
Sweden: Citizens with university degree			
(average emigration, 1961–62)	(average annual re-immigration, 1958–59)		
	198	75	123
United Kingdom: (a) Holders of Ph.D. in a science			
(total outward movement, 1957–61)	(return of those on fellowships & temporary appointments)		
	1,548	910	638
(b) Degrees issued by British universities in 1965 – engineering and technology and science			
Engin. and Tech.	230	75	155
Science	460	345	115
Total	690	420	270
(c) High degrees in engineering and science			
Engin.	106	16	90
Science	477	152	325
Total	583	168	415
Canada: Citizens with economics degrees			
(moving to or trained in the U.S., now in Canada or U.S.)	(U.S. trained, now in Canada)		
	107	63	44

SOURCE: Sweden, Goran Friborg, "A First, Preliminary Report . . . Regarding the Migration of Scientists to and from Sweden," Committee on Research Economics, Swedish Research Council, Stockholm, Report No. 20, (mimeographed). United Kingdom (a), rearranged from *Emigration of Scientists from the United Kingdom,* Report of a Committee Appointed by the Council of the Royal Society, London, the Royal Society, 1963, summarized in *Minerva,* 1, Spring, 1963, pp. 358–60; (b) and (c), *The Brain Drain,* p. 24. Canada, Estimates from Anthony D. Scott, and Herbert G. Grubel, "Flux and Reflux: The International Migration of Canadian Economists" (forthcoming).

around 50 per cent of the emigration that might be recorded by statisticians who depend on official returns, such as those published by the United States Immigration Service.

WAVES: THE SOCIAL AND ECONOMIC DIMENSION OF
MIGRATION BEHAVIOR

Some useful study has been made of the social influences on migration, quite apart from those characteristics of national economies strengthening influential determinants mentioned previously. In particular, it is worth noting that brain drains do not seem to have been steady flows, but irregular and cumulative movements. There are some obvious reasons for this, but here it may be useful to mention some unexpected aspects of the flow.

First, because in theory the brain drain is caused by a disequilibrium, we should expect it to be spasmodic, commencing in response to some change in the international economy's factor or goods markets and ending when population movements are no longer required. (However, this is a simplistic and static view. It is possible to imagine countries steadily supporting the education of their sons in preparation for occupations abroad. Scottish marine engineers, Nepalese mercenaries, French cooks, and Swiss watchmakers may be examples. But such steady flows would hardly be the subjects of brain-drain complaints.)

Furthermore, emigration or immigration may be interrupted or prevented by war. Thereafter the migration may be twice as large as the initial disequilibirum would indicate. Similarly, a potential brain drain may be delayed by shortages of people of the right age or sex. This is a "bottleneck," exogenous but otherwise similar to the endogenous bottlenecks to be mentioned later.

Second, considering the brain drain simply as an adjustment to an international factor disequilibrium, we might expect the flow to be largest at the outset, then to diminish as the gap or disequilibrium was remedied. However, factor flows are rarely as monotonic as this because the absence of communications, institutions, or transportation systems is not remedied until the first units of flow are completed. Thereafter uncertainty is reduced, communications with home are improved, and removal becomes simpler. (Marco Polo may move first, but not much time elapses before his cousins and their mothers-in-law follow.) We expect all migrations to be cumulative, at least until the disequilibrium is adjusted.

Third, the brain drain cannot become large until supply bottlenecks have been removed. An important brain drain must depend heavily upon the products of local universities and professional schools. If the labor markets were in equilibrium before the drain began, the subsequent perceived excess demand abroad will be transformed into a large emigration only after (a) drawing down existing stocks of scientists and professionals, raising their local demand prices, reducing their incentive to move during the waiting period (when the price mechanism is attracting additional students through the necessary training and experience), and (b) expanding local education facilties, if the excess demand overseas is larger than can be supplied by these facilities at attractive incomes.

Fourth, demand bottlenecks may also have to be removed. Prior to the migrations, the countries of destination may have been "making do" with substitute skills or inputs. The actual creating of vacancies for the newly discovered sources of professional and scientific manpower may take time, as may the removal of legal, customary, trade union, or cultural barriers to their employment.

Fifth, emigrants with particular skills or national characteristics may by their presence create new roles for themselves and their kind which were foreseen neither by the original professionals or scientists nor by their employers.

Sixth, the countries of destination may be gradually building up their educational, industrial, or scientific establishments. Consequently, their excess demand for qualified persons may grow rather than be satisfied.

In addition to these microeconomic aspects of adjustment to international disequilibria in the markets for various kinds of educated persons, two particular categories of large and general flow should be picked out for special mention.

The first of these comprises refugee intellectuals. It goes without saying that the fleeing of intellectuals from Russia, Germany, Italy, China, or Hungary at various times in this century can hardly be properly classified with other categories of brain drain. The motives for removal are entirely different, and the permanence of their emigration may depend upon the permanence of the conditions which drove them abroad. Nevertheless, so different are the motivations, that the existence of a stream of refugees ought to have created some useful opportunities for economic research on the brain drain. One interesting circumstance, for example, is that some countries of destination were merely able to offer liberty, not necessarily large schools, institutes, or research facilities. Hence, the capacity of emigré intellectuals to change the environment of technology or education should be open to study *ceteris paribus* (instead of mutatis mutandis, as is so often the case when a brilliant scientist is invited abroad to work in an already productive environment.) A second, symmetrical circumstance is that the country of emigration may have provided all the physical and intellectual environment and facilities necessary to hold and use the refugee productively. His expulsion, therefore, may illustrate *ceteris paribus* the effect of the departure of isolated individuals or groups on an otherwise fruitful scientific atmosphere. Indeed, it has often seemed to me that the time is ripe for a wise scholar to compare science in Stalinist Russia, from which emigration of dissatisfied scientists was impossible, with science in Nazi Germany, where emigration was, for all practical purposes, compulsory.

In any case, it is to be expected that waves of refugees have also created environments favorable to subsequent migrations. This is not so much because the potential employers will seek more scientists or engineers from the refugee's country (indeed, the refugees may prevent the employment of new generations with different beliefs), but because the refugees may have established openings or vacancies for men with certain types of ability or training found only in that country. An obvious example is the boost given to German and classical literary studies in North America by German refugees; similar remarks could be made about Chinese studies in western universities, originally strengthened by scholars unable or unwilling to return to their homeland, now perhaps awaiting a stream of younger Chinese archeologists, historians, artists, and literary specialists trained on the mainland. Similarly, it should be noted that refugee scholars are somewhat less willing to make concessions to the educational or scientific traditions of their new countries, because their migrations have not involved a voluntary surrender of their own traditions and approaches, and because they have often been forced to migrate at a later age than is usual among brain-drain migrants. Unhappy and stubborn, they may actually make a larger impact than if they expunged parts of their own past in adjusting to their host's culture.

The discipline of economics can count many such scholars, from the greatest to the most ordinary recruit of a small college or government research branch.

The second category comprises the "wave" of educated migrants accommodating to long waves of economic development, land shortage, demographic forces, and factor movements across the Atlantic and national borders. We are almost completely indebted to Brinley Thomas for this information. Summarized by Walter Adams in his recent book, it runs as follows:

> Why, then, do we view the international flow of talents and skills in a different perspective from earlier observers? In the first place, as Brinley Thomas points out, the great outpouring of human capital in the 19th century from Europe to North America was complementary to an export of physical capital and unskilled labor. Flowing from the developed countries, it created an infra-structure in the developing continent and had important feedback effects on the exporting countries. It resulted, according to Thomas, in a progressive narrowing of the gap between countries in different stages of development, benefiting both sending and receiving countries.
>
> The current wave of migration, in contrast, has moved in the opposite direction from that of physical capital.[11]

THE SOCIAL VALUE OF HUMAN CAPITAL EMBODIED IN MIGRANTS

MEASUREMENT

The study of migration generally, and that of the brain drain in particular, has made much of the "human-capital" approach. By analogy with capital theory, this approach regards each person as having attached to him an amount of wealth equal to the present value of his net future earnings. While he cannot usually realize this wealth, as he would by selling a machine or farm that he owned, he can increase its future earning power by investment in his schooling, on-the-job training, and occupational and regional mobility.

[11] Walter Adams, ed., *The Brain Drain*, p. 3.

The importance of the approach lies in the fact that it is the source of hypotheses about behavior: people's investment in themselves should be in forms, amounts, and periods which will maximize the value of their human capital, after making allowance for nonpecuniary types of income and for leisure. This application is clearly positive. It should lead to the prediction of decisions about schooling, location, and jobs, and in aggregate, can help to explain group behavior or attitudes to investment in educational facilities, migration, and to collective bargaining for working conditions, pensions, and retirement provisions.

At the same time, the human capital approach has been used in a quasinormative manner in determining rates of return to buttress claims that too little (or too much) is being spent in aggregate on certain types of educational facilities, as opposed to social spending on physical capital and other forms of public goods.

In migration studies, both these approaches are present, and they ought to be clearly distinguished. Among the positive studies, Sjaastad, Myers and a number of other writers have explained how migration is to be regarded as investment in human capital, and have attempted some measurement of its payoff or rate of return. The estimation of personal rates of return is difficult, chiefly because it is difficult to discover what migrants expect certain values to be. The aggregate rate of return, however, is just as difficult to estimate as an aggregate rate of return to schooling because of the impossibility, short of a complete (planning) model, of knowing what rates of pay would exist if all categories of educated persons were to be changed. In migration studies, it is comparatively easy to learn or guess what personal incomes are believed to be in a certain region, but it is impossible to guess what the pay levels would, in fact, become if everyone moved where his human wealth would be maximized.

Normative studies of migration suffer not only from the same difficulties (of data, and of aggregation) as the positive or behavioristic studies, but also from a perceptible tentativeness in the relevant welfare theory. As with similar problems in land and real estate appraising and valuation theory and practice, the measurement of the quantity of migrating human capital must, in a world of adjustment to disequilibrium in goods and factor markets, depend upon the purpose for which the measurement is to be used. A few examples are: (1) the value of exports of human capital, analogous to the balance of trade or similar values of exports of machines and other capital goods; (2) the "debt" of a migrant to his homeland; (3) the "balance of indebtedness" between two countries exchanging migrants; (4) the "supply price" of a country training additional migrants for "sale"; and (5) the "demand price" of a country importing additional migrants instead of training its own people.

In the absence of human-capital markets and during disequilibrium in labor markets, the values of these concepts will differ, though impatient economists may reason that in the long-run with perfect markets the differences would disappear.

Closer examination of the differences reveals that their source is in different assumed conditions in which some hypothetical transaction is to take place. We must ask, for example, if there were a *stock* of nuclear scientists for sale, what short-run price would emerge from competition among the nations? Second, if nuclear scientists were produced for sale, what long-run price would be determined by interaction of both supply and demand? Third, if potential emigrants were to buy their right to leave from their remaining countrymen, how much would they offer, and how much would their countrymen demand?

As will be discussed later, a number of such questions can be posed and indeed have been suggested as bases for international compensation in brain drain exchanges[12] and as variables in explaining total community outlays on education.[13] When the problem of finding quantitative answers is faced, however, only four actual techniques have been suggested:

1. Cost-saving to the country of destination for the human capital received.

2. Present value of the human capital migrating.

3. The dead-weight, or consumers'-surplus, loss from migration.

4. The reduction in the flow of savings, taxes and public spending.

These techniques will be reviewed in the following section, emphasis being given to "cost-saving" estimates.[14]

---

[12] See Harry G. Johnson and others in Walter Adams (ed.), *The Brain Drain.*

[13] See Burton A. Weisbrod, *External Benefits of Public Education,* Princeton: Industrial Section, Princeton University, 1964.

[14] A review of (1) and (2) will be found in Bowman and Myers, *op. cit.*

1. *Cost-saving measures.* This approach can best be summarized by suggesting the question which it directly answers: if an immigrant brings a certain education and experience with him, what are the direct resource costs and foregone earnings which are avoided by his new country? The answer, obviously, requires discovering that country's costs of schooling at various levels (average or marginal costs depending on whether or not the immigrant is part of a stream); his foregone earnings (on the assumption that he might otherwise have migrated before his period of schooling and worked in his new country); or his maintenance costs (on the assumption that his new country might have sent someone to his homeland for an education); and making allowance for the degree to which he worked part-time.

In fact, such estimates follow very closely the methods pioneered by T. W. Schultz in estimating the human capital embodied in the U.S. labor force.[15] Difficult questions arise about whether or not to use domestic or foreign values, reflecting differences between alternative approaches to building up or importing elements of skilled local manpower. But most of the complexities of the method, which has been extensively used by Grubel and Scott, Parai, and Wilkinson,[16] lie in problems of data.

Grubel and Scott, basing their estimates on the gross *flow* of 43,000 scientists and professionals to the United States from 1949 to 1961, found that the gain to the United States was about $1 billion, or $23,000 per immigrant, considering both full education costs and earnings (production) foregone.

The same authors made a more detailed analysis of the influx and return of foreign students to the United States. In 1963, 75,000 students, about evenly divided between undergraduates and graduates, absorbed American educational, maintenance, and travel resources of about $4,300 per student, or a total of $325 million. However, after allowing for self-support for foreign students, this sum declines to about $175 million. After further subtracting the "gain" to the United States from the 10 per

[15] See especially T. W. Schultz, "Capital Formation by Education," *Journal of Political Economy,* 68, December 1960, pp. 571–83; and *The Economic Value of Education,* New York, 1963.

[16] References are given in succeeding footnotes for Grubel and Scott, and Louis Parai. For B. W. Wilkinson, see *Studies on the Economics of Education,* Occasional Paper No. 4, Economics and Research Branch, Department of Labour, Ottawa, July 1965.

cent of foreign students who remain there, and from the studies of American students abroad, this United States contribution is converted to a *gain* of about $16 million per year.

In another study of the economics profession in Canada and the United States, Grubel and Scott compute the contribution made by migration, training abroad, and return of students and mature economists to the stock of academics in the two countries. Here it is found that, although there are more Canadian economists in American universities than Americans in Canadian universities, the American contribution to graduate training of students who eventually returned to Canada outweighs in value the net American gain from Canadian migration.

The value of the "reflux" or return homeward of migrants and students is therefore one of the most important aspects of the brain drain question. As Swedish, British, and Canadian studies have shown, there

TABLE 4

"Gains" and "Losses" to Canada
from Professional Migration, 1953–63
(in millions of Canadian Dollars at 1961 prices)

	Gain	Loss
Replacement costs of education of professional manpower	532	292
Replacement cost of foregone earnings during migrants' schooling	455	240
Total	986	531
Student exchange: cost of educating net excess of 6,500 Canadians abroad over foreigners studying in Canada – @ $1,800 per student	12	
Net Gain to Canada from migrations and study abroad (balancing item)	–	(467)
Total	998	998

SOURCE: Based on data in L. Parai, *Immigration and Emigration of Professional and Skilled Manpower During the Post-War Period*, Special Study No. 1, Economic Council of Canada, Ottawa, 1965.

may indeed be such large homeward flows (i.e., not merely flows of immigrants to offset emigration) from previous emigration as to nullify the prevailing impression that emigration amounts to a significant proportion of the home output or stock of qualified persons. Furthermore, to the extent that other persons have been students (in graduate and professional schools), undertaking postdoctoral research or on-the-job training, they may not have been registered in *any* statistical compilation as migrants. However, their return may produce a more substantial change in the stock of human capital in their native land than the better documented flow of permanent migrants.

This may be illustrated by adjusting some calculations by Louis Parai.[17] Confining himself to the flows to and from Canada of "professional" manpower, for the period 1953-63, he estimated the gains and losses shown in Table 4.

The extent to which emigrants eventually return home can be illustrated by a sensitivity analysis. The "loss" column in the table measures the value of emigrant professional human capital for the period 1953-63 to be $531 million (for about 56,000 emigrants). If, as may easily be the case, the number of emigrants is overstated—through the neglect of subsequent returns to Canada—by 10 per cent, the residual calculation of Canada's net gain could also be out by more than 10 per cent.[18]

A striking illustration of the extent to which neglect of returning emigrants can invalidate gross cost-saving estimates is provided by Göran Friborg.[19] Using the Grubel-Scott technique, he first values the gross annual Swedish loss of scientists and engineers to the United States at $1.8 million in 1960. "Re-immigration" of highly qualified Swedes

---

[17] Louis Parai, *Immigration and Emigration of Professional and Skilled Manpower During the Post-War Period*, Special Study No. 1, Economic Council of Canada, Ottawa, 1965, pp. 82–122.

[18] For the most part, Canadian emigration measures are residual estimates after net natural increase, and immigration have been added to census counts. Hence, *professional* emigration figures must depend on U. S. Immigration data. But these do not count immigrants as Canadian if they are recent arrivals in Canada. Furthermore, nobody counts U. S. immigrants of Canadian citizenship who return to Canada. See Parai, Technical Note 8, Table 11 and Table A-45.

[19] Göran Friborg, "International Movement of Scientific and Technical Personnel," Part IV of Meddelande Nr. 27, Kommitten för Forskningsorganisation och Forskningsekonomi, (Committee for Research Organization and Economy), Stockholm, December 1966.

TABLE 5

Revision: "Net Gain to Canada" from Student Exchange

Canadian Contribution to Schooling		
of Foreign Students in Canada		
1 Total students[a]	55,760	
2 Graduate students	11,152	
3 Undergraduates	44,608	
4 Education resource costs — grad.		
@ $4,143		$ 46,200,000
5 Education resource costs — under-		
grad. @ $1,800		80,300,000
6 Maintenance costs — 50 per cent of		
students (grad. + undergrad.) @ $1,700		47,400,000
7 Total Canadian contribution		
(4) + (5) + (6)		$173,900,000
Foreign Contribution to Schooling		
of Canadian Students Abroad		
8 Total students in U. S. and U. K.[a]	62,307	
9 Graduate students	12,329	
10 Undergraduate	49,978	
11 Education resource costs — grad.		
@ $4,143		$ 51,100,000
12 Education resource costs —		
undergrad. @ $1,800		90,000,000
13 Maintenance costs — 50 percent of		
students (grad. + undergrad.) @ $1,700		53,100,000
14 Total foreign contribution		
(11) + (12) + (13)		$194,200,000
Net Gain to Canada		
(14) − (7)		$ 20,300,000

SOURCE: Total students, L. Parai, *Immigration and Emigration of Professional and Skilled Manpower During the Post-War Period,* Special Study No. 1, Economic Council of Canada, Ottawa, 1965. Education resource costs — graduate students, A. D. Scott and H. G. Grubel, "The International Migration of Canadian Economists" (forthcoming), p. 42; undergraduate students, Parai, *op. cit.,* p. 123. Maintenance costs, Scott and Grubel, *op. cit.,* p. 52.

[a]Graduate/undergraduate ratio assumed similar to United States (see *Doctorate Production in U. S. Universities,* 1920–62, National Academy of Sciences, 1963, p. 204) and adjusted for nonreturns.

from the United States, however, reduces this figure by *80 per cent*, to $350,000, after making allowance for the fact that the returnees are more highly trained than the emigrants. Friborg suggests that the $80 million per year found by Grubel-Scott for all scientific and engineering emigration to the United States may also be subject to a similar reduction to 20 per cent of its gross amount.

Obviously, what is required is a frequency distribution of the numbers of migrants returning homeward in each subsequent year. Bowman and Myers do set up a formal individual decision model for the decision to return, in which they think that the probability of return home will decline with the increase in the number of years absent.[20] This would mean that the distribution of returns by one year's group of emigrants would be heavily concentrated in the early years and would trail out with a large number never returning. There is, however, little evidence against which to test these hypotheses. We must be content—if a second-best can be achieved—to count the actual returners.

The importance of studies abroad by nonmigrant students requires further examination of the $12 million figure in Table 4. Parai obtained this estimate by multiplying 6,500, the "net" number of student-years abroad (the excess of foreign student-years in Canada over Canadian student-years abroad), by $1,800 each. This cost-saving to Canada is obviously understated. Allowance should also be made for the difference between the costs of graduate and undergraduate schooling, for maintenance costs while away, and for the degree of student self-support. In Table 5 the recalculation is shown. It assumes that students everywhere are divided in the same proportions between graduate work and undergraduate studies as they are in the United States; that 50 per cent of students are self-supporting; that maintenance cost rather than foregone earnings is the relevant concept for the calculation; that Canadians studying abroad are concentrated in the United States and the United Kingdom (i.e., not in France); and that 10 per cent of graduate students do not return.[21]

---

[20] Bowman and Myers, p. 893.

[21] The bulk of these calculations was made by Mr. L. Brown, and are merely summarized here. The chief problem was to get workable assumed proportions for students in graduate work and college. Parai assumes neither maintenance costs nor foregone earnings are relevant, saying that the latter, for the student abroad, are in effect "borne by Canada."

These student-exchange modifications nearly double Canada's gain from Parai's $12 million to $20 million. The most important adjustments are, of course, the inclusion of maintenance cost and the greater weight given to the higher education resource costs in graduate work. It is likely that most Canadians abroad are in graduate work, whereas many foreign students in Canada are undergraduates. If this is true, then the $20 million represents Canada's gain or "indebtedness" on student exchange. It is also likely that, with a large number of Canadians abroad doing graduate work in the United States, the assumed 50 per cent of self-supporting students is too high. If these likelihoods are correct, then the Canadian gain is about $22 million, or over $1 million per year, on student exchange alone.

On the whole brain-drain calculation, after making some allowance for returning Canadians and for student exchange, Parai's $467 million should be raised to at least $485 million, or an average of $44 million per year over the eleven-year period.[22]

2. *Present value of human-capital migrating.* The techniques of estimating the present value of the human capital embodied in migrants working, from expected future earnings, are already well examined in the M. J. Bowman and R. G. Myers article cited[23] and are best known in their employment by Weisbrod in his attempt to measure the gain and loss of human capital by Clayton County.[24] More recently, Rashi Fein has made a similar calculation for the American South,[25] and Myers himself has made interesting application of the technique to the decisions of Peruvian students in the United States about where to live permanently.[26]

As with the cost-saving approach, it is necessary to know the numbers of persons migrating and their schooling. Their age becomes particularly important, because the method attempts to measure the value of

[22] The returning-Canadian factor is credited above with only $10 million. If, as suggested in the text earlier, it is really underrated, and should be $100 million, then the total annual Canadian brain-drain *gain* on professionals and students would be over $50 million per year in 1961 prices.

[23] Bowman and Myers.

[24] Burton A. Weisbrod, *op. cit.*

[25] Rashi Fein, "Education Patterns in Southern Migration," *Southern Economic Journal,* 32, 1965–66, pp. 106–24.

[26] R. G. Myers, *op. cit.*

income in the remaining working years. Obviously one of the most important questions for any particular study is the decision whether to use expected future incomes in the country of destination or the country of origin. If the aim is to estimate the incentive to migrate (as in the Grubel-Scott formulation reproduced earlier), present values in both places may be used, and increasing degrees of disaggregation (by age, sex, and profession) will then be found to increase the understanding of migratory behavior.

However, the normative or policy usefulness of present-value estimates of migrating human capital is not clear. Rashi Fein, indeed, draws no conclusions from his briefly reported valuation of southern migrations.[27] Bowman and Myers appear to place most stress on the capacity of the technique to weigh accurately the differing age and skill compositions of a region's inflows and outflows, thus measuring migration's contribution (in comparison to schooling) to the formation of human capital. This role can be approximated by cost-saving measures; Wilkinson and Parai, for example, both make much of the fact that Canada's net gain from immigration is not merely in differences in the numbers of skilled or professional people coming and leaving, but in the fact that the immigrants on the average embody more schooling than the emigrants.[28] Bowman and Myers,[29] and Fein, therefore, can be regarded as taking this examination one step further by turning from relatively insensitive cost-of-years-of-schooling estimates to more finely detailed expected earnings of various skills and professions. With their approach, therefore, it is possible to test the "paradox" that an equal exchange of equally schooled persons could raise the value of the stock of human capital in *both* regions; with the years-of-schooling approach it is not possible to do this. But I am not convinced that this paradox is the kind of proposition that needs rigorous confirmation, except as propaganda to convince noneconomists that specialization, the division of labor, and mobility can be beneficial generally, not simply to the "net gainer" of educated persons.

---

[27] Fein, *op. cit.* See the reference to his measurements in Bowman and Myers, p. 879.

[28] Wilkinson, *op. cit.*, p. 69; Parai, *op. cit.*, p. 82.

[29] Bowman and Myers, *passim,* especially p. 880. These authors are also rightly concerned to include remigration and with on-the-job training. The effect of the latter, of course, is much more easily dealt with by present value, than by direct cost, estimates.

3. *The dead-weight, or consumers'-surplus loss from migration.* This approach, not strictly in the human-capital stream of migration studies, is more in the tradition of the cost-of-monopoly and cost-of-tariff studies associated with A. C. Harberger and H. G. Johnson.[30] It does not place a value on the gross amount of human capital migrating, but only on the "loss of welfare" from a nonmarginal emigration.

Consider a simple competitive economy in which the income of a certain skill is determined by supply and by the (derived) demand. Then migration, by reducing the supply of this skill, will: raise the average and marginal revenue product of this skill; raise its price; alter total income distribution in its favor, depending on the elasticity of demand for it; and leave a small dead-weight loss of product (consumers'-surplus) which does not accrue to the migrants, to the survivors, or other factors. It is this last concept which, in principle, may be measured.

The concept itself has been fully discussed by Grubel and Scott,[31] Berry and Soligo,[32] and by H. G. Johnson.[33] Only Mishan has attempted to measure it for the United Kingdom. (See footnote 38.) He is responding to the brief and disappointing Chapter IV of the 1967 *Brain Drain* report on "The Cost of the Brain Drain." (See source to Table 1.) Here the working group briefly reported on the cost of training professionals and scientists and the "loss of investment" when they migrate. However, "the true measure of loss to the community is indicated by the value that might be placed on the productive career of the individual concerned. . . . The significant point is that for every young high quality engineer who emigrates to the United States, the British economy in effect presents the American economy with a gift of the magnitude indicated in these figures." The figures are that the cost of training for engineers and Ph.D.'s, respectively, are £6,000 and £16,000, but the present values of the

---

[30] A. C. Harberger, "Using the Resources at Hand More Effectively," *American Economic Review*, 49, May, 1954, pp. 134–46; and H. G. Johnson, "The Economic Theory of Customs Union," *Pakistan Economic Journal*, 10, March, 1960, pp. 14–32.

[31] Herbert G. Grubel and Anthony D. Scott, "Theory of Migration and Human Capital," 1967, based on 1965 version (mimeo.).

[32] R. A. Berry and R. Soligo, "Some Welfare Aspects of International Migration," Yale Economic Growth Center Discussion Paper No. 8, July 7, 1966, (mimeo.).

[33] Harry G. Johnson, "Some Economic Aspects of the Brain Drain," *Pakistan Development Review*, 7, Autumn, 1967, pp. 379–411.

value placed on the careers by employers—i.e., salaries—are £ 30,000 and £ 78,000.[34]

In other words, the working group valued the British "gift" at the present value of future foreign income. (This position was heavily criticized by Johnson,[35] with particular reference to taxes and to externalities, by Grubel and Scott,[36] and later by other "internationalist" writers in W. Adams' *The Brain Drain*. (See footnote 2.) Bowman and Myers appear to accept this measure of loss, externalities aside.)[37]

Mishan, in a semipopular analysis, in effect rejects the gift as a measure of British loss and proposes the present value of the area under the demand curve not accruing to migrants nor survivors—the consumers' surplus. He makes a rough estimate of this sum, assuming a unitary elasticity of derived demand.[38]

4. *The loss of the flow of savings and of taxes.* For completeness it is necessary to report on two proposed rough measures of national loss from emigration. The first of these is the loss of future savings, investment, or capital, and the second is the loss of transfers of public goods and expenditures from scientists to other citizens.

Consider a growing economy depending on savings and capital inflows for future per capita income growth. Such an economy may well attach more importance to the size and timing of these flows than to the dead-weight loss of current output. The brain drain will be seen as an outflow of capital which may be regarded as a "regrettable necessity," either unpreventable or desirable for reasons irrelevant here. The drain, however, is capable of producing future capital benefits via emigrant remittances homeward. The statistical problem of the "cost" of the drain, therefore, is to estimate the difference between the flow of savings, if the emigrants had remained at home (their income minus their consumption

---

[34] *Ibid.*, p. 16. Footnotes suggest that some economic calculations had been made for the working group, but the whole discussion of "cost" is confined to one page.

[35] Harry G. Johnson, "The Economics of the 'Brain Drain': The Canadian Case," *Minerva*, 3, Spring, 1965, pp. 299–311.

[36] Grubel and Scott, "The International Flow of Human Capital," *American Economic Review*, Papers and Proceedings, 56, May, 1966, pp. 268–74.

[37] Bowman and Myers, pp. 892–93.

[38] E. J. Mishan, "The Brain Drain: Why Worry So Much?" *New Society*, 10, November 2, 1967, pp. 619–22.

and transfers) and the flow via remittances (the recipients' income minus their consumption and transfers). This has actually been attempted.[39] The underlying theory is also discussed by Charles Kindleberger.[40]

Indeed, many growth models[41] are, to the extent they are quantifiable, capable of measuring absolutely or comparatively the impact of an outflow of human capital on the growth path and the equilibrium growth rate.

Second, it would seem possible to undertake a study of the tax-and-transfer consequences of the brain drain for nonmigrants. Harry Johnson, in an attempt to discourage the use of the present value of future incomes as a measure of national loss, has been particularly emphatic in stressing this valid alternative.[42] What is required is a benefit-cost, or with-and-without-migration analysis of the tax and transfer mechanism within the economy. In static terms, the emigrant will pay certain taxes from his expected income and receive certain specific benefits (i.e., with positive marginal cost). The difference between these two expected flows is a measure of the loss or gain of the nonmigrating population. It is possible to make specific assumptions about whose taxes will increase and what benefits will be altered in the economy's post-migration adjustment; these will enable the benefit-cost analysis to determine which identifiable income groups, among the surviving population, will actually gain or lose.

In less static terms, the economist may be able to concentrate his attention on the impact of the migration on certain generations. To do

[39] Constantine Michalopoulos, "Labor Migration and Optimum Population," *Kyklos,* 21, 1968, Fasc. 1, pp. 130–46.

[40] Charles Kindleberger, "Emigration and Economic Growth," *Banca Nazionale del Lavoro Quarterly Review,* 18, September, 1965, pp. 235–54.

[41] See, for example, the models of H. Uzawa on economic growth with a labor force with embodied capital. Models with vintages of capital goods can shorten their assumed lives to allow for the emigration of a certain percentage of each vintage of educated people. The to-be-published paper by Berry and Soligo also has a section on a dynamic economy, using saving propensities. But it is difficult to see how it could be used to discuss future growth rates, since it is intended to elucidate the dead-weight approach above.

[42] H. G. Johnson, in Walter Adams (ed.), *The Brain Drain,* pp. 83–84, and his earlier contributions in *Minerva.* Johnson has, of course, also considered the general sources of loss: externalities and changes in factor proportions; see the appendix to his article in the *Pakistan Development Review.* Brinley Thomas' *Minerva* article makes much of this loss.

so, however, requires that he make assumptions about the adjustment in the tax-and-transfer mechanism to reduce or maintain the net payments to older people (and *their* adjustments in retiring later and working harder); and to reduce or maintain the flows of payments for the welfare and education of younger generations. It is difficult to know how to make such assumptions satisfactorily, yet, in the absence of the correct assumption, it is all too easy to bias such analyses to show that the burden is borne entirely by any of the three generations: old people, contemporaries, or children.[43]

So far, only two clear facts are known: that brain-drain migrants earn more than average taxpayers, and so presumably make a net fiscal contribution when they reside in a country with a progressive fiscal system; and that their removal carries both a tax source and an expenditure burden to a new fiscal economy.

POLICY QUESTIONS ABOUT MIGRATION

Behind the schemes for measuring the cost of migration lies the implicit aim of increasing and maximizing the Gross National Product, or the GNP per capita.[44] It is argued, for example, that a statement similar to the balance of payments or the national accounts would enable nations to adjust schooling, incomes, and migration policies so as to make the best of the brain drain.

The maximization of GNP, however, is not the only conceivable policy. Alternative aims may accompany or displace the more conventional income-per-head goal. Four such goals are briefly examined in this section. A review of the literature on marginal vs. large flow emigration,[45] and on long-run effects vs. short-run adjustment costs[46] is deemed unnec-

[43] An exchange between Thomas, Johnson and myself has already utilized our respective implicit assumptions on how society would react.

[44] Whether income-per-head, or income, is the best variable for maximization is discussed in Grubel and Scott, "The International Flow of Human Capital." See also Berry and Soligo, and Bowman and Myers.

[45] Grubel and Scott, "The Theory of Migration and Human Capital"; Berry and Soligo; and Johnson, "Some Economic Aspects of the Brain Drain," make the most of the marginal-vs.-large-scale-flow distinction, and the loss of GNP to the survivors of an emigration in the latter circumstances.

[46] See Grubel and Scott, "The International Flow of Human Capital"; Johnson, "Some Economic Aspects . . ."; and Berry and Soligo.

essary. The goals surveyed are: (1) the "export" of brains; (2) income redistribution; (3) achieving external effects; (4) aiding economic growth.

1. *The "export" of brains.* The human-capital approach automatically leads economists to compare the brain drain to capital movements, and to frame questions about preventing or assisting it in terms similar to those applied to the gold drain or to direct investment. Furthermore, some of the literature has demonstrated that (leaving externalities out of consideration) circumstances are conceivable in which a brain drain may even benefit the average surviving nonmigrant.

None of this literature has gone so far as to recommend that, in certain circumstances, a country selfishly gear up its educational and on-the-job training systems to *assist* the highly advantageous migration of young professionals. For example, some human-capital literature on the manpower programs of less developed countries compares rates of return in education with rates on physical-capital projects, but misses the opportunity to take account of the open nature of the manpower market, under which rates of return on "exported" schooling may be still higher than any domestic alternative. Conceivably the best course for some country might even be to educate all its people to take jobs elsewhere.

This raises the general question: the brain drain is desirable for the migrants' own "Scottish" reasons,[47] may a brain drain not also be a desirable social policy for a whole country, either to empty the place and

[47] "The noblest prospect which a Scotchman ever sees is the highroad that leads him to England." James Boswell, *Life of Samuel Johnson,* Chicago, Encyclopaedia Britannica, 1955.

Underdeveloped countries may also have a ruling élite which extracts a good schooling for its children from the treasury. This policy allows such children to migrate, or escape, if domestic political, social, or economic policies should suddenly become hostile. This point is not often mentioned, although Grubel and Scott, 1966, did stress that education is provided by the older generation for the benefit of their children, however it is used. Allied points are that the scramble of able intellectuals to get ahead of "the mob" of candidates for B. A. degrees in India does create an incentive to be trained and emigrate (Dandekar, p. 227); and that political unrest is often a reason for leaving—but education of one's children is an insurance policy for middle-class people in case of the inevitable unrest in many countries (Myint, p. 237). Both these discussions are in Adams, *The Brain Drain.* But neither these nor other writers seem to recognize that the brain drain may also be part of a planned export of talent.

allow everyone to do better abroad, or to set up as a profitable, steady exporter? It is difficult to find large scale examples of assisted brains-export policies, but the world is full of migrated specialists whose education must have been provided in contemplation of their probable emigration. Scottish engineers, Norwegian sea captains, and Viennese psychoanalysts, for example, all appear to be products of schools so large that their founders could never have believed that the home labor markets would absorb all the graduates.

Of course, the conditions under which an unrequited exodus of brains could benefit the per capita income of the survivors are already well laid out in the literature. Roughly, the emigrant must carry with him less capital (human or physical) than the per person endowment of the nation as a whole. This condition is fairly easy for unskilled emigrants to meet, but it is more difficult for the brain drain; by definition, professional people embody a good deal of capital. (A separate condition under which emigrants should expect to pay a larger net fiscal contribution than survivors also works against the desirability of the brain drain as opposed to unskilled emigration.)

Even if these general static conditions weigh against brain exports as a national policy, are there not conditions under which it may be desirable? It is not good enough to rule the drain out by *assumption,* as is done by Bowman and Myers[48] and by Berry and Soligo.[49] All these authors, following the logic of other parts of their models, assert that the social return on educational outlays becomes zero when the manpower in which it is embodied moves abroad. Thus they accept Leacock's identification of migration with death.[50] If we reject this assumption, are there circumstances under which export would pay off socially?

In the first place, it is by no means inevitable that such export of highly qualified persons be unrequited or uncompensated. The discussions of the value of migrants in this paper suggest at least that appropriate numbers could be found for a pricing process. A number of contributors to the *Brain Drain* volume and symposium speculated on the most promising international compensation scheme; a consensus would have favored payments from the receiving country to the losing country

---

[48] Bowman and Myers, p. 892.
[49] Berry and Soligo, p. 21.
[50] Stephen B. Leacock, *Sunshine Sketches of a Little Town,* London and New York, 1912, p. 239.

rather than from the emigrant to his homeland. Either of these flows of payment could, as with the network of small colleges in New England, justify an investment in teachers and facilities to export professionals for profit.

Second, even if a swollen drain of brains is uncompensated, it may bring benefits to the home economy. Chief among these are the benefits of scientific research and discovery, expedited in the foreign environment, that will spill back to producers and consumers in the home environment to a greater extent than if the emigrant scientists had attempted to work at home. Against these benefits should be set the losses of specific discoveries about methods and products which are unlikely to be undertaken, or undertaken successfully, in foreign environments. (For example, a medical benefit might best emanate from a western economy laboratory investigating drugs; but the dispersion abroad of medical scientists, who would be instrumental in discovering such drugs, might hinder research in public health techniques, in mass treatment of disease, in population control, and so on, since these activities depend on the scientists' presence in the society itself.)

Third, a redefinition of national advantage, rejecting the "emigrants have no national payoff" assumption of Berry, Soligo, Bowman, and Myers, may implement parents' willingness to pay for children's schooling and cause them to view with complaisance their children's leaving home to prosper in the best environment available, whether overseas or in their own country. While it is difficult for economists to calculate the domestic gain from such a flow abroad, which betters not only the emigrant generation but also its descendants, with no gesture of thanks or spillover of benefit toward the old country, it is clear that many parents' behavior does require economists' agreement that some national, social benefit does exist. If educational investment is to be public, then it behooves economists to find ways in which to measure this gratification in the overseas success of children, not to deny that the gratification offsets whatever costs the drain may also produce.

This is not the place to argue these three points fully. However, they should be sufficient to indicate that, quite apart from the impact on survivors now deprived of the complementary inputs from some scientists and engineers, it is possible to conceive of circumstances in which the survivors might encourage the export of brains.

2. *Income redistribution.* Each nation has a distribution of incomes brought about by the pricing of its inputs and outputs, and most nations have government policies which alter this distribution. The redistributive policies mostly involve tax rates, transfers, and incomes in kind which differ from person to person. However, each nation can also utilize the earnings structure of organizations and corporations directly controlled by the government, and, less effectively, it can invoke government controls on wages and conditions of work.

In connection with the brain drain, for example, the government can influence the incomes paid to scientists and engineers by either of two approaches on distinct levels: It may utilize such broad policy measures as the imposing of income tax rates and exemptions, the fixing of the average burden of total taxation for real and welfare purposes, and the provision of free or cheap government services such as hospital services; or it may adopt special policies such as the manipulation of the level of incomes in universities, laboratories, and the civil service, and the level of incomes paid by private employers to scientists and engineers. As discussed in an earlier section, both approaches may have important effects on professionals' decisions to remain or leave; a social resolve to remove the incentive to migrate might therefore well begin by making sure that the incomes of potential migrants were favorably treated by these income redistribution mechanisms.

General redistributive policies involving some degree of progression in the total fiscal burden on successive income groups are usually not aimed at professionals and scientists but at "rentiers," those receiving "unearned incomes" or "surpluses." However, it is difficult to distinguish those inheriting intelligence from those inheriting real estate; both have had schooling and both may have similar occupations. Hence, it would be unusual to exempt scientists and professionals from the higher levels of taxation levied on entrepreneurs and capitalists of similar incomes; indeed, collection may be stricter and avoidance more difficult on their institutional incomes.

It follows that the more keenly the nation adheres to general redistribution policies of an egalitarian nature, the more probable is the migration of its scientists and engineers, given the net income alternatives abroad.

Special income policies may work either way. Dandekar, in an interesting survey of India's brain drain, blames the carryover of a British policy of paying scientists, civil servants, and professors at European rather than Indian levels. This policy, he says, now attracts "mobs" of students to courses preparatory for these occupations and so eventually creates an excess supply of better men seeking jobs abroad.[51] In a less extreme fashion, the European custom of appointing one highly paid professor in each field at each university may well attract more students and low-rank faculty than can be absorbed. This discriminatory policy of favoring a few incumbents is bound to create a stock of young or unsuccessful aspirants available for employment abroad.

Special income policies may also work against all members of a profession and may, therefore, be even more potent as a brain-drain stimulant. Harry Johnson, in particular, has pointed out that, although two professions may yield the same rate of return on costs paid by the student (fees and employment foregone), and hence be equally attractive, special income policies may ordain that the first should have high fees and high lifetime incomes, while the second has cheap (subsidized) schooling balanced by low lifetime salaries. In a closed economy, such an income policy may succeed in allocating acceptable flows of students to both occupations; but the low lifetime incomes of the second profession may, in an open economy, drive professionals to migrate to the higher levels abroad.[52]

Since it is natural for an economist to suppose that migration is motivated by income differences, it is not surprising that general or specific policies which alter these differences, whatever their rationale for redistribution, should be viewed as conflicting with mobility policy and on the whole contributing to the brain drain rather than reducing it.[53] Such reasoning, however, should not be allowed to obscure the income differences which are simply the result of over-all national poverty. For

---

[51] V. M. Dandekar, "India," in Walter Adams (ed.), *The Brain Drain,* pp. 203–32.

[52] Johnson, "Some Economic Aspects. . . ." Johnson takes as his example the low fees, low incomes, and high rates of migration of British doctors.

[53] For example, in my own work on federal finance, without challenge, I assumed that regional income redistribution reduced interregional movement by those people who, by education and wealth, were the least mobile anyway. If such people are assumed to have less-than-average incomes, then such policies will increase the mobility of more-than-average-income persons. See "The Goals of Federal Finance," *Public Finance,* Vol. 19, No. 3, 1964, pp. 241–88.

example, it is quite likely that some poor agricultural countries have much the same income *structure* as wealthier countries. If migration were opened up by a relaxation of border restrictions, the same percentage differences would exist between occupations at all levels of each nation's income structure, presumably raising the likelihood of migration per thousand, more for the poor than for the rich.[54] All experience suggests, however, that upper-income, professional, academic, and skilled people will actually move more readily than low-income, low-skill people. The point of the example is simply that a brain drain may exist in the absence of any income redistribution policy in either country.

3. *Achieving external effects.* Most concern over the brain drain stems from worry about the loss (or nonrepayment) of the cost of the education embodied in the migrants, and about the effect on the general welfare of the survivors. The former is the subject of the schemes of measurement suggested in the previous section of this paper. The latter may be the "dead-weight" loss of consumers' surplus, but this is a technical, economists' concept not even intuitively obvious to laymen. The remaining explanation of the latter is that men with brains (professionals, scientists) are different in kind from other men, not just in degree. Like public goods in the theory of public expenditure, it is their nature either to exhibit powers of invention, leadership, and organization which are not diminished by their employment or application, or, more modestly, simply to produce uncompensated services (externalities).

The literature on the brain drain has analyzed pretty thoroughly the possible external diseconomies of a man's departure for economic reasons. All of them depend on his having been expected to render public services in excess of his expected income. Such externalities can be grouped into three classes. First, the economies of scale from his membership in a research team, a medical group, or small profession whose output varies in greater proportion than the change in its membership. Second, spillovers from his practice of a particular profession, such as public health medicine, agricultural engineering, or acting as judge or policeman. However, such spillover benefits are resumed as soon as he

---

[54] If marginal utility diminishes, a given percentage increase in income will be more important to poor than to rich people.

is replaced, in contrast to the third class—social benefits spilling over from the personal capacity of a particular professional or scientist of such quality that they will not be replaced by his routine replacement. This class is important, but is it likely to be significant? Why should the emigrants be more socially fertile than their replacements? The case seems to require a decline in quality from one generation to the next.

Full comments on these three cases are unnecessary in view of their discussion in the literature. Note that in all of them these external losses differ from and add to losses of consumers' surplus, taxable capacity, or embodied capital, and that the wholesale departure of many educated people may, in addition, lower the whole national average level of political, cultural, and social aspiration, discussion, adjustability, and progressiveness.

How seriously they are to be rated depends on one's point of view. A "cosmopolitan" will argue that each of them is likely to be balanced by an equal gain in the country of destination,[55] while a "nationalist" will be sensitive only to his own country's status in a science or art. Furthermore, a cosmopolitan will point out the increased extent to which a nation can be helped by its former scientists and innovators working in the more productive environment of the richer nations, relying on the international transmission of ideas[56] to send the techniques back home, while a nationalist will insist upon the extent to which less developed countries require local research and practice in domestic agricultural, industrial, medical, social, and cultural problems. Finally, a cosmopolitan will point to the gains in better or cheaper imports and from the flow of advisers and experts, while a nationalist will maintain that economic development cannot flow from improved imports but only from improved production, and that the technical assistance of uncommitted visiting experts is of value only for specific projects such as dams and canals.

The entire externalities-of-emigration literature is useful in raising questions about educational "requirements" now being studied in the educational planning of less developed countries. Otherwise, its value lies chiefly in suggesting categories for the analysis of the contribution of education to economic growth.

---

[55] Johnson, in "Some Economic Aspects . . .," investigates the extent to which the losses and gains will balance each other.

[56] Johnson, "The Economics of the 'Brain Drain': The Canadian Case."

4. *Aiding economic growth.* Each nation, in addition to maximizing, by allocation and combination, the amount of national output per head, seeks to grow—especially when suffering from the brain drain. A nation's concern about the emigration of highly qualified people, therefore, may not be a reflection of its static losses of consumption or of capital, but a manifestation of its belief in a slowing down of its development.

That the outflow of human capital could cause a slowing down of economic growth is not in doubt. On the one hand, statistical analyses of national growth rates have been forced to attribute part of economic growth to the "residual factor," which is presumed to be knowledge, or education. On the other hand, it is plausible to construct neoclassical growth models in which investment in human capital, at the same rate of return as investment in capital goods, produces an equilibrium growth rate which is a function of the common rate of return. At the most basic level of theory, expanding population requires more capital, even to stand still. A brain drain, by definition, spills more capital than people. All this is commonplace in growth theory and development economics.

What is less investigated is the cause. To what extent is the presence of a group of scientists and engineers a cause of growth, as opposed to being either a precondition, or a consequence, of growth? Professionals organize, adjust, apply, and innovate. Both to reach the production-possibilities frontier and to advance it require sophisticated and trained personnel. Does the drift of such personnel toward richer countries actually prevent this optimizing and shifting? Or does the drift merely symbolize a failure of energy and will in the economy, so that the trained personnel, as a group, lose interest and incentive?

We must leave this question to developmental specialists, with two observations. First, it is possible that the emigration and scarcity of professionals trained to deal with the *specific* technical problems of a country —its soils, insects, diseases, climate, and so forth—may actually slow down a growing country's growth rate. A drain of potential local experts, in other words, may create a series of bottlenecks which will impede progress for generations. Health questions apart, however, it is difficult to think of convincing illustrations.

Second, the most serious source of some countries' brain drain is the leakage of students who train abroad. If the students did not go abroad, the country would gain no specialists at all, and growth would presumably fail. Hence, unless all training is to be undertaken at home, growth is impossible without some seepage abroad from the training program.

However, it has not yet been proved that economic growth requires *any* technical experts from the growing country. A nation determined to grow, putting more weight on growth than on having its own corps of experts, professionals, and scientists, and having the will to work and save, can import engineers and scientists, either as immigrants or as short-term consultants, in unlimited numbers. What it then may lack are middle-level technologists, nurses, midwives, high school teachers, civil servants, and entrepreneurs; but these are not the raw materials of the brain drain. Preventing the brain drain, and encouraging economic growth, are not the same policy.

IS THERE A BRAIN-DRAIN POLICY QUESTION DEPENDING ON HUMAN CAPITAL MEASUREMENTS?

IN these concluding paragraphs, I turn to the justification of some recent research in which, along with Herbert Grubel, Burton Weisbrod, Rashi Fein, Robert Myers, and Mary Jean Bowman, I have been involved. My general point is that the values obtained have little or no value for justifying policy about migration of highly qualified persons.

Elsewhere, Grubel and I have argued that what *should* be important to a nation is the maximization of income per capita, either of all members of the society, or of those remaining after emigration of a few. Originally, we meant merely to assert this aim against those who would claim that, regardless of population, "bigger GNP is better" in a nation's policy. We were surprised to find that some contemporaries do not agree with us, especially those who attempt some kind of decision-making calculus using as a measure of benefits the total of private incomes (for simplicity we assume there are no spillovers). Although they sometimes make little use of it, this assumption is found in the work of Weisbrod, Bowman and Myers, Holtmann, and Berry and Soligo.

In any case, an income, or income per capita, maximization is assumed to be the chief policy aim in the brain-drain literature. My brief references to policy in the earlier parts of this paper have implied a belief that most countries and most authors accept this aim.

Now, what is gained by measuring the value of the human capital in migration? When one realizes that human-capital evaluations require full information about training, age, and other factors, it is obvious that policy-makers must already be aware of the flows involved. Little that is new can come out of the total or its parts.

For example, consider the theoretical studies referred to earlier. They conclude that the remaining population gains or loses by emigration depending on whether each emigrant has more or less human capital embodied in him than the capital (of all types) per head in the national endowment. A paper by Grubel and Scott has actually attempted some rough measurement to determine whether the United States gains or loses by immigration. But to what purpose? No one has argued that U. S. immigration policy should be such as to admit only migrants who have more than the average existing capital per head; and an abstract argument about the aims of migration policy, were it to be staged, would not be clarified by such measurement. Nor does any country's schooling or emigration policy now turn on the capital-embodied characteristic of the emigrants.

In another example, I have myself measured the balance of indebtedness in the exchange of academic economists between the United States and Canada, in an attempt to discover which country has made the greatest gift of human capital to the other in rearing costs, schooling, and foregone output. (A similar calculation could be made in terms of expected future income.) The results show that Canada owes more to the United States than the United States to Canada—an interesting and, to most brain-drain conscious Canadians, unexpected result. However, this fact has no importance; Canada will train more or fewer of its own economists for reasons other than to try to correct this imbalance. And so it goes. When the primary aim is the simple one of maximizing income per head, the net value of moving human capital is not a useful guide.

If one now considers other aims, such as achieving a favorable distribution of income before or after a migration, or avoiding undesired external effects, one comes to the same conclusion about the calculation of the amount of migrating human capital: it simply is not important.

(And nobody has yet advanced the hypothesis that the value of migrating human capital would be a better dependent variable than the number of migrants to be explained in an econometric study.)

In short, I believe that human-capital migration valuations have only two useful purposes, and these are not very urgent.

First and less important, countries which have a guilty conscience about the numbers of trained men they are receiving as "gifts" or as "loot" from poorer countries may be better able to persuade themselves to aid the sending nations if they can value the human capital in the brain drain than if they cannot. This statement is hardly open to argument— it is merely a hypothesis about what voters and statesmen find persuasive or compelling. Thus, Grubel and others have been publicizing the value of human capital embodied in foreign students who decide not to return home. It has been found that such estimates help to bring the loss of the sending countries into some kind of perspective, although this perspective must surely be inappropriate for policy formation.

Second and more important, countries which receive highly qualified emigrants from other countries may be inclined to enter into negotiations to compensate the senders for their gift or loss. The bargainers will certainly look for some standard estimates which can be easily understood and verified; the cost-of-human-capital figures meet these requirements. Thus, the sending country might argue that the capital embodied in the migrants is an estimate of the amount of capital which might have been used for other purposes and therefore is at least a rough indicator of the present value of future incomes it lost (forgetting that most of it would have been consumed by the emigrant and his children). Or the sending country might take a more grimly commercial view and offer to "export" brains and skills at average cost. Finally, on some theoretical model or other of economic growth, or of economies of scale, the sending country might argue that the absence of the embodied capital has delayed or prevented the growth of the incomes of the remaining population by a certain fraction of the estimate of the gift.

No one can deny that hard figures, available to both sides, or in an international clearinghouse, would expedite and simplify such negotiations and might also help countries of origin, not only to agree to, but also to encourage further migration. But is there any reason why the compensation *should* be made at these valuations? If we assume that the bargaining is bilateral, and both parties agree that migration is not to be obstructed whatever the outcome of the bargaining, there is no reason why the gaining country should ever pay the full value of the embodied capital, or *any* particular fraction of it. If we assume instead that the losing country threatens to stop the migratory flow unless it is compensated, it may well be willing to accept something less than the full value of the embodied human capital, for this full value is much more than the remaining citizens (in the absence of spillovers) would expect to receive from the emigrant if he stayed at home. On the other side, the gaining country in the long run may be willing to pay whatever is needed to get "brains" cheaper than by rearing and training them itself (and in the short run to pay even more than this). Thus, the full value of embodied capital might well be the upper limit of the range within which the bargain will be struck. Only if the losing country regards itself as an "exporter" of human capital would its similar estimate (at its own prices and costs) also form the lower limit.

If the bargaining is multilateral, the different aims or problems of each country cannot easily be handled through a single clearinghouse for international human-capital compensation, and it is not very profitable to speculate on how the nations might resolve to value the flows and crossflows. Practice in a few international treaties on other subjects, however, does suggest the diplomatic attractiveness of valuations "at cost." Here again, then, one might see sums exchanged, and even see schooling and migration policies adjusted on the basis of the message of the values of human capital migrating.

These export or compensation schemes are remote and fanciful possibilities. Any other benefit-cost calculation about educational expansion or migration policy will not, in my opinion, involve human-capital valuations.

COMMENTS

A. G. HOLTMANN
FLORIDA STATE UNIVERSITY

Anthony Scott has done an exceptional job of synthesizing the elements of the human-capital approach to international migration, and, in most cases, I will merely add emphasis to points made, but not thoroughly discussed. First, with respect to the question of the determinants of the decision to migrate and the question of a subsequent return home, we may gain some insight by investigating the intentions of migrants. This technique has already been adopted by demographers to predict future population growth, and it might be a useful tool in estimating permanent migration. In one such study concerning intentions of Canadian students in the United States, it was found that approximately 30 per cent of the sample planned to remain in the United States after they completed their studies.[1] In this study by Ronald Pavalko, the reasons given for planning to remain in the United States were mainly associated with better job opportunities, as in the studies cited by Scott. Of course, plans may change, and there is the question of what influences a person's plans. Pavalko finds that the length of time the student is in the United States is related to his plans to remain. For all male students, 20 per cent of those who were in the United States less than one year plan to remain after their schooling, but over 50 per cent of those who were in the United States four or more years plan to remain after their schooling. When students are classified as graduate students and undergraduate students, there is still a strong relationship between length of time spent in the United States and plans to remain in the United States.

These findings seem to support the general type of model set up by Bowman and Myers which suggests that the probability of returning home decreases with the number of years spent away from home. In any case, more detailed studies of migrants' attitudes would help in reducing the

---

[1] Ronald Pavalko, "Talent Migration: American Students in the United States," *International Review of Education*, No. 3, 1968, pp. 300–24.

Figure 1. "Dead-Weight" Loss Resulting From Migration of Factor of Production.

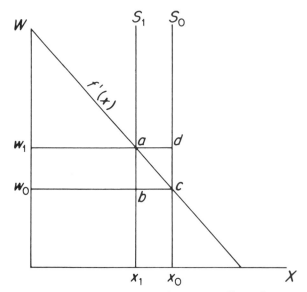

NOTE: Loss is triangle abc described by (1) linear decreasing marginal physical product function $f'(x)$; (2) shift in supply of factor x from S_0 to S_1, x_0–x_1; and (3) factor payment w_0–w_1, equal to marginal product.

statistical overestimation of permanent migration, and would offer more evidence on the determinants of the decision to migrate.

The environmental factor influencing migration, mentioned by Scott, might be approached by considering the studies of intranational migration. For example, a study of new migrants to the Cape Kennedy area showed that health and climate considerations were most important after those factors associated with jobs were considered. However, better schools were given a very low rating.[2] One can, of course, suggest a whole host of reasons for these results, but my purpose is not to explore the study in detail. It is interesting to note that the findings might suggest that there is little in the controlled environment that influences

[2] Charles M. Grigg, *et al., NASA Impact on Brevard County*, Tallahassee, Institute for Social Research, 1966, pp. 106–09.

migration after job opportunities have been considered. But the important point is that economists might more often consider available attitude studies in developing and testing their models concerning migration.

I should now like to turn to Scott's discussion of the theory of migration and human capital. In this discussion, and in several of the studies cited, a good deal of attention has been given to the "dead-weight loss" associated with the migration of a factor of production. Figure 1 depicts this loss assuming: two factors of production; a shift in the supply of the factor, X from S_0 to S_1; a linear decreasing marginal physical product function, $f'(x)$; and a factor payment, W, equal to the marginal product. Then, the well known dead-weight loss is the triangle abc. Others have shown that diminishing returns and a nonmarginal change in supply assures the loss. My purpose is not to debate the importance of the dead-weight loss in any absolute sense, but to show that a small weight given to the income distribution effect of migration may make the dead-weight loss relatively unimportant.

In Figure 1, the income distribution of the nonmigrating owners of factor X has been increased by $X_1 \Delta W$, and this has come at the expense of the other factor of production. Now economists are not able to determine the proper income distribution, but a country may be concerned with this shift in the income distribution from one factor to another. If we consider the ratio of the dead-weight loss to the income distribution effect, we see that the ratio is rather small, except when the marginal product function is rather elastic. Writing the dead-weight loss as $1/2 \Delta W \Delta X$ and substituting e for the elasticity, we have the ratio of the dead-weight loss to the income distribution effect, $1/2 (\Delta W / W_1) e$. Therefore, except when e is large, the ratio is rather small. At least in some cases, then, the importance of the dead-weight loss will be swamped by the importance of the income distribution considerations. In general, this point has been ignored in the international migration literature, even though it has been considered in the general economic literature.[3]

Considering Figure 1 again, there is another point worth noting. If we take the marginal product before migration as the loss associated with a migrant, we underestimate the total loss by abc, but if we take the

---

[3] See: O. E. Williamson, "Economies as an Antitrust Defense," *American Economic Review*, March 1968, p. 28.

marginal product after migration as the loss associated with a migrant, we will overestimate the total loss by *adc*. While it is the underestimate that has been stressed in the literature, we may have little knowledge about the direction of the bias in our empirical estimates of the loss. Of course, either bias disappears in the limit. All of this also neglects the question of the divergence between earnings and the marginal product of a factor.

While my previous points may go beyond Scott's remarks to some extent, they are in no way in conflict with his position as I see it. However, I believe his position on the nature of external effects is somewhat different from mine. Scott seems to feel that if the external effects generated by an emigrating professional can be replaced by training another professional, there is no further problem. There may or may not be a loss to the home country when external effects are involved, but it has nothing to do with simply retraining another man. In fact, the country may refuse to train another professional.

Assume that the country increases the subsidy to a given profession until the subsidy to the last man is just equal to the marginal external benefit that he confers on the country. Then in equilibrium we have

$$K_0 = \sum_{t=1}^{n} \frac{EB^t}{(1 + r)^t}$$

where K_0 is the subsidy given in the initial period; EB^t is the marginal external benefit conferred on the country in all future periods t; and r is the discount rate. If the individual migrates immediately after the initial period, the loss to the country is K_0. Migration, in this case, may be motivated by rewards offered by other countries to capture the external effects. Then, the home country will continue to lose subsidized individuals. However, if all countries offer rewards to attract foreign professionals, this will be part of the price that all countries must pay for a professional. In this case, individuals may be willing to pay for their own training, and countries merely buy professionals at the "market price."

The loss to the country may only be a short-run problem. As a country starts to find its trained men lured away, it will discontinue the subsidy. This, however, assumes that the problem is just one of misjudging the market mechanism at work. In fact, the problem may be political.

Through the ballot, one group may force a subsidy for their training and, then, leave the country to maximize the private return to the profession. The nonprofessionals in the home country will continue to sustain losses in the latter case. Scott's example of free training of British physicians fits either case. Nonetheless, it becomes clear that there is more than a replacement problem.

Lastly, I would like to consider Scott's prognostication about the usefulness of measures of human capital as an aid to policy concerning the brain drain. At the outset, I should indicate that having a capital-value measure of a migrant would eliminate some of the problems in measuring the brain drain that he discussed in his paper. For example, he states that children, no matter how intelligent, will not be counted as part of the brain drain. But, of course, they should be counted as some sort of drain if they embody certain capital investments in either themselves or their parents. Weisbrod has made a convincing case, in my opinion, for considering the human-capital element in migration. He has shown that the per capita capital value of a population may be a better guide to its welfare status than a per capita income measure.[4]

In my judgment, the emphasis at the conclusion of Scott's paper was too greatly influenced by the brain drain or manpower approach to international migration. If one considers the amount of human capital that a migrant represents, and not just the particular occupational label that we attach to the individual, we may see that the measurement of human capital is crucial. Such an approach will move us into questions concerning capital theory, aggregate production functions, and economic growth. Much of this, however, may not take us far from the question of externalities. It is my guess that investments in human capital raise the marginal product of all the factors of production. In this case, a decision to migrate based on the private return to human capital may not be optimal for society. Here, I rely on the type of theory of the production function, of the modifier, and of income distribution developed by Frankel.[5] Simply stated, the private return to human capital or physical capital is low because part of this return goes to labor as a sort of auto-

[4] Burton A. Weisbrod, "An Expected Income Measure of Economic Welfare," *Journal of Political Economy,* August 1962, pp. 355–67.

[5] Marvin Frankel, "The Production Function: Allocation and Growth," *American Economic Review,* December 1962, pp. 995–1022.

matic transfer payment. Without trying to develop any analytical framework here, I suggest the aggregate production function analysis of Solow, Frankel, Griliches, Nelson and Phelps, and others, will more and more introduce concepts of human capital to explain growth in output. Measures of the stock of human capital will be needed to test the theory, and the loss of human capital through migration may be found to be critical in determining the economic growth of a country. In fairness to Scott, I feel he is discussing the limited use of human-capital measures in present policy decisions, but this should not be generalized to future policy decisions as if economic theory will have no influence.

LARRY A. SJAASTAD
UNIVERSITY OF CHICAGO

Anthony Scott's style in his brain-drain paper is reminiscent of Lyndon Johnson's March 31 speech. Nothing in the previous fifty-one pages prepares one for the sudden conclusion that prior research on the brain-drain issue has "little or no value for justifying policy about migration of highly qualified persons." I believe that this conclusion has a great deal of merit; much of the manipulation of statistics found in the brain-drain literature has little relevance for policy, nor do the policy recommendations of Walter Adams, *et al.*, seem to be based upon hard estimates of costs and benefits. I further believe that this state of affairs derives from an overemphasis on the construction of estimates of population and human capital flows and a neglect of the identification of the real economic issues and end use for the figures by the manipulators of statistics. The issues have been laid out rather clearly by Harry Johnson and others, and Professor Scott certainly does draw attention to them, although I wish he had added some elaboration. It is in this direction that I cast this brief comment.

In the first place, data on the numbers of warm bodies and the amount of human capital involved in the international migration of professionals are largely irrelevant until one has some measure of their significance. Is a flow from Britain to the United States of one million dollars of human capital per annum small, and one of 100 million large?

I don't see how one can judge until some estimate of the true transfer is made.

There are, I believe, only two economically interesting measures of the effect of the brain drain. The first is the (largely irrelevant) direct transfer and the second involves externalities. When the state causes the private costs of acquiring an advanced degree to be less than the social costs, the ultimate effect is that earnings of persons holding those degrees will be lower than they would be if the private costs equalled the social. To the extent that social costs and the discrepancy between private and social costs of training differ among countries, incentives are set up for immigration. If, as appears to be the case, the private and social costs of training are both lower in poorer countries (due to lower alternative costs) and if, as also appears to be the case, the poorer countries indulge themselves in larger (relative) subsidies to the training of professionals than do the richer countries, one has a situation in which the poorer countries have a comparative advantage in (at least partial) training of professionals—this effect being reinforced by very high rates of public subsidization of that training—and the richer countries offer the more lucrative markets for the finished product. The resultant population flows stemming from these incentives cause alarm when they reach the high levels claimed to have accompanied the United States' great scientific leap forward since Sputnik. The alarm would appear to be a result of certain people collecting rents that the bureaucrats had not anticipated. Governments that lament the outflow of trained professionals and simultaneously ensure that an ample supply (via free education) be available at "fair" or even fixed prices require instruction to be sure, but that instruction does not require the benefit of brain-drain research. I believe that this is part of the message of Scott's last five pages.

The direct transfer, then, is not between nations, as a superficial reading of much of the brain-drain literature would lead one to believe, but rather it is a transfer from one subgroup of individuals of one nation to another subgroup of that same nation. Although public education imposes upon us the collective burden of paying for the education of our children, it does not require us to repay the costs of our own training, hence the transfer. (As this transfer is usually made quite willingly, it strains the language somewhat to refer to it as a burden.) The transfer calls forth complaints only when the beneficiaries seek out—at home or abroad—higher rates of remuneration. In the case of immigration, which usually involves partial or total shift of political allegiance from one state to another, the transfer becomes a burden in the sense that it would not be freely made if they had it to do over again. But in any case, the transfer remains between individuals rather than between nations (except in some accounting sense). That is, the fact that British taxpayers have financed the education of a Manhattan physician need not directly enhance the welfare of the United States taxpayer. Hence a measure of the brain drain made in terms of training costs is relevant as an estimate of the transfer from taxpayers to students and does reflect to some extent an international capital flow, but does *not* reflect an international *income* flow in any economically relevant sense. A recent reading of the Preface and Foreword to Adam's *Brain Drain* moves me to state this banality.

We are left then with the externality, or rather the two externalities. First, a brain drain of any importance will presumably have as one consequence some internal redistribution of income via changes in factor prices in both the sending and the receiving countries. We know virtually nothing of the nature and magnitude of this redistribution, but perhaps we can learn something by a production-function approach of the Griliches type. This internal redistribution, however, has little to do with the glamor of the brain drain, as the sex appeal of the latter lies largely in the alleged international redistribution of income (and wealth) it promotes. The second and more interesting externality is the effect on per capita output of the changing factor proportions—the familiar triangle economics. Here we have for the first time some real possibility of international transfers of income, as a brain-drain induced decline in per capita income of nonimmigrants of the one country will tend to be matched by an induced increase in the per capita income of nonemigrants of the other. Here again our ignorance is impressive, as we have as yet neither the tools nor the numbers to make a good estimate (except possibly for the work of Mishan, which I have not seen).

In summary, I concur with Professor Scott's conclusion that brain-drain research to date has turned up little of significance, particularly for policy, but I am less pessimistic than he seems to be concerning the usefulness of potential research in this area. Estimation of the extent and magnitude of brain-drain induced international income transfers of the type mentioned in the immediately preceding paragraph would be an interesting research undertaking, one which could be carried out independently of the nationalist-internationalist controversy, which I find to be both stale and distracting from the relevant issues. Such research will probably come as little comfort to those who emphasize the strategic importance of professionals in the growth process; my only comment in this connection is that one spin-off of the brain-drain event has been a wider recognition of the international character of the market for professionals. If professionals are indeed important to growth, then there is little to prevent the country in need from meeting its requirements in that market.

CONFERENCE OVERVIEW

THE RECKONING OF EDUCATION
AS HUMAN CAPITAL • T. W. SCHULTZ •
THE UNIVERSITY OF CHICAGO

The mainstream of the analytical work on human capital pertains to the economic properties of education. My reflections on this and related work are threefold. I shall begin with a comment on the advances in economic knowledge from this work coupled with some observations on its apparent shortcomings; I shall, then, consider briefly aspects of the aggregation problem in the treatment of human capital, whatever its source, in analyzing costs and returns, economic growth, migration, educated labor in a production function, and of human capital in explaining the personal distribution of income. Thirdly, I shall direct attention to some major omissions.

AS ECONOMIC KNOWLEDGE

THE advances are mainly a joint product of theoretical and empirical analysis. Those that stem from theoretical analysis are predominantly the work of Gary S. Becker. Beginning in the area of investment in human capital, Becker distinguished between specific and general human-capital forms. Next he recognized the importance of earnings foregone in an array of economic activities and developed a theory for the allocation of time to cope with such earnings, and recently, he rediscovered the production activities of the household,[1] for example, in the formation of a substantial part of human capital.

---

[1] See Margaret G. Reid, *Economics of Household Production,* New York, 1934.

Clearly, in economic thinking and measuring, the concept of human capital is a source of many new analytical insights with respect to particular classes of economic behavior. Seminal economic properties are being attributed to human capital. Mark Blaug in his *Economics of Education*,[2] reviews the progress in this area[3] and then presents the major papers that have been published. His annotated bibliography lists literally several hundred contributions.[4] In determining the role of human capital in the comparative advantage of nations, we turn to Kenen.[5] Human capital has received even more attention in analyzing international migration as is clear from the survey by Scott.[6] The findings of Krueger,[7] in her pioneering paper on factor endowments and per capita income, attributes an important new dimension to human capital. Her conclusion is "that the difference in human resources between the United States and the less-developed countries accounts for more of the difference in *per capita* income than all of the other factors combined."[8] While we await confirmation of her findings, it behooves us to begin thinking through the radical economic implications of her conclusions for economic development. In explaining the personal distribution of income, first Mincer,[9] and more recently, Becker[10] and Chiswick[11] have turned to human capital. Advances in economic knowledge pertaining to internal migration keyed to education and to costs of migrating as a form of human capital are

[2] M. Blaug, editor, *Economics of Education,* Baltimore, Maryland, 1968.

[3] *Ibid.,* "Introduction," pp. 7–9.

[4] M. Blaug, *Economics of Education: A Selected Annotated Bibliography,* Oxford and New York, 1966. Also, see, more recent mimeographed supplements by Blaug, bringing this bibliography up to date.

[5] See paper by Peter B. Kenen in this volume.

[6] See paper by Anthony Scott in this volume.

[7] A. O. Krueger, "Factor Endowments and *Per Capita* Income Differences Among Countries," *The Economic Journal,* 78, September 1968, 641–59.

[8] *Ibid.,* p. 658.

[9] Jacob Mincer, "Investment in Human Capital and Personal Income Distribution," *Journal of Political Economy,* 66, August 1958, 281–302.

[10] Gary S. Becker, *Human Capital and the Personal Distribution of Income,* W. S. Woytinsky Lecture No. 1, Department of Economics, Institute of Public Administration, University of Michigan, 1967.

[11] Barry R. Chiswick, "Human Capital and the Distribution of Personal Income," unpublished doctoral dissertation, Department of Economics, Columbia University, 1967.

also impressive (Sjaastad,[12] Bowman and Myers,[13] Schwartz,[14] and others). Needless to say, there are also other classes of economic behavior and approaches that stem from human capital.

But when we turn to the other side of the coin of these discoveries, there are growing pains, omissions, and a generation gap between those who espouse human capital and those who guard the establishment. Although the guardians of capital theory and economic growth theory may be defending a weak fort, the walls have not come tumbling down.

The beauty of accounting and discounting is that we can take the cost of education or we can transform the earnings from education and call it human capital. But this acquired beauty only conceals the difference between them where there is economic growth. Then, too, the fine art of capital aggregation hides the key to the economic information that makes for economic growth. The aggregation of human capital from education is no exception. As an input, it is well behaved in a production function and it contributes to the output, thus adding to our confidence that educated labor matters in production. But it does not tell us whether all or only a part of this education is worthwhile. Studies of international migration have not been designed to determine whether a well behaved international market for particular high skills is emerging. The going prices for high skills are not made explicit. Nor has the introduction of human capital in analyzing international trade revealed the effects that trade has upon the prices of high skills. Then, too, we consider only a part of education and find it convenient to neglect other parts, notably the large investment in the education of women. By concentrating on education, we are in danger of losing sight of other sources of human capital and, not seeing their contributions, credit some of them to education.

[12] Larry A. Sjaastad, "Income and Migration in the United States," unpublished doctoral dissertation, Department of Economics, The University of Chicago, 1961. Also, "The Costs and Returns of Human Migration," *Journal of Political Economy,* October 1962, Supplement, 70, No. 5, part 2, 80–93.

[13] Mary J. Bowman and Robert Myers, "Schooling Experience and Gain and Losses in Human Capital Through Migration," *Journal of the American Statistical Association,* 62, September 1967, 875–98.

[14] Aba Schwartz, "Migration and Life Time Earnings in the U.S.," unpublished doctoral dissertation, Department of Economics, The University of Chicago, 1968.

AGGREGATION AMBIGUITIES

IT will not do to continue to bypass the ambiguities of capital theory or of capital in economic growth models because human capital as a part of it is subject to the same ambiguities. The different faces of capital, both theoretically and empirically, lack analytical integrity. What they tell us about economic growth, which is a dynamic process, are inconsistent stories. As the alternative investment opportunities change over time, it alters the difference between the factor cost of a particular form of capital and the discounted value of the stream of services that it renders. But worse still is the capital homogeneity assumption underlying capital theory and the aggregation of capital in economic growth models. As Hicks[15] would have it, capital homogeneity is the disaster of capital theory. This assumption is demonstrably inappropriate in analyzing economic growth in a dynamic world that is afloat on capital inequalities, whether the capital aggregation is in terms of factor costs or in terms of the discounted value of the lifetime services of its many parts. Nor would a catalogue of all existing models prove that these inequalities are equals. But why try to square the circle? If we were unable to observe these inequalities, we would have to invent them because they are the mainspring of economic growth. They are the mainspring because they are the compelling economic force of growth. Thus, what is interesting and what matters in economic growth is concealed by capital aggregation.

One of the major advances of recent years in economic knowledge is the approximate solution of the problem of the residual. Jorgenson and Griliches have shown us a way of explaining productivity change.[16] The improvements in the quality of labor is an important part of the explanation and this part is a consequence of investment in human agents, restricted in their empirical work to education. A decade ago the then growing awareness of investment in human capital followed the observed rise in the quality of labor, and now we have fortified the quality approach in explaining productivity change. The improvements in the

---

[15] John Hicks, *Capital and Growth,* Oxford, 1965, Chapter III, see page 35.

[16] D. W. Jorgenson and Z. Griliches, "The Explanation of Productivity Change," *The Review of Economic Studies,* 34, (3), No. 99, July 1967. The references listed in this paper cover the recent relevant literature.

quality of nonhuman capital have, also, been large, perhaps a good deal larger than the best available estimates indicate. But the investment activities that account for this part of the additional quality have not been adequately clarified. In large measure, these activities pertain to advances in scientific and technological knowledge, advances which are truly, in some ultimate sense, a consequence of investment in the scientific skills of man.

Now that we have disposed of the residual, where do we go from here? Clearly, so it seems to me, the real unfinished business is to reckon the costs of and returns to each of these quality components along with the traditional components. But it cannot be done with the family of growth models that presently dominate the literature in economics. These models, including capital theory, begin with the wrong questions for the purpose at hand. What we want to know is the relative rates of return to investment opportunities and what determines the change in the pattern of these rates over time. To get on with this analytical task we must build models that will reveal the very inequalities that we now conceal and proceed to an explanation of why they occur and why they persist under particular dynamic conditions. The solution obviously is not in the art of producing ever larger capital aggregates.

The growth problem, thinking in terms of economic decisions, requires an investment approach to determine the allocation of investment resources in accordance with the priorities set by the relative rates of return on alternative investment opportunities. It is applicable not only to private decisions but, also, to public decisions guided by economic planning. The production and distribution of public goods (services) are a necessary part of the process, for example, the investment in research where the fruits of it do not accrue to the researcher or his financial sponsor but are captured by many producers and consumers. Thus, we move toward Harry Johnson's "generalized capital accumulation approach."[17]

While this approach may be paved with good economic logic, it is in fact a rough road with many detours. For particular investments, and

[17] H. G. Johnson, "Towards a Generalized Capital Accumulation Approach to Economic Development," *The Residual Factor and Economic Growth*. Paris: OECD, 1964, pp. 219–25.

there are many such in the domain of human capital, the value of the resource added (services rendered) is exceedingly hard to come by. It is all too convenient to leave the hard ones out, yet each and every omission falsifies the true picture of the full range of alternative investment opportunities. In analyzing education, we cling to differential earnings and leave aside differential satisfactions with no more than a pious acknowledgment that they exist. Another rough feature of this road is the determination of the investment sources and the price of each. The facile assumption of a well behaved capital market serving the formation of human capital is, I am sure, far from true. When it comes to private investment in human capital, poor people are subject to a great deal of capital rationing. Bruce Gardner's analysis of farm family income inequalities in the United States suggests that neither schooling nor migration has been a solution because of the inability of those poor people to respond to shifts in the structure of demand for skills by migrating or acquiring additional skills.[18] The explanation is to be found in capital rationing.

SOME OMISSIONS

Let me turn to some major omissions in the work on education, thinking in terms of the formation of human capital. If one were to judge from the work that is being done, the conclusion would be that human capital is the unique property of the male population, that the only services rendered by it are earnings, that the instructional activities of the educational enterprise are the only source of the educational capital produced by formal education, that the response to changes in educational investment opportunities is restricted to the private decisions of students or their parents, and that advances in knowledge are not altering the quality and value of instruction. There is enough substance to this image of what is being done for us to be troubled by the implications.

If it is true that investment in human beings is only for males, we would do well to drop the term "human capital" and replace it with

[18] Bruce L. Gardner, "An Analysis of U.S. Farm Family Income Inequality, 1950-1960," unpublished doctoral dissertation, Department of Economics, The University of Chicago, 1968.

"male capital." It would serve notice that human capital is sex-specific! Despite all of the schooling of females and other expenditures on them, they appear to be of no account in the accounting of human capital. If females are capital-free, in view of all that is spent on them, we are in real trouble analytically, unless we can show that it is purely for current consumption. There is no way of hiding the fact that females attend elementary and high school to the same extent as males and probably perform a bit better than males. In college attendance they fall behind somewhat; of the 4.9 million enrolled, October, 1966, about two-fifths were women. Even so, in terms of median years of school completed, of all persons twenty-five years and older in the United States, females are ahead of males slightly and the difference in favor of females has been increasing over time.[19] Surely, it cannot be denied that the factor costs of all this schooling of females is real and large. Nor is it plausible that all of these direct and indirect costs are only for current comsumption. The investment component must be large. But if there is little to show for it, how do we patch-up the economic behavioral assumption underlying the investment in education?

Mincer[20] and Becker[21] have each devoted a couple of pages to women. Mincer found that on-the-job training is not for women. Becker observes that the rate of return to female college graduates may not be lower than for males "because direct costs are somewhat lower and opportunity costs are much lower for women."[22] But differential earnings are a small part of the story. The two main reasons for the failure to get at the returns to schooling of women are, it seems to me, (1) concealment by aggregation and (2) the lack of any accounting of the differential satisfactions that correspond with the differentials in schooling.

There are many puzzles about the economic behavior of women that can be resolved once their human capital is taken into account. Young females leave the better parts of agriculture more readily than young males; these females have a schooling advantage and they are not

[19] U. S. Bureau of the Census, *Statistical Abstract of the United States, 1965,* Table 147, p. 112.

[20] Jacob Mincer, "On-the-Job Training: Costs, Returns and Some Implications," *Journal of Political Economy,* 70, October 1962, Supplement, see pp. 66–68.

[21] Gary S. Becker, *Human Capital,* New York, 1964, pp. 100–102.

[22] *Ibid.,* pp. 100–102.

held back by any specific on-the-farm training as are males. The explanation of the preponderance of women in most Negro colleges before school integration is to be found in the differences between the job opportunities open to Negro women and Negro men graduates. At a more general level, there is the slow, yet real, economic emancipation of women. It may be viewed as a consequence of growth and affluence. But it is also true that a part of this growth and increase in family income is some function of the rise in the education of women, much more than is revealed by the increasing participation of women in the labor force. At the micro level of the household, there is the shift from household work to work for pay; while a part of the explanation is undoubtedly the relative decline in the price of the services rendered by consumer durables, an important part is a consequence of the rise in the value of the time of women which in turn is in large measure the result of the education of women.

Turning now to another major component that is omitted in our work, there is the human capital represented by human agents without any education or by children before they enter upon schooling. The distinction between people with some schooling and those with none, educated labor versus raw labor, is useful for some analytical purposes as Welch has shown.[23] But children before they are old enough to attend school are also a form of human capital. I find it hard to believe that there is no economic rationality in the acquisition of this form of human capital. Surely parents derive satisfactions from their children; in traditional societies children provide old age security for their parents, a substitute for retirement "bonds." But the acquisition of children has its price. An approach that treats the production of children, viewed as human capital, in all probability will tell us a great deal about the economics of family planning.[24] In determining the costs of children, it is already clear that the level of schooling of women and changes in job

---

[23] Finis Welch, "The Determinants of the Return to Schooling in Rural Farm Areas, 1959," unpublished doctoral dissertation, Department of Economics, The University of Chicago, 1966.

[24] T. Paul Schultz, *An Economic Model of Family Planning and Fertility,* The Rand Corporation, P-3862-1, Santa Monica, California, July, 1968; also, *A Family Planning Hypothesis and Some Empirical Evidence from Puerto Rico,* The Rand Corporation, M-5405, Santa Monica, California, November, 1967.

opportunities for women—or more generally, the economic emancipation of women—and the required school attendance of children, whether cultural or legal, are among the important cost factors.

My conclusions are in two parts. First, there is a class of research, which I have not discussed, in which the very idea of reckoning priorities violates the essence of the process of discovery. It is not possible to reckon priorities for this class because the problem to be solved is one of the unknowns awaiting to be discovered. Consider the original theoretical analysis of investment in human capital by Becker.[25] I think it is fair to say that he started with the aim of estimating the returns to college and high school education in the United States. In pursuing this aim, he discovered that the investment activities associated with education were akin to other investments in people and that all these activities had basic attributes in common for which received theory, tailored to investment in structures and equipment, required reformulation.[26] Then, later in pursuing the many implications of earnings foregone, he discovered the problem that could be solved by a theory of the allocation of time.[27] I find it intuitively plausible that advances pertaining to this part will come largely from microanalysis, mainly, in response to puzzles and paradoxes revealed by economic data, for example, Telser's modification of specific human capital and its formation by firms in his search for the determinants of the differences in the rates of return in manufacturing.[28] Thinking in terms of the activities of the household, it may prove especially rewarding in coping with human-capital formation by the family to approach it as a part of the production activities of the household and, also, in getting at the satisfactions that it renders to the family in consumption.[29] The differences in the motivation of students

[25] Gary S. Becker, "Investment in Human Capital: A Theoretical Analysis," *Journal of Political Economy,* 70, October, 1962, Supplement, pp. 9–49.

[26] Here I have drawn upon my "Reflections on Investment in Man," *Journal of Political Economy,* 70, October, 1962, Supplement, p. 2.

[27] Gary S. Becker, "A Theory of the Allocation of Time," *Economic Journal,* 75, September, 1965, pp. 493–517.

[28] L. G. Telser, "Some Determinants of the Rates of Return in Manufacturing," unpublished paper, Department of Economics, University of Chicago, September, 1968.

[29] My reading of an unpublished paper by Gary S. Becker modifying consumption theory is an approach along these lines.

in their school work associated with the differences in job-market discrimination, following the approach of Welch, is another case in point.[30]

Turning to the second part of my conclusions; a good deal can be said for a reckoning of priorities. Specifically, from this limited endeavor at reckoning priorities, my conclusions are as follows: (1) As a device for preliminary exploration, it is not wrong to use national aggregates whether it be to determine the costs and returns to higher education or to secondary schooling, or to ascertain the amount of human capital in commodities entering into international trade or that which highly skilled people who migrate possess or as a quality input in a national production function, *provided that such use is viewed as exploratory.* In fact, it has been a necessary first step in discovering whether or not there is any economic value in education or in other forms of human capital. (2) Now that it is established that human capital is both real and important, the question becomes: where does it stand within the full range of alternative investment opportunities? In entering upon this analytical task, we are beset by the ambiguities of capital theory and of capital, including human capital aggregates, in economic growth models and in national accounting of change in the quality of labor. It is, also, true that the art of capital aggregation conceals a critical part of the information that we must have to understand and explain the dynamics of economic growth. (3) An investment approach, not only to the many different forms of human capital but also to research activities and to traditional nonhuman forms, is in principle the next analytical step. (4) In the work that has been done, the omission of human capital in females and in children before they enter upon schooling should give us pause. But this troublesome omission, so it seems to me, can be taken on, and the rewards in terms of additional knowledge are likely to be large.

[30] Finis Welch, "Labor-Market Discrimination: An Interpretation of Income Differences in Rural South," *Journal of Political Economy,* 75, June, 1967, pp. 225–40.

NOTES ON CONTRIBUTORS

ROBERT E. BALDWIN, born in 1924, is professor of economics at the University of Wisconsin. He is the author of "The Case Against Infant-Industry Tariff Protection," *Economic Development and Export Growth,* and *Nontariff Distortions of International Trade.*

YORAM BEN-PORATH, born in 1937, is a lecturer in the department of economics at Hebrew University, Jerusalem. He has recently published *Arab Labor Force in Israel* and "The Production of Human Capital and the Life Cycle of Income."

SAMUEL BOWLES, born in 1939, is assistant professor of economics at Harvard University. His publications include "The Efficient Allocation of Resources in Education," "The Determinants of Scholastic Achievement—An Appraisal of Some Recent Evidence," and *Planning Educational Systems for Economic Growth.*

MARY JEAN BOWMAN, born in 1908, is a professor of economics and of comparative education at the University of Chicago. Some of her major recent publications include: "Principles in the Valuation of Human Capital," and (as coauthor) *The Communicative Nexus and Mountain Development* and "Human Capital and Economic Modernization in Historical Perspective."

JOHN E. BRANDL, born in 1937, is Director of the Public Affairs Institute at the University of Minnesota after recently serving as Deputy Assistant Secretary for Education Planning, with the Department of Health, Education and Welfare. Mr. Brandl is author of "Education Program Analysis at HEW," "On the Treatment of Incommensurables in Cost-Benefit Analysis," and "Constrained Maximization and Decision Rules in Government: An Analysis of an Investment Allocation Formula."

BARRY R. CHISWICK, born in 1942, is an assistant professor at Columbia University. He is the author of "Inter-regional Analysis of Income Distribution," "Minimum Schooling Legislation and the Cross-Sectional Distribution of Income," and co-author of "An Economic Analysis of State Support for Higher Education."

JOHN CONLISK, born in 1939, is associate professor of economics at the University of California in San Diego. He has recently published "Some Cross-State Evidence on Income Inequality," "A Neoclassical Growth Model with Endogenously Positioned Technical Change Frontier," and "The Equilibrium Covariance Matrix of Dynamic Econometric Models."

D. J. DALY, born 1923, is professor of economics in the Faculty of Administrative Studies at York University in Toronto. His works include "The Impact of Monetary Policy," *Scale and Specialization in Canadian Manufacturing,* and "The Postwar Persistence of Business Cycles in Canada."

DUNCAN K. FOLEY, born in 1942, is assistant professor of economics at M.I.T. Two of his major recent publications are "Monetary and Fiscal Policy in a Growing Economy" and "A Negative Tax Primer."

ZVI GRILICHES, born in 1930, is professor of economics at Harvard University. Among his publications are "Production Functions in Manufacturing: Some Preliminary Results," "The Explanation of Productivity Change," and "Distributed Lags: A Survey . . ."

W. LEE HANSEN, born in 1928, is a professor of economics and of educational policy studies at the University of Wisconsin. He is coauthor of *Benefits, Costs, and Finance of Public Higher Education* and "Schooling and Earnings of Low Achievers."

JOHN C. HAUSE, born in 1935, is an associate professor at the University of Minnesota. He has recently published "Leads, Lags, and Spectral Analysis" and "The Welfare Costs of Disequilibrium Exchange Rates."

A. G. HOLTMANN, born in 1936, is associate professor of economics at The Florida State University. Mr. Holtmann is the author of "A Note on Public Education and Spillovers Through Migration," "Linear Programming and the Value of an Input to a Local Public School System," and "Migration to the Suburbs, Human Capital and City Income Tax Losses: A Case Study."

PETER B. KENEN, born in 1932, is Provost of Columbia University. He is coeditor of *The Open Economy,* coauthor of *Money, Debt and Economic Activity,* and author of *International Economics.*

ANNE O. KRUEGER, born in 1934, is professor of economics at the University of Minnesota. She has recently published "Factor Endowments and Per Capita Income Differences," "Balance of Payments Theory," and "Some Economic Cases of Exchange Control."

JACOB MINCER, born in 1922, is a professor at Columbia University and a senior staff member at the National Bureau of Economic Research. He is the author of *Human Capital and Income Distribution, Economic Forecasts and Expectations,* and *Labor Force and Unemployment.*

RICHARD R. NELSON, born in 1930, is professor of economics at Yale University. Mr. Nelson, whose research has focused on the economic growth process has recently published *Technology, Economic Growth, and Public Policy.*

THEODORE W. SCHULTZ, born in 1902, is Charles L. Hutchinson Distinguished Service Professor at the University of Chicago and a past president of the American Economic Association. He has recently published "Resources for Higher Education: An Economist's View," "Institutions and the Rising Economic Value of Man," and *Investment in Man and Research.*

ANTHONY SCOTT, born in 1923, is professor and head of the department of economics at the University of British Columbia. Some of Mr. Scott's recent publications include "Investing and Protesting" and "Immigration to North America."

LARRY A. SJAASTAD, born in 1934, is an associate professor at the University of Chicago. His published work includes "The Costs and Returns of Human Migration" and "Argentina and the Five Year Plan."

LESTER C. THUROW, born in 1938, is associate professor of economics at M.I.T. He has recently published *The Economics of Discrimination and Poverty* as well as numerous journal articles.

AUTHOR INDEX

SUBJECT INDEX